LAWYERS FOR HIRE

Lawyers for Hire
Salaried Professionals at Work

EVE SPANGLER

YALE UNIVERSITY PRESS
New Haven and London

Designed by Margaret E.B. Joyner
and set in Galliard with Optima type
by Eastern Graphics, Binghamton, N.Y.
Printed in the United States of America by
Halliday Lithograph, West Hanover, Mass.

Library of Congress Cataloging in Publication Data
Spangler, Eve, 1946–
    Lawyers for hire.

    Bibliography: p.
    Includes index.
    1. Lawyers—United States. I. Title.
KF297.S47   1986   340'.023'73   85-14339
ISBN 0-300-03462-8 (alk. paper)

The paper in this book meets the guidelines for
permanence and durability of the Committee on
Production Guidelines for Book Longevity of the
Council on Library Resources.

10   9   8   7   6   5   4   3   2   1

To my mother and father

Now these are the Laws of the Jungle,
and many and mighty are they;
But the head and the hoof of the Law
and the haunch and the hump is
—Obey!

Rudyard Kipling
The Second Jungle Book
The Law of the Jungle, refrain

CONTENTS

PREFACE

This book tells the story of how salaried attorneys do their work in a variety of settings: in law firms, in the law departments internal to corporations, in the civil service, and in the Legal Services program. It focuses on the many ways in which staff attorneys reconcile accountability to their employers with their own professional judgment.

To date, most popular commentary about lawyers has addressed other concerns: for example, the economic costs of producing "too many" lawyers and "too few" scientists, or the social costs of allowing lawyers to exacerbate a sense of "rapacious individualism" that rends the social fabric. These criticisms are certainly worth considering, but in fact they tell us little about lawyers' everyday work, and so they cannot show how lawyers come to produce the effects attributed to them. The present book focuses precisely on the question of how lawyers order their work and on the corollary issue of how such organization affects both the lawyers' own interests and those of their clients.

To understand the experience of staff attorneys, it is necessary to comprehend something about the fate of professional people more generally. Two forces shape the current experiences of experts: the rapid growth in their numbers and the transformation of their work from self-employed to salaried forms. The increasing importance of experts results from a century of corporate policy that systematically separates task planning from task execution. Such policy creates two groups: a class of professional people who design, coordinate, and supervise the work of others, and an industrial working class who do the jobs assigned to them. Lawyers, of course, are professional people and therefore members of the more privileged group of task planners. Like many other experts, however, attorneys are finding themselves increasingly in salaried staff positions.

Much speculation has been devoted to the fate of professional people in complex organizations. Some theorists predict that professionals will use their knowledge to take over the organizations that employ them. This argument is typically based on the importance of the tasks that professional people perform. Others predict that experts can be subordinated just as craft workers were before them. This argument concentrates less on the expertise of professionals and more on the organization of their work, which makes them answerable to their employers. Still others see professional people as near-permanent captives of their ambiguous, contradictory position between labor and capital. This argument assumes that status considerations will prevent staff professionals from making common cause with other workers and that a lack of effective political action will likewise keep them out of the ruling classes.

These predictions differ in their depictions of winners and losers, but they share the assumption that staff professionals and their employers are locked in a struggle to control the life of the workplace. More specifically, all predictions about the fate of salaried experts turn on such questions as the following: Who sets the ideological agenda, the definitions of institutional purpose, in organizations that employ professional people? How are assignments of particular work tasks negotiated? Who controls the day-to-day minutiae of the labor process itself, the routines by which work is accomplished? Finally, who makes the bureaucratic rules by which the life of the workplace is organized?

The experiences of staff attorneys are examined in light of these questions. Specifically, ideological control is revealed by inquiring how policy is made, technical control is manifested in the use of standard forms (boilerplate), and bureaucratic control is studied by ask-

ing how the processes of recruitment, training, evaluation, and reward are organized.

Data for the study reported here are drawn from a larger research
effort funded by the National Institutes of Mental Health (Grant
1R01 MH35893) and directed by sociologists Charles Derber and
Morris Schwartz. The larger Project on Professionals was designed
to explore the changing work life of doctors, lawyers, and engineers.
Doctors were chosen as research subjects because they are so often
used as a point of reference in discussing the professions. Lawyers
and engineers were chosen because they represent two of the most
populous professions and also because they present an interesting
contrast: engineers traditionally have been salaried employees,
whereas lawyers more commonly have been independent practitioners. The comparison of lawyers and engineers, therefore, is also a
comparison of a more recent and a long-standing adaptation by the
professions to salaried employment.

The present book, although confined to reporting lawyers' experiences, seeks to accomplish two things: to anchor speculation about
the future of experts in an examination of lawyers' work, and to place
the study of lawyers within the broader discussion of changes in the
professions.

The first chapter discusses in detail the larger social issues raised
by the experiences of staff professionals. Chapters 2–5 concern, re-
spectively, the work life of associates in large law firms, house counsel in business corporations, civil service lawyers in the federal government, and Legal Services attorneys. Each chapter begins with a
description of the particular organizations that participated in the
study. Then follows a fairly detailed account, in the words of the
lawyers themselves wherever possible, of the daily routine, the work
life, in such places. Relationships with managers are examined to see
how employers attempt to control staff professionals and how professional people, in turn, respond to such attempts. Relationships
with clients are examined to test the argument that "knowledge
is power." Each of these chapters concludes by considering what
particular individuals can tell us about the experiences of salaried at-

torneys in general. (Appendix A discusses the comments of a small number of private practice attorneys who were interviewed for the contrast their experiences might provide to those of their salaried brethren.)

Finally, the concluding chapter returns to the debate that surrounds the experiences of salaried professionals. Some thirty years ago C. Wright Mills said of the salaried middle class, "On the political market-place of American society, [they] are up for sale; whoever seems . . . strong enough can probably have them. So far, no one has made a serious bid" (1951, p. 354). Now, it seems that corporations and government in fact are making a serious bid to bring independent professionals under their control.

ACKNOWLEDGMENTS

This book could not begin more fittingly than with an expression of thanks to Charles Derber, who designed the larger research project of which this study is a part. To those who know his work, the effects of Charlie's intelligence, interest, and friendship will be clearly discernible throughout the pages that follow.

Thanks are due also to the National Institutes of Mental Health for their three-year-long support of this research and to Elliot Liebow and Maury Lieberman for their resourceful administration of the grant. Dean Donald White of Boston College's Graduate School also deserves thanks for administering the Boston College Faculty Research Support Program, which provided additional funding for my research during the summer of 1982.

My colleagues in the larger Project on Professionals have been consistently insightful in their ideas and generous with their time and attention. In addition to Charles Derber they are coprincipal investigator Morris Schwartz, Steven Brint, Ann Cordilia, Peter Meiksins, Jerry Boren, Rich Campbell, Cheryl Gooding, Avery Gordon, Andrew Herman, Helen Madfis, Madelyn Rhenisch, Sara Schoonmaker, and Bill Schwartz.

Dean Richard Huber of the Boston College School of Law was an invaluable source of advice and encouragement. His introduction to strategically placed members of the New England bar made it possible for the Project on Professionals to realize its goal of interviewing a number of individuals in several settings for each type of organization that employs staff attorneys. Without Dean Huber's contribution the sampling in this study would have been no more than a haphazard, catch-as-catch-can exercise.

As the reader will soon discover, the lawyers who consented to be interviewed were, without exception, cooperative, reflective, and articulate. I regret that the requirement of safeguarding their anonymity makes it impossible to thank them except in this collective and faceless way. I hope they realize that my appreciation of their willingness to speak candidly about their work is not less for being expressed so elliptically.

My efforts to complete this book have been immeasurably aided by Janet Brown, Kathy Randal, and Barbara Walsh, who gracefully discharged the exacting task of transcribing more than 100 two-hour interviews, and by Shirley Urban, Alice Close, Sara White, and Anne Young, who typed the first draft of the manuscript and then retyped seemingly endless revisions and amendments with unfailing courtesy and good cheer.

A number of friends and colleagues have been kind enough to read all or parts of this study. Peter Berger, John Donovan, Cynthia Epstein, Scott Fitzgibbon, William Form, Richard Huber, David Karp, Jack Katz, Peter Lehman, Michael Lewis, Sheldon Messinger, Richard Moran, Charles Page, Peter Rose, Kay Schlozman, Richard Schwartz, Rita James Simon, Ronnie Steinberg, Gladys Topkis, Sidney Verba, John Williamson, and Dan Woods have all accomplished the delicate and difficult feat of combining intellectual rigor and even occasional polite skepticism with unfailing personal warmth. For their many comments and suggestions I am most grateful; were it not for their contributions, my work would contain many more flaws than it does. A very special vote of thanks is also owed to Professor Charles Page for his extraordinary efforts in editing the first draft—much of whatever cogency this manuscript possesses is a direct result of his patient, meticulous, and painstaking editorial work.

In the book that follows I have tried to illuminate the experiences of contemporary staff attorneys by combining the best of three major traditions in the sociological study of work. From the functionalists I derive the question: How do changes within occupations ultimately affect the fabric of life in a whole society? Specifically, in the case of lawyers, what is the larger significance of the transformation of an "independent" profession into a profession of employees? How does this change affect the life of the law and the struggle for preferment among various occupations and classes? From Everett Hughes and his students I have learned that in order to answer such questions one must go out into the field; one must listen attentively and observe astutely to hear and see beneath the surface appearances of social life. From the Marxists I have learned that one of the crucial, though largely hidden, sources of occupational change is the class struggle—the conflict between labor and capital that is enacted in myriad forms.

Some readers will conclude that my attempts at weaving together these diverse strands of the sociological tradition have failed: that I have said too little about the connection between lawyers' experiences and the life of the law; that my capacity for disinterested observation has been compromised by the deductive character of the study; that to study the fate of privileged employees is to trivialize the issues of class inequality. Others, perhaps, will feel that I have achieved an interesting and useful synthesis: that the law is largely what lawyers make of it in the midst of their mundane concerns; that predetermined questions do not inevitably impair an interviewer's ability to get at what really is out there; that the subordination of people with a strong sense of entitlement is an important though ominous process.

Whatever the reader's opinion, however, I want to acknowledge here my indebtedness to the one person who most encouraged my efforts to bring together a number of sociological perspectives without being limited to any one of them. I thank Dean Albertson, not just for the usual hand-holding that the author's spouse is called upon to perform (although for this, too, I am grateful), but for sustaining, by example and encouragement, my efforts to write the book I thought should be written.

LAWYERS FOR HIRE

CHAPTER 1

COUNSELOR OR SERVANT?
The Work Life of the Salaried Lawyer

Some years ago, a businessman addressing a group of lawyers summed up his reservations about their profession in an anecdote:

> Two men were up in a balloon. They became lost in a fog and wandered for several hours. Finally they hit a break in the fog and discovered that they were only about fifty feet from the ground. Immediately below them they spied a man who was looking up at them. One of the men in the balloon leaned over and shouted, "Hello down there. Where are we?" The fellow on the ground shouted back: "You're up in a balloon." At this point the other chap in the balloon said, "There's no point in asking him anything. He's obviously a lawyer." His partner asked, "How do you know that?" The other replied: "Well, everything he told us is exactly true, and we're no better off than we were before." (American Business Lawyer, 1978, pp. 843–844)

Negative stereotypes such as this have a venerable history. Lawyers were the butt of barbed jokes ("a lawyer is someone who gets two other men to strip for a fight and then takes their clothes" [Blaustein and Porter, 1954, p. 1]) long before they reached prominence in American life. Both the Bible and the works of Shakespeare, for example, contain sneering references.[1]

---

1. Luke 11:46: "And he said, Woe unto you also, ye lawyers! For ye lade men with burdens grievous to be borne, and ye yourselves touch not the burdens with one of your fingers." Perhaps the best-known derogatory remark about lawyers is Shakespeare's: "The first thing we do, let's kill all the lawyers. . . . Is not this a lamentable thing, that of the skin of an innocent lamb should be made parchment? That parch-

1

But the recent spectacular growth in the number of lawyers in America has been a source of renewed concern. The figures are indeed startling. Today approximately one U.S. citizen in every 364 is a lawyer (Curran, 1984, p. 2). Our nation has about twenty times more lawyers per 1,000 people than Japan (Reich, 1981, p. 22); each year we graduate more than twice as many lawyers as there are in that entire society (Bok, 1983, p. 41). Likewise, our society has three times as many lawyers as Germany and ten times as many as Sweden (ibid., p. 40). We have, however, correlatively fewer engineers and scientists than they do. Japan, for example, produces proportionally almost six times as many technically trained people as America does (Reich, 1981, p. 22).

Comparing the proportion of lawyers in the American population with the proportion in Japan, Sweden, and Germany suggests one obvious source of concern: there are economic costs that attach to our preoccupation with the law. We direct an exceptionally high percentage of our most talented and educated people into work that, in the words of the Japanese, "does not make the pie grow, but only serves to carve it up" (Bok, 1983, p. 41). Our precarious economy, then, is in some measure the result of all those processes that produce "too many" lawyers and "not enough" of other kinds of educated labor.

If the deluge of lawyers has economic costs, other commentators, such as historian Jerold Auerbach, fear the social costs even more. Ours, Auerbach argues, is already a society beset by "rapacious individualism" (1976, p. 44). Both in law and in popular culture the individual's interest is clearly preferred to the collective well-being. Lawyers reinforce this tendency; in some ways, they are its perfect embodiment. By their very presence they suggest that all social relations should be regarded as potentially adversarial in character; that a rigorous calculation of self-interest is the most orderly way to conduct social life; that any appeal to the collective good which requires selflessness or altruism is suspect. The more committed to this com-

---

ment, being scribbled over, should undo a man? Some say the bee stings; but I say 'tis the bee's wax; for I did but seal once to a thing, and I was never mine own man since" (*Henry the Sixth, Part II*, act 4, sc. 2, line 68).

bative view we become, the less able we are to bring to bear any other standards for organizing public life. Yet every viable community must be able to rely on a level of commitment from its members that goes beyond the purely instrumental calculation of self-interest (Goldner et al., 1977, p. 539). Lawyers, Auerbach fears, impair our collective capacity to make such commitments. The relentless pursuit of self-interest leads by a relatively direct route to the war of each against all.[2]

Some commentators do not agree that legalism breeds excessive combativeness and inflames conflicts of interest. Instead, they argue that law promotes orderliness and rationality. Yet even these people acknowledge the point made by the classical French sociologist Emile Durkheim: "Society cannot exist simply by rational agreement . . . because agreements are not possible unless each partner trusts the other to live up to them" (Collins and Makowsky, 1984, p. 104). For their viability, specific contractual relations rely on a more generalized goodwill, which Durkheim called "pre-contractual solidarity." This very solidarity, in turn, is undermined by the spirit of legalism, which takes nothing on trust.

Such concerns about our national obsession with lawyers are echoed in yet another strand of cultural criticism. Reservations are being expressed about the growing influence not only of lawyers but of experts in general. An increasing number of writers are turning their attention to the rise of a "new class" of educated workers to positions of political and economic power and social prominence.[3] These writers are propounding an updated version of the managerial revolution theories of the 1930s and 1940s.[4] Then it was ar-

2. Auerbach (1976, p. 44) makes the further point that a war of each against all will not long confine itself to purely legal forms of competition. Lawlessness and litigiousness, he argues, are two distinct aspects of the same underlying phenomenon of "rapacious individualism."

3. Intellectuals from all parts of the political spectrum have speculated about the significance of a "new class." Among the better known commentators are, on the right, Berger, 1978 and 1979; in the center, Bell, 1973; and, on the left, Gouldner, 1979. For a summary of the debate, see Bruce-Briggs (ed.), 1979.

4. The two classical statements of the managerial revolution position are Berle and Means, 1932, and Burnham, 1941.

gued that the separation of the management of an enterprise from its ownership portended vast changes in corporate behavior. Today a similar argument is being made about the separation of expertise from ownership. The experts, we are told, are taking over the corporation, the government, the society. And experts, being what they are, will be more inclined to respect the claims of knowledge than the claims of property; they will opt for order and rationality and planning; they will be intrinsically hostile to the unpredictable and competitive discipline of the market. Lawyers are seldom mentioned explicitly by any of the new class theorists.[5] However, their numerical weight among the educated and their central role in structuring business deals are such that their experiences cannot be ignored in any argument about a new class of experts.

Of course, speculations about the origins, political intentions, and overall significance of highly educated people are now new. Almost from the time that modern industry grew out of the small, individually run business described by Adam Smith into the complex corporate form we know today, commentators of every political stripe have cast educated labor in a significant role. As the turn of the century, the Progressives in America, the Fabians in Great Britain, and the academic socialists in Germany all hoped that the systematic application of knowledge to the affairs of the state and the economy might produce a more rational, just, and conflict-free society (Bruce-Briggs, 1979, pp. 1–18). They therefore accorded educated workers an especially valuable role in the advancement of the community. Thorstein Veblen (1921), for example, had high hopes that the same skills that engineers used to manipulate the physical world could be deployed to plan and manage the social world.

Dissenting and skeptical voices were also heard. Anarchists such as Bakunin deplored the development of a new elite.[6] Even the more traditional defenders of working-class interests were suspicious of programs that made a tiny privileged group the guardians of the

5. A notable exception is Glazer, 1979.

6. For a discussion of Bakunin's contribution to this debate, see Bruce-Briggs, "An Introduction," p. 11, and Harrington, 1979, p. 127, in Bruce-Briggs (ed)., 1979.

common good. In the view of such men as Samuel Gompers, working-class organization, not enlightened social management, was the most reliable means of promoting justice.[7]

The deeply pessimistic German sociologist Max Weber had still other reservations. Science, he warned, is intellectually imperialistic. By refusing in principle to recognize a realm of the unknowable, it discredits all nonscientific forms of knowledge, particularly religion. But while science can destroy the plausibility of religion, it cannot adequately replace it, according to Weber. Scientists can answer many "how to" questions, but they cannot, as scientists, address themselves to questions of values. They cannot tell us who we should be or how we should live our lives. Therefore, science is an inadequate, even a dangerous, basis for social action. There is little reason, in Weber's view, to hail the advent of the scientific age, the expert society (1958b, pp. 77–128). "Not summer's bloom lies ahead of us, but rather a polar night of icy darkness and hardness," he said of the future (1958c, p. 128).

Each of these positions has its intellectual descendants today. John Kenneth Galbraith (1958, 1967) and Daniel Bell (1973), among others, foresee a post-industrial society in which a technocratic elite (or an "educational and scientific estate") controls strategic decisions in society for the benefit of all. Recent calls for industrial planning, notably by Felix Rohatyn (1984) and Robert Reich (1981; Magaziner and Reich, 1982), are more sophisticated in that they leave some room for interest-group politics; nonetheless, they look to expert planning to play a key part in industrial recovery.

Ivan Illich (1977) and Christopher Lasch (1978) echo the anarchist position. They deplore the destruction of folk wisdom by the wrongheaded, debilitating, and self-serving cant of experts. Their brand of commentary, however, mostly criticizes expert domination of ordinary or even weak and dependent people. It has less to say about the competition of old (property) and new (knowledge) elites. Nevertheless, like union people on the left and neoconservatives on

---

7. For a discussion of Samuel Gompers' contribution to this debate, see Bruce-Briggs, p. 2, in Bruce-Briggs, 1979, and Ratner, 1980.

the right, the anarchists are suspicious, not to say contemptuous, of reform efforts initiated by the privileged. Defenders of traditional working-class organization like Stanley Aronowitz (1983) still look to the revitalization of the union movement as the key to social progress. Neoconservatives call for a return to the discipline of the market to secure the public good (Kristol, 1978). And even experts in some cases are wary of the role of experts. For example, the ecology and antiwar movements have their own highly educated advocates, but by and large these movements have understood the Weberian critique: they distrust "the best and the brightest."[8]

Most of these positions also appear in popular discussions of lawyers. There are those who on the whole admire the American penchant for legalism. They are apt to applaud "the steadfast defense of individual freedom and civil liberties, the constant elevation of reason over prejudice and passion, the protections afforded to minority and disadvantaged groups" (Bok, 1983, p. 38), which, they say, are the objects of our legal system. These people are quite likely to feel that the most serious fault in the system is the limited access it affords, despite its size, to poor and middle-income individuals. And, indeed, some of the facts support them. If one in 364 Americans is an attorney, only one attorney seems to be available for every 7,000 *poor* Americans. In the Chicano community, the ratio is one to 14,000 (Auerbach, 1976, p. 44).

Not only is the sheer quantity of legal talent available to the poor restricted. Such legal help as they do receive often confirms the worst fears of the anarchist critics of the professions. In this vein, studies of both the public and the private defense bar suggest that defense lawyers routinely compromise defendants' rights to all-out, full-strength advocacy. Sometimes a vigorous defense is curtailed by inadequate funds. Worse, just as often it is vitiated by the defense attorney's desire to maintain cordial relations with other members of the legal community (judges, district attorneys, clerks of court), who will

8. The first person to use the term "the best and the brightest" with extreme skepticism was David Halberstam in a book of the same name criticizing U.S. policy in Vietnam (1969).

continue to be part of his or her work life long after any particular defendant has come and gone.[9] Similarly, lawyers who serve the poor in civil matters are accused of sometimes slighting the unique needs of a client to further their own acclaim at the bar through law reform efforts. For example, a recent study of a midwestern Legal Services office shows how changes from a case-by-case legal aid philosophy to a preference for class action suits have as much to do with the career aspirations of the staff attorneys as with the legal needs of clients (Katz, 1982). Even middle-class private clients may find that their goals are transformed by their lawyers' preconceptions of what is legally feasible and socially appropriate. One study, for instance, has shown how private matrimonial lawyers dissuade their clients from using their divorce settlements to attain emotionally valued but punitive ends (O'Gorman, 1963). Similarly, another study shows how consumer complaints against local business merchants are pursued only as far as the private bar's sense of "reasonableness" permits. Most troublingly, this study reveals how private-practice attorneys' views of reasonableness are often colored by their desire to maintain amicable relations with local business people (McCaulay, 1979). Yet another study shows that, despite contingency fee arrangements, lawyers representing personal injury plaintiffs often find it economically advantageous to urge their clients toward early and relatively meager settlements (Rosenthal, 1976).

Although the organized bar rejects the notion that its interests may diverge systematically from those of its clients, the general public seems to have understood or anticipated many of the studies cited above. As a result, lay people distrust lawyers and seek ways to avoid or control them. Jurist Bryant Garth (1983) captures this point when he shows how differently the legal and lay communities respond to criticisms of the bar. Lawyers focus their attention on issues of competence by calling for reforms such as further in-service education, which, while making lawyers better trained, would also

---

9. Numerous writers have documented the organizational constraints that curtail a vigorous defense effort. See, e.g., Blumberg, 1967; Eisenstein and Jacob, 1977; Gilboy, 1981; Skolnick, 1976; and Sudnow, 1965.

make their services costlier and less intelligible to laymen. The public, on the other hand, calls for accountability, for greater control over the actions that experts undertake on its behalf. Where such control eludes them, people attempt to remove as many human problems as possible from the purview of lawyers. Hence the support for no fault divorce and car insurance. Other movements attempt to construct new, quasi-legal, and semiprofessional arrangements to substitute for the law. "Alternative dispute resolving" mechanisms such as mediation projects grow out of such efforts.[10] Still other strategies would empower lay people to act directly for themselves within the legal arena. Norman Dacey's bestseller, *How to Avoid Probate*, typifies this approach.

What is common to all these otherwise diverse positions, in the discussion of both experts generally and lawyers in particular, is the shared belief that experts are important. Whether this importance is described in glowing or somber terms, all the views mentioned above assume that experts are people who can make their understandings of reality prevail. In short, there is very wide consensus that knowledge is power and that therefore experts are powerful people.

Clearly, some experts (social workers, teachers, doctors) have more credibility than the lay people (troubled families, st...
patients) who are their clients. Despite our nominally
ethos, professionals often speak with more authori...
the street. It does not follow, however, th...
tinely able to translate their credibility...
workers, teachers, and even d...
from their point of view...
And, more to the point,
credibility of experts tha
wealthy patrons.[11] The no...

10. For a discussion of the alternat...
see Abel (ed.), 1982. Auerbach (1983) a
Private mediation services aimed at a busi...
Homer, 1984.

11. For a classification of all possible...
professionals, see Johnson, 1972.

differently, that the possession of knowledge confers as much control over the conduct of others as the possession of property— is an idea whose truth cannot simply be assumed to follow from the growth of expert knowledge. The extent to which power has passed from an older, propertied business elite to a newer, knowledge elite (the new class) is a matter that requires empirical investigation as well as conjecture.

The notion that experts have become increasingly essential to industry and government gives rise not only to theories about the development of a new elite but to an opposite set of speculations as well. Do experts truly play a vital role in modern institutions? Then, might it not follow that, far from deferring to experts, owners and politicians would seek to subordinate them? Certainly the organizational settings in which many professional people work suggest the possibility of their subordination.[12] The independent, self-employed practitioner is no longer the prototypical doctor or lawyer, as table 1.1 reveals. Within a single generation the legal profession has been transformed. At mid-century, 87 percent of the bar was in private practice, 59 percent in solo practice. By 1980 only one-third were solo practitioners, and for each lawyer still practicing alone another now held a salaried position in industry, in government, or in a law firm.

Both the extent and the recency of this transformation suggest a number of questions. From the salaried professional's point of view: Is the exercise of professional judgment compatible with accountability to management? From management's point of view: Why hire professional people? Why not use them as consultants instead? Experts are, after all, expensive employees. They add to corporate overhead not only their own fairly substantial salaries but also the cost of additional office space, support staff, research tools, pension

12. Derber (1982, pp. 5, 193) writes: "Between 1900 and 1950 . . . the number of salaried professionals increased tenfold, almost three times more than the total number of professionals. . . . Professionals for the first time share with other workers the fundamental necessity of selling their labor power on a labor market. This change implies a loss of control rather than an expansion of authority. . . . This new perspective does not deny the importance of the authority that professionals exercise over clients, but suggests that it is increasingly a delegated authority that professionals exercise in the service of interests defined by their new employers."

Table 1.1. Status in Practice of Lawyers in the United States

	1951	1960	1970	1980
Government	9.7%	10.0%	11.0%	13.0%
Federal	4.0	5.1	5.7	4.2
State	1.7	1.7	2.9	8.7
Local	3.9	3.2	2.4	8.7
Private Practice	86.7	76.2	72.7	68.3
Solo	58.9	46.3	36.6	33.2
Partner	23.2	24.1	28.5	26.3
Associate	4.6	5.8	7.6	8.8
Salaried	6.3	9.9	12.4	14.0
Industry	5.5	8.9	10.3	10.0
Education	0.6	0.7	1.1	1.2
Other	0.2	0.3	1.0	2.8
N =	221,605	285,933	355,242	622,000

Sources: For 1951–1970: U.S. Department of Commerce, Bureau of the Census (1975), *Historical Statistics of the United States From Colonial Times to 1970*, series H: 1028-62, and American Bar Foundation (1972), *The 1971 Lawyer Statistical Report*, "Status in Practice"; for 1980: Barbara Curran, "The Legal Profession in the 1980's: Selected Statistics From *The 1984 Lawyer Statistical Report*," paper presented at the annual meeting of the Law & Society Association, 1984.

Note: Percentages in this table do not total to 100, because lawyers listed as "retired and inactive" or as members of the judiciary are not included. Some included individuals have been counted twice because the reporting procedures of the original source do not prevent this error.

funds, and bonuses. In the realm of intangibles, professionals often have loyalties to occupational groups outside the corporation and expectations of workplace autonomy that may become an object of envy to more conventional staffers. For a corporate or governmental entity to incur these costs, it must anticipate some substantial benefit: specifically, that of *control*. Whereas clients have relatively little control over experts, employers have a considerable amount of control over employees. The rise of the staff professional, then, may be seen as suggesting not the emergence of a new elite but, rather, the subordination of a former elite.

This view is supported by a considerable amount of historical research which shows that big business has long been adept at securing control over key factors of production. Today educated labor is one such key factor. A precedent for its absorption and control by industry already exists. In the late nineteenth and early twentieth centuries, American corporations succeeded in transforming the craftsmen of an earlier age into the industrial wage labor force we know today. This transformation was fraught with bitter conflicts between labor and management (Edwards, 1979). For our purposes it is sufficient to note that, in the end, management succeeded in subordinating craftsmen. This was done by a variety of means. The technology available to workers was manipulated, as were the social relations of the workplace, primarily for the purpose of enhancing management control. For example, David Noble (1977, 1979) and Harry Braverman (1974) describe how industrial management financed the development of "smart" machine tools. Such tools were designed by engineers rather than master craftsmen and could be used by workers only in those ways that their engineering and design permitted. This development represented a major shift away from the enhancement of craft skills among workers. Instead, it established the separation of task design from task implementation. As a consequence, task design became a professional or managerial prerogative. Workers were relegated to carrying out tasks that were planned elsewhere. De-skilled workers were, of course, replaceable workers, hence subordinated.

In a similar vein, Richard Edwards (1979) and Stephen Marglin (1975) have shown how highly skilled workers can be subordinated by the manipulation of the social relations at work. For example, Marglin points out that the development of factories in the cotton industry preceded the development of high-speed mass-production technologies. Initially, factories were preferred to cottage industry only for social reasons: they permitted greater control over the labor force. "If you don't come in Sunday, don't come in Monday," read the sign on the factory gate. It was only after a pattern of factory labor had been institutionalized that industrialists began to appreciate the economies of scale available to them. Edwards goes on to suggest that, in general, the systematization of personnel relations characteristic of large bureaucracies is designed to limit the scope of labor-management conflict to those few, narrow channels that management can control.

The preceding argument, however, can be taken to mean two

things. First, it can be used as a straightforward analogy: as crafts-men were once subordinated, so too shall staff professionals be brought to heel.[13] But another conclusion is possible as well. The very strategy of controlling craft workers by de-skilling them creates almost as many problems as it resolves. If craftsmen are limited to performing jobs designed by others, who does the job planning? By their very nature, worker-control strategies, whether technological or social in character, create specialized positions for those who de-sign, coordinate, supervise, and manage the work of others. These positions necessarily have a built-in structural ambiguity. In some measure, people in these positions exercise the prerogatives of own-ers: they command and direct the labor of others. In other ways, however, they are like workers: they are dependent upon capital for their jobs, their wages, their evaluations.[14]

A number of sociologists, most notably C. Wright Mills, portray professional people as near-permanent captives of their contradic-tory position between labor and capital. On the one hand, Mills doubts that "the class that is indispensable in fulfilling the major functions of the social order . . . is slated to be the next ruling class" (1951, p. 298). If that were the case, he argues, there could never have been societies in which slaves performed the essential tasks while freemen disdained work as unfit for gentlemen. Hence it is incorrect to claim that power follows from indispensability. Yet if Mills doubts that experts will be the next ruling class, he likewise doubts that they will become simply another component of the working class. Class consciousness, he insists, does not follow in any neat and orderly way from objective class position (1951, pp. 294, 324–327). However much the position of salaried professionals may "objectively" resemble those of workers, Mills predicts that ex-perts will opt for a status rather than a class consciousness. By this he

13. This position is sometimes referred to as proletarianization theory. Its leading exponents are Aronowitz, 1973, 1979; Aronowitz et al., 1970; Mckinlay, 1973; and Oppenheimer, 1973.

14. For a discussion of the general point see Wright, 1979, 1980, Wright et al., 1982, and Ehrenreich and Ehrenreich, 1979. For a particularly insightful application of this argument to the experience of engineers, see Meiksins, 1982.

means that professionals are likely to concentrate on the ways in which they enjoy a more privileged position than other workers. Correlatively, they will ignore their relative powerlessness vis-à-vis employers (1951, pp. 353–354).

This second line of analysis suggests that the fate of staff professionals would be better compared with that of managers than with that of craft workers.[15] This brings us back to the twin theories of managerial and professional revolution. Upper-level expert employees of necessity enjoy a certain latitude in their work. Do they use this autonomy to further some distinctive program of their own? Do they do the job the owners want done? Whom do the servants serve?

A well-known study by Rosabeth Moss Kanter (1977) touches on this point tangentially. She confirms what novelists have long suggested: in the large corporation, "the man in the grey flannel suit" is extremely conformist (Wilson, 1955). He needs to be because he has, in fact, no personal history in common with the people whose interests he serves. The national job market is such that corporate employers are forced to put people in positions of trust, with access to sensitive, "backstage" information, without knowing them personally.[16] Old-boy networks and job interviews are, at best, meager substitutes for long personal acquaintance or family connections in ensuring an employee's loyalty. In this context, managers reassure employers with demonstrations of conformity—dress and demeanor that say, in effect, "You may not know me personally, but you can count on me." Kanter's data thus flatly contradict the managerial revolution theories. Far from subverting the corporation, managers promote themselves by promoting the owner's interests.[17]

Kanter's work, along with the work of Braverman, Noble, Edwards, and others, suggests that the long-heralded revolution against the traditional prerogatives of ownership is not likely to arise either from skilled craft workers or from managers. Will professionals suc-

15. For empirical studies on this point see Brint, 1981, 1984, and Wuthnow and Shrum, 1983.

16. The concept of "backstage" and "frontstage" areas of social life was developed by Goffman, 1959.

17. For a more detailed discussion of this point see Useem, 1984.

ceed where others have failed? Will they take command directly through government programs and regulations—or indirectly by subverting the organizations that employ them? If they do become the new power structure, what will be the content of their programs? In large measure, the controversy about the political efficacy of experts boils down to three distinct sets of questions. The first concerns the success of professions in winning direct government action favorable to their interests; the second is about the success of professionals in dealing with the mass public, whom they encounter as clients; the third and most recent is about the success of professionals in dealing with government and private-sector employers.

In answer to the first question, it can be said that the professions have had some success in getting the government to enact their interests into law. Indeed, almost by definition, professions are those occupations to which the government has granted licensing privileges. Accreditation and licensure, in turn, create the distinction between authorized and illegitimate practice, and thereby a sheltered market for particular services. Several histories of this process have been written. Political scientist Corinne Gilb (1966), for example, stresses the role of professional associations in lobbying for licensing monopolies. Sociologists Magali Larson (1977) and Terence Johnson (1972) locate the success of professional organizations in the larger historical setting of emerging capitalism. Historian Barton Bledstein (1976) describes how the middle classes of the late nineteenth century embraced the process of professionalization to further their own ambitions.

In another sense, however, the significance of these findings should not be overstated. Taken together, they demonstrate that both the internal organization of an occupation and its rhetoric are significant resources. Some groups have been outstandingly successful in pursuing their own economic and status interests by the use of these mechanisms. Nevertheless, these studies also show that professional organizations harbor few if any politics except those pertaining to their own relatively narrow interests. They do not show that there is a general political agenda common to the professions on broad public policy issues. Indeed, insofar as professional associations are effective, one would expect them to be divisive of a new class politics. If, for example, social workers are generally antimilitary because they believe that public spending will not stretch to cover both guns and butter, then, by the same logic, engineers should be in favor of elaborate military hardware.[18]

Professional politics, in sum, do much to advance the interests of professional groups. However, the power, prestige, and income that accrue to the professions are hardly wrested from older elites. Rather, they are secured through the subordination of clients. It is in relation to the lay public that experts most clearly exercise real power. All professions, George Bernard Shaw once commented, are conspiracies against the public (Mayer, 1966, p. 9). A number of studies of lawyers, for example, suggest that it is rare for professionals merely to "translate" an individual client's demands into a legally and technically correct transaction (Cain, 1979). More commonly, the "translation" process also involves some elements of transformation (Berends, 1981). Even if a lawyer says only, "We don't care about what happened, we only care about what is going to happen" (Hosticka, 1979), he or she already is doing violence to the client's sense of a unique and richly nuanced complaint. The literature on lawyer-client relations is not unanimous, but, in general, it suggests that lawyers do exercise a great deal of power over individual clients, especially when they are of poor or working-class background.[19]

In contrast to this pattern, however, stands the lawyer's relationship to business clients. In their definitive study of the Chicago bar, John Heinz and Edward Laumann (1982) recently have shown that the corporate and individual service bars are two almost entirely separate spheres of the legal profession. One important point of contrast is the degree of control over clients. Lawyers who serve individuals may enjoy considerable control, but business lawyers do not. Business lawyers are retained by clients of commanding wealth and considerable sophistication in the legal dimensions of their business

18. For a discussion of social worker politics see Cohen and Wagner, 1982. For a discussion of engineers' conflicting views, see Leventman, 1981.

19. Jerome Carlin's work is the best-known illustration of the degree of control that lay people in the role of clients exercise over lawyers (1962, 1966).

transactions. Such clients often function almost as patrons in relation to their attorneys. They clearly are able to maintain control over the goals toward which their lawyers work.

One of the primary means by which powerful clients—large corporations, government agencies—control their "hired guns" is by putting them in staff positions. Indeed, so common is this pattern that it seems anomalous only because we are used to thinking of law and medicine, the last bastions of the independent practitioner, as the protoypical professions.[20] Doctors and lawyers are unusual, however. More typical are the engineers, clergy, scientists, and professors, most of whom have been employees from the beginning. Moreover, in any number of continental European countries, membership in the salaried classes is the typical pattern even for doctors and lawyers. Concern about bureaucratic encroachment on professional autonomy is therefore as distinctive in American and British sociology as is the independence of professionals that this train of thought presupposes.[21]

Despite the historical and cultural limitations of the argument, however, much has been made of the difficulties of absorbing professional people into bureaucratic organizations. Professionals reputedly require a substantial degree of autonomy in order to do their work. Their expertise is such that it seems to be "in the very nature of things" that outsiders cannot judge them. Professionals therefore cannot be supervised; their work can be assessed only by their peers. If experts are to be loyal to their clients' interests, such loyalties must be ensured by a subtle process of socialization. Large and bureaucratic organizations, on the other hand, depend for their efficiency on routine rule-following and hierarchical coordination. Thus, at the level of both structural principle and individual motivation, bureau-

---

20. Of this choice, Larson writes: "This singularity of medicine is important. For, indeed, to choose it as an occupational model when neither the advantages of its market structure nor in many cases the advantages of its cognitive basis can be reproduced is an *ideological* choice. As such, it suggests the general ideological functions of the professional model" (1977, p. 38).

21. On this point see Friedson, 1983, and Rueschemeyer, 1973, 1983.

cracy and professionalism would seem to be incompatible ways of marshaling work commitments.[22]

A number of studies of salaried engineers and scientists have suggested ways in which professional and bureaucratic styles can be accommodated to one another. Staff professionals can be segregated in their own departments, where evaluation and career advancement are determined by professional standards (Kornhauser, 1962; Ritti, 1971); bureaucracies can emphasize rationality and fairness while deemphasizing deference to arbitrary authority (see, for example, Gouldner, 1964; Hall, 1963, 1968; Montagna, 1968; Stinchcombe, 1959; and Udy, 1959); the profession as a collectivity can dedicate itself to business ends, as engineers have done (Perucci and Gerstl, 1969). Less appealing but nonetheless effective means of integrating professionals into bureaucracies are also available. Recent retrenchments in public spending have certainly succeeded in putting teachers and social workers on the defensive.

More significantly, perhaps, several writers have pointed out that bureaucracies and professions differ more in emphasis than in absolute terms. They arise in the same historical context.[23] They are similarly antidemocratic in animus: both the people who speak from the authority of knowledge and those who speak from the authority of office expect to prevail over "mere uninformed opinion." Most important, professions and bureaucracies often work in tandem. In many instances, professional people prevail over clients as much because of the power that emanates from their office as by their persuasiveness and expertise. Arlene Kaplan Daniels (1972, 1975) has shown how military psychiatrists derive much of their authority from their rank. More generally, doctors' orders are carried out because of their formally recognized authority to prescribe treatment even when patients are skeptical or unpersuaded (Freidson, 1970b).

22. Davies, 1983. This argument has been applied to lawyers by Schwartz, 1980.

23. Larson (1977, p. 199) writes: "Both professions and bureaucracy belong to the same historical matrix: they consolidate in the early twentieth century as distinct but nevertheless complementary modes of work organization."

The preceding discussion indicates that the relationships among professionals, their employers, and the public are highly complex. What emerges from the literature is less a sense of certainty about the future of experts than a series of questions. As noted earlier, some predict that experts will become a new ruling class. Others foresee the opposite: that business will tend increasingly to subordinate staff professionals, thus depressing their status until they resemble skilled workers. Still others argue that staff professionals will continue to occupy an intermediate position between labor and capital. For the general public, such opposing predictions must seem to cancel each other out.

But if scholars differ in their predictions, they agree on certain fundamental assumptions. The workplace is seen by all as a "contested terrain" (Edwards, 1979). For management, the goal of the contest is to ensure that the potential labor power contracted for in the wage relationship is in fact expended in accomplished work. For the staffer, the goal is to ensure that the labor process is carried out under acceptable terms of autonomy and reward. Whichever party wins the contest, certain issues of workplace organization must be resolved.

Charles Derber (1982) has identified three such "contested terrains" in which both management and educated labor seek to prevail. First, each wants to be instrumental in developing the ideology of the organization: the definitions of institutional identity and purpose, products and services. For example, in Legal Services programs, fierce battles have been waged over which philosophy should guide the organization. Law reform and legal aid proponents have each had instances of success in capturing the organization for their camp. The difference between legal aid and law reform is not intrinsically one that need divide managers from staff, but it often does so when a younger generation of law reformers enters an organization in which managers have spent much of their work life in legal aid activities (Katz, 1982).

Second, both managers and professionals want control over the specifics of the day-to-day labor process, the technical aspects of the job. This issue is especially significant to professional people who do the most complex work in an organization and therefore have perhaps the largest investment in their own work product. In general, lawyers have a good chance of protecting their autonomy in this area from the encroachment of business people and administrators. Few lay people feel able to dictate legal strategy or legal language. However, when lawyers have managers who are also lawyers, much of their elbow room evaporates. For example, the emergence of the law clinic that dispenses legal services in conjunction with such places as H & R Block or Sears Roebuck depends upon highly standardized, routinized work products. In such settings, individual staff attorneys have little control over the basic forms they are to use or the kinds of tasks they are assigned.

Finally, both management and staff professionals want to control the bureaucratic aspects of the organization, the formal and informal rules governing the life of the workplace. In a number of different settings, salaried attorneys have come into conflict with management over what are essentially due process issues. Law firm associates want some say in the number of hours they are expected to work. Legal Services attorneys want clearly specified grievance procedures. Corporate staff attorneys want executive training programs and job posting rules so that they can more readily move from the legal to the business side of the corporation.

All this suggests that the relatively harmonious relationship between staff attorneys and their employers is a somewhat provisional achievement snatched from the jaws of potential strife. Much has been written about educated labor in general, little of it about staff attorneys. Much has been written about lawyers, little of it about their experiences as employees. The present study seeks to bring these two topics together—to anchor the discussion of the new class in an empirical study of lawyers' experiences and to set the study of lawyers in the context of what is happening to experts generally.

A total of 103 lawyers—33 in five large law firms, 26 in five corporate law departments, 21 in four civil service agencies, 18 in three Legal Services programs, and 5 in solo practice—agreed to be interviewed for this study. All were practicing law in the New England area, where the research project was located. The choice of location (made for economic reasons) is significant because the culture of the bar is said to have pronounced regional variants. The truth of this observation was borne out in the interviews when a number of law firm associates contrasted their experiences with those of their counterparts in Wall Street firms. Government lawyers likewise saw a significant difference between the experiences of regional (New England) and home office (Washington) attorneys. The regionalism of the bar means that, at least in detail, the findings of this study may not be directly applicable to salaried attorneys throughout the country. In general, New England lawyers seem to feel that their offices are smaller and more conservative or traditional than offices in other parts of the country.

After electing to confine the study to the New England region, the second step in the sampling strategy of the Project on Professionals called for specification of the kinds of settings in which lawyers were employed as staff counsel. Previous research on lawyers (Abel, 1980) described four sets of salaried attorneys: associates in large law firms (Nelson, 1981, 1983; Smigel, 1960, 1964); house counsel in business corporations (Donnell, 1970; Slovak, 1979, 1981); attorneys in the various branches of government (Spector, 1972, 1973); and attorneys who worked for local affiliates of the Legal Services Corporation (Girth, 1976; E. Johnson, 1974; Katz, 1978, 1982). It was decided to interview staffers in all these diverse settings because they are more than a miscellaneous collection of research sites. Taken together, the range from law firms to Legal Services forms a continuum: from right to left on the political spectrum, from rich and prestigious to poor and beleaguered, from settings in which employees are almost totally identified with their employers to settings in which they have formed an organized opposition to management. To have omitted any of these settings would have been to lose a significant portion of the story of the lawyer-as-employee.

Once the project had decided where to find salaried attorneys, our plan for arriving at the final sample of 103 respondents was developed in two further steps. While we were able to study all the *types* of settings that employ staff lawyers, clearly we could not be equally exhaustive in entering particular research sites. We chose to rely on a panel of experts to identify specific research sites, and thereby we created a purposive sample.[24] Ten law school professors in the New England area agreed to advise us about the managerial style and accessibility of particular law offices. With their help we were able to locate five law firms, five corporate law departments, four government law offices, and three Legal Services programs that showed a diversity of management styles and philosophies. Initial contact with each of these sites took the form of an introduction, arranged by the consulting professors, to one of their former students, now employed in the place to which we sought entry. The alumnus then carried our request to the appropriate decision makers in his or her workplace. In all but one firm the research project received a cordial welcome and unstinting cooperation.

Finally, within each research site, we selected a random sample of individuals for our interviews. We began the study in large law firms. In New England in 1982, this meant firms of 75 or more lawyers.[25] In the first firm, our random selection procedures netted a set of businesses, tax, and real estate lawyers as respondents. Since these specialties (along with litigation) constitute the core departments of most large law firms, we confined our sampling to these areas in the other firms as well.

Next we turned to interviews in the office of the corporate general counsel. Again, we wanted to explore the impact of a complex management system on staff professionals and so opted for only the largest New England law departments, employing 30 or more lawyers. We tried to maximize diversity among these departments by targeting a wide variety of host industries. The final sample of five corporations with large in-house legal capacities contains a broad range of business types, from financial services to heavy industry. Within the office of the general counsel we tried to locate those law-

24. In using an expert panel, we were following the precedent of Laumann and Heinz (1977), who used such a panel in their study of the Chicago bar.

25. Higgins (1985, p. 31) notes that the largest New York law firms number more than 400 lawyers and the largest Chicago law firm over 600. The relatively small size of large New England law firms confirms our respondents' sense that New England's regional culture tends to be conservative.

yers who were most nearly comparable to our law firm respondents. To accomplish this, we confined our sampling to the business and real estate divisions of the corporate law department.

Much of the work of the business lawyer, both in the law firm and in the corporation, is created by the activities of government lawyers in their regulatory capacity. Having interviewed a number of private-sector business lawyers, we sought next to find their opposite numbers among civil service attorneys. We therefore selected two business-regulating agencies as the sites for our initial government interviews. Then, because we also anticipated conversations with reform-minded Legal Service lawyers, we selected two more government agencies whose mandate required them not to regulate business but to implement social reform legislation.

Finally, on the advice of our expert panel, we approached three Legal Services programs in the New England area. Again, we chose particular programs with an eye to covering the range of administrative styles (from highly professional to highly industrial) to be found among Legal Services agencies. We soon discovered that during the time of the study all affiliates of the national Legal Services Corporation were facing massive funding cuts and therefore were shrinking in staff size. As a result, and contrary to our initial plans, we interviewed in some programs employing only a handful of attorneys. Somewhat to our surprise, we found that program administration remained a complex matter even when program size had been drastically reduced. Both the highly politicized environment surrounding the Legal Services Corporation and the presence of staff unions within it ensured that management had unusual challenges to face. Moreover, although we were interested in the possible subordination of salaried experts, we were no less intrigued by their resistance to subordination. For this reason the presence of staff unions in the Legal Services affiliates made these settings especially interesting for the study.

At the very end of our research, we contacted five solo practitioners randomly selected from a Boston-area lawyers' directory (Martindale-Hubbell, 1982). They were interviewed for the contrast their comments provided to the experiences of staff attorneys.

Our sample, in sum, resulted from four successive decisions. First, this is a regional study, tapping the experiences of lawyers in the New England area. Insofar as there are real geographic differences in the life of the bar, our findings may not be precisely replicable in other parts of the country. Second, we were exhaustive in studying the types of settings—law firms, corporate counsel's staffs, civil service departments, Legal Services affiliates—in which attorneys hold staff positions in the region. Third, we used a panel of experts to help us identify specific research sites. This stage of the sampling was a purposive one intended to secure the greatest possible diversity in managerial styles for each type of employer. Finally, we randomly sampled individuals within each setting to arrive at the panel of 103 respondents. We were refused an interview by only one organization (a law firm) and by only one person, so that 17 or the 18 sites and 102 of our final 103 respondents are the people we originally set out to interview. The interview schedule appears in Appendix B.

As with most interview studies, the design of this research falls somewhere between the extensive, systematic data gathering of a large survey and the richly textured, intimate approach of participant observation. The middle position has a number of advantages. Open-ended interviews typically allow people to talk about their lives at greater length and in more detail than surveys do; they also allow the researcher to enter a larger number of settings than can usually be studied by participant-observation techniques. Despite their strengths, however, research interviews suffer from one great weakness: they tell us what people say about their lives but not whether these statements are true or false, self-deluded or perceptive. For this reason, interview studies often buttress their conclusions, as this one does, with references to public sources of information and with the researcher's own reflections and observations.

More important, the validity of the present inquiry is protected by the sampling strategy, which called for interviews with a number of people in both staff and management positions in every office that participated in the study. Clustering respondents in this way guaranteed that observations made by a particular individual could be checked not only against public sources but also against the perceptions of other people in the same office. Generally, the comments of office-mates reflect both the common environment and the differing positions of speakers—for example, respondents agree in characterizing particular offices as "friendly" or "troubled," but within this shared view young lawyers worry more about evaluation than their superiors do. Such convergent accounts tend to confirm the candor and perceptiveness of the men and women who were interviewed.

Wherever possible, the respondents speak in their own voices —for three reasons. First, compellingly, because *they are there*. There is no substitute for hearing a business lawyer express his glee and scorn by saying, "If you've ever seen a settlement agreement written by litigators, it's hysterical. It assumes that everything is going to happen. There's never any provision in it for what happens if the contingencies don't happen." Nor could the stratagem that managers refer to as overdelegation be more vividly described than in the words of the corporate counsel who was asked to take over a closing on her first day on the job. "Now, I kid you not, I knew not the meaning of the word 'closing.' And I thought, 'Hm, I'm going to learn this by jumping in, but I don't think I should do this.' And I went to about three attorneys and said, 'Could you just give me a clue as to what happens in a closing? Do I light candles and wear black robes?'" Likewise, the harried atmosphere of the Legal Services office is suggested by the lawyer who complained that "everything's a fucking emergency." Finally, the lawyer's own words best describe one civil servant's thinking about moving from a regulatory agency to a regulated industry. "Would I be promoting justice to be on the other side? [That] is really not a concept I'm thinking about. I don't even think about it on this side."

I have also let the respondents speak for themselves with readers in mind. Probably many of the latter will be lawyers, law students, and pre-law students, not social scientists. They may have little interest in the more theoretical opening and closing discussions, but they will want an unobstructed view of what really is out there in the work settings that may someday be their own. This I have tried to give them.

To do so, I have of course had to do a great deal of picking and choosing (and mostly deleting) from my more than 4,000 pages of transcripts. To be sure, some trust is required from the reader that I have chosen appropriately,[26] but the deductive nature of the study greatly simplified the task of identifying common sentiments among the respondents. In technical parlance, the interviews that provide the basis for this study were semistructured and open-ended. The open-endedness allowed respondents to discuss in their own idiom issues of workplace control. However, the structure imposed by the interview schedule ensured that I would cover the same topics with each person. This strategy undoubtedly prevented me from discovering information about topics not included in the interview guide. Many readers will be disappointed by the lack of "sexy" material: inside stories about the famous and the infamous, whistle-blowers and wheeler-dealers. But the tight control imposed on the interviews also created a situation in which all the respondents addressed themselves to the same issues. Thus, when I came to edit the transcripts, I had a reliable basis for judging how common or atypical any particular opinion might be. When there was substantial agreement among the respondents, I chose the most succinct or the most evocative statement of a position. When I quoted a highly unusual idea, I identified it as such and, given other data from the same workplace, speculated about the reasons for a discrepant opinion.

Even in relatively controlled, deductive interviews, however, respondents do talk about more topics than appear in the final study. In the chapters that follow I have opted to keep the focus on the ways in which lawyers are treated as employees and on the responses they make to such treatment. I have omitted much material about the motivations of people who choose legal careers, which might interest the psychoanalytically inclined. Suffice it to say that, in re-

26. On the subject of trusting experts, Horobin writes: "All experts claim legitimacy for their contribution. . . . This is not, or at least not primarily, a confidence trick. . . . It is rather an inherent feature of the division of labor. If we have to agree to others performing tasks in exchange for the tasks we perform, we at the same time grant license to them to become expert and to use their expertise on our behalf" (1983, p. 102).

trospect, the respondents spoke less about having made an affirmative choice of law as their life's work than about their belief that a law degree would provide a generic job-market credential for either a professional or a business career. Fully 60 percent of the respondents indicated such sentiments. A sizable minority, about 10 percent, indicated that they had chosen among different professions; law versus medicine, architecture, city planning, or political science. Only 2 of the 103 respondents said that they had always wanted to be lawyers. One remembers being so argumentative that his father took to addressing him as "Perry Mason," and the other was enchanted by the biographies of Oliver Wendell Holmes and William O. Douglas he had read as a young teenager.

Also missing from this book are the data that would intrigue historians; narratives of events specific to particular firms, corporations, government bureaus, and Legal Services programs. This material had to be omitted in order to preserve the anonymity that was promised not only to the individuals but also to the organizations that participated in the study. Yet, while the study is not historical in the conventional sense, neither is it set in the timeless present inhabited by so many sociological studies. Rather, it reveals the dilemmas of professional work at a particular point in time when the accommodations between staff attorneys and administrators are just beginning to be established. There is every reason to suppose that the same study undertaken twenty years ago or twenty years hence would produce very different results.

Perhaps the topics most conspicuously absent from the following chapters are explorations of sex and race differences in staff attorneys' experiences as employees. Early in the project, the research team posited sexism, racism, and worker subordination as three conceptually (if not always empirically) distinct processes. Because we were interested only in the last of these, we originally planned to limit our sample to a population of white men, thus holding constant the confounding effects of race and sex on our small sample. Further, we were aware that most project members favored the proletarianization theories which predict the subordination of experts to new class theories that predict their empowerment. To counteract our own prejudices, we sought out the data least hospitable to our views. This criterion strengthened our preference for a white male sample since we assumed, for reasons too obvious to dwell on, that white men would have a better chance of escaping domination than women of any race or nonwhites of either sex.

In any case, in the field we found that it would have been all but impossible to include black attorneys—only two were found in all the research settings we visited. On the other hand, we soon discovered that we could not realistically omit women from our study, since they constituted more than half the work force in certain settings. We therefore abandoned the aim of an exclusively white male sample. Chapters 2–5 identify female and nonwhite respondents as such so that readers interested in sex and race differences can judge for themselves whether men and women, whites and blacks, talk about work commitments differently. Overall, it is the impression of the interviewers that they do not. The largest sex difference arose when many of the women but only a few of the men mentioned making accommodations to a two-career family. The one black attorney who was interviewed spoke of using his legal training to build a political career, whereas most whites who were contemplating a career change were preparing for business positions. Generally speaking, however, the interview did not seek to elicit information about the interplay of gender, race, and career, and the respondents themselves seem not to have felt compelled to introduce the topic.

The astute reader will notice that many of the excerpts from the interviews read more like written than like oral language. I have achieved this effect by editing out the redundancies and tangential remarks characteristic of the spoken word whenever it was possible to do so without changing either the substance or the flavor of a quoted passage.

Finally, I have used quotations liberally as an aid to those social scientists who may read the book. They will be interested in both the data and the theoretical ideas that frame this inquiry about the relationship of knowledge to power, about the accommodations between employers and employees, about the relationships of work experiences to political beliefs. Presumably, they will wish to judge for themselves how well the data fit the ideas. I have tried to give them ample opportunity to do so.

CHAPTER 2

HIRED GUNS
Partners and Associates in Large Law Firms

Calvin Coolidge once said that "the business of America is business." To this, many observers have been quick to add that the business of law is also business.[1] It should therefore come as no surprise that, as American business has changed, so too have legal services. In business, small family-owned enterprises gave way first to ever larger corporations and later to multinational conglomerates. In similar fashion, business lawyers moved out of their small-town offices into lucrative downtown law firms that are now often multicity operations with branches in New York, Washington, and abroad. The development of the law firm thus parallels the growth, intensification, and rationalization of business. The present chapter describes the work life of the large, free-standing law firm as it exists today in the New England area.[2]

THE LARGE LAW FIRM: OLD WEALTH AND NEW

The large law firm began to assume its present institutional form in the early years of this century. In New York, the center of the Ameri-

1. Heinz and Laumann (1982) estimate that about half of the bar's efforts are devoted to the service of big business. The other half is done for small businesses and individual clients with business needs. Mayhew and Reiss (1969) similarly conclude that the law is best suited to facilitating the acquisition, maintenance, and transfer of property.

2. Two accounts of the growth in large law firms are by Lewin (1982, 1983a). The limits to growth are discussed by Higgins, 1985.

can bar,[3] Paul Cravath set out deliberately to transform his venerable but personalized law firm into an organization whose structure would transcend the life of its individual members. According to Paul Hoffman, chronicler of the Wall Street firms, Cravath "had a definite philosophy about the organization of his law firm. First, like a symphony orchestra, it should be tyrannical; one man would call the tune. . . . Second, the firm would prosper on . . . what it knew; it would live by merit" (1973, p. 6). Third, practice for the firm was to be the exclusive professional activity of its members. Fourth, association with the firm was ideally a lifelong commitment: the highest positions were to be occupied by incumbents promoted from within. For those who began their professional life in the firm and did not rise through its promotion scheme, other employment was found with satellite (highly specialized) firms or in the law departments of corporate clients. "Nobody starves," said Cravath (p. 7). He might also have insisted, "And nobody rocks the boat either." Clients were to be provided with legal counsel that was "safe, sound and steady" (p. 9) rather than distinguished. The elite of the American legal profession was a place "for a man to make money, not to make his mark" (p. 52).

The Cravath model of law firm organization soon predominated. Law firms came to be structured as pyramids: the bottom two-thirds occupied by support staff (secretaries, messengers), the top third by varying proportions of partners and associates. Partners owned the firm. They attracted multiple-matter clients—business clients who required ongoing legal advice and who brought in more work than partners could do alone. Partners therefore surrounded themselves with associates—employees to whom the simpler aspects of a client's business were delegated. The law firm, in its fully mature form, was therefore more than a space-sharing arrangement among equals. It was a guild-like organization in which senior craftsmen supervised apprentices and served a business public.

The exploits of its members have been chronicled not only by

3. The business character of the bar is underscored by the fact that its capital is located not in Washington, D.C., near the seat of government, but in New York City, near the stock exchange.

journalist Paul Hoffman but also by insider James Stewart (1983) and by innumerable fiction writers from Louis Auchincloss (1963, 1977) to John Jay Osborne (1979). Cynthia Epstein (1980) has written about the very few women lawyers on Wall Street. Joseph Goulden (1972) has followed the Wall Street lawyer from New York City to Washington, D.C., where he represents business clients before congressional committees and executive agencies. All these accounts abound in well-known names, allusions to posh private schools, elite universities, law review editorships, swank suburban homes. They generally depict a world of frenetic activity and highly skilled if not often reflective legal work. Perhaps it was journalist Martin Mayer who best captured the ambience of the large, prestigious New York law firm with its genteely disguised but nonetheless single-minded pursuit of profit.[4] Large firm partners, says Mayer, are rather like building contractors. Having no fixed annual wage, they charge too much for the work they do and take too many jobs for fear of turning things down (1966, p. 25).

In successful law firms, as the Wall Street firms proved to be, work begot more work. And the growing work load, in turn, produced ever larger numbers of lawyers working together within a single administrative structure. The pyramidal form developed by Cravath was maintained. But growth could not continue indefinitely as more of the same, only bigger. Eventually, the size of the law firm required some systematic attention to administrative rationalization and coordination. Early attempts by the Wall Street law firms to achieve administrative orderliness were chronicled by sociologist Erwin Smigel. He found the development of a committee structure among the partners and the designation of a managing partner, who, while practicing law, also became responsible for overseeing firm operations (Smigel, 1964). At present, some New York firms are experimenting with an even sharper differentiation between administrative and professional functions. They employ a business-trained manager to organize the entire administrative machinery of the firm

---

4. The single-minded pursuit of profit continues, although of late its genteel concealment seems to be slipping. See, e.g., the following articles in the popular press: King, 1983; Lewin, 1983d; Taylor, 1983c; and Aric Press et al., 1984.

while the lawyer-partners return to an exclusive concern with their professional practice.

Regional law firms outside New York City have traditionally patterned themselves on the Wall Street model, although with a time lag. For example, recent research by Robert Nelson (1981, 1983) on the Chicago bar suggests that large law firms in that city are less bureaucratic to this day than Smigel's New York City firms. Nelson concludes that Chicago lawyers continue to be "professionals"; they have not become "organization men" (1981, p. 139). In the five New England law firms that furnished data for the present chapter, both bureaucratic and professional elements are clearly visible, reinforcing the idea presented in the first chapter that bureaucratic and professional principles for ordering work are less antithetical than is sometimes supposed. On this point Eliot Freidson, a leading scholar of the professions, writes:

> For at least a century we have been treated to the use of the word "bureaucracy" as an epithet. Indeed, we have tended to take as self-evidently true the assertion that the rationalization and systematization of work, governed by formal administrative authority and written rules, lead to a fragmentation of experience and a loss of meaning, a sense of alienation. . . . In contrast to the negative word "bureaucracy" we have the word "profession." This word is almost always positive in its connotation, and is frequently used to represent a superior alternative to bureaucracy. . . . It seems to be assumed that technical expertise is . . . so self-evidently true as to automatically produce cooperation or obedience in others as well as the efficient attainment of ends. . . . But . . . the authority of expertise is in fact problematic, requiring in its pure . . . form the time-consuming and not always successful effort of persuading others that its "orders" are appropriate. As a special kind of occupation, professions have attempted to solve the problem of persuasion by obtaining institutional powers and prerogatives that at the very least set limits on the freedom of their prospective clients and that on occasion coerce their clients into compliance. (1970b, pp. 129–131)

In short, professional people often rely on bureaucratic procedures to accomplish their ends. Therefore, the distinction between a professional organization of men and a bureaucratic organization of offices is often more apparent than real.

Of course the lawyers of New England do not spend their time debating the relative merits of "professionalism" and "bureaucratization" as concepts to describe their firms. Rather, their sense of history leads them to distinguish between long-established firms and partnerships only recently arrived among the large firms, to distinguish between firms still under the sway of dominant partners like Cravath and those that, having lost their patriarchs, must create new arrangements among the partners. Of the five firms that participated in this study, three are of considerable age with well-established positions in the market for legal services. One of these remains dominated by a firm patriarch; the other two operate in a more participatory and collegial mode. The remaining two—which I have called the entrepreneurial firms—are new to the ranks of large law firms and still in the process of securing their market positions.

The traditional, Cravath-like firm continues to operate in the patriarchal mold with a powerful senior partner who dominates the partnership group, delegates little power, and generally maintains control over the firm, firing off memoranda on even such minutiae as Friday afternoon office attire. As one senior partner described the beginnings of his own career: "When I came to work we had all these dumb rules. You were always supposed to wear a hat, for example. I wasn't supposed to go out on State Street without my hat. That's crap, and I knew it then, but that was the rule. There was one point in time, a long time ago when the associates all wore little white coats, kind of reminded me of the clerks in the counting houses of Dickens." Another lawyer described the atmosphere in this firm as "byzantine." It is no coincidence that in the patriarchal firm associates perceive the route to advancement to require the sponsorship of an individual mentor rather than broad exposure to a substantial number of partners. Significantly, the patriarchal firm agreed to participate in this study because of perceived employee disgruntlement: "We want to find out why everyone is mad at us," said one very influential partner.

In contrast to such a traditional firm stands the collegium: the large law practice in which policy-making and administrative duties, more or less systematized, are widely shared among the partners but not the associates. Typically, the collegium arises when the founding or dominating partner of a traditional law firm retires, leaving no one of sufficient will or energy to control the partnership. The partners in a collegial law firm are therefore often younger than those in a patriarchal firm, the atmosphere is more informal, and advancement for associates is perceived to be the result of broad exposure within the firm rather than individual sponsorship. Firm administration is frequently somewhat haphazard, with every partner having his say and no one clearly designated to implement decisions. "We recreate the wheel too many times," says one member of such a collegium. "That's one clear weakness. There's not enough integration of thoughts and ideas and processes which would benefit others." Or, in the words of an executive committee partner: "There's a constant statement of the need to get organized. Constant statement of the need, and a constant resistive chaos."

Different as they may be in tone, however, the more autocratic and the more participatory law firms share a market niche. Their clients are institutionalized: they have brought their legal work to these firms for many generations and are unlikely to switch allegiances because of personnel changes in either the law office or the corporation. Established firms in Boston, said one lawyer, "represent Harvard, the Mass General [Hospital] and the estates of the Pilgrims who died three hundred years ago."

The established firms cannot rest on their laurels, however. Increasingly, they are being challenged by newer, entrepreneurial firms—partnerships in which personal relationships remain the chief connection between lawyers and their corporate clients. "If I leave here tonight and get hit by a truck, are my clients going to stay?" asks one partner at an entrepreneurial firm. And, if they stay, he adds, will they bring all of their multifaceted legal business to the entrepreneurial firm or only those matters that fall within the competence of the partner who is their contact person? Recently, Robert Nelson (1981) distinguished among the various roles lawyers play within the law firm, identifying "finders," "minders," and "grinders." The finders are the rainmakers, the client getters; minders to the administrative work of the firm; grinders, as the name suggests, are the associates who do the research work that involves little client contact and has the least glamour. The entrepreneurial firm, then, is the firm in which the finder is still king.

Two of the five law firms in this study are entrepreneurial in character, although they respond to their market position differently: one with a very heavy emphasis on competitive, up-to-the-minute technology, the other with an aggressive marketing and business stance. The more technocratic firm prides itself, for example, on having not only the standard office technology (a computerized case retrieval system, word processors, printers) but also computers compatible with those of its major clients, thereby drastically reducing the need for messenger services.

The other entrepreneurial firm is dominated by a business spirit in two senses. In relation to clients, it has a reputation for doing business that others might shun. One partner recalls:

> We have one fairly senior partner who was heard to say, "We're all whores. We work for whoever will pay us." And I said, "I disagree with you. I will agree we are hired guns, but we choose who we want to work for." Difference, big difference. If someone walked through the door today and said, "I've gotten the rights [to] put up a high rise [on the waterfront] and I want you to represent me," I'd look at that and say, "That's $100,000 in legal fees. Fine, I'll be an advocate." Would I say, "No, that's not good for Boston"? The answer is, he'll go upstairs, or downstairs, or someplace else and they'll do it. That's the hired gun concept. I have to make the decision whether it's going to happen, and maybe I can be a good influence.

The hustling, "bottom-line" attitude of this firm is also reflected in its internal affairs. It is here that the partnership is seriously considering a corporate management structure that would delegate all administrative chores to a management team and would reduce the partners to the status of stockholders.

Despite the fact that the large Wall Street-type law firms of the New England area differ among themselves in history and tone, their similarities far outweigh their differences. They exist in essentially the same economic environment, providing counsel to big business and fearing the development of the corporation's in-house law department. To meet this challenge, individual law firms offer increasingly specialized legal services.[5] They buttress their claim to expertise by recruiting the top graduates of the best law schools,[6] by having a prestigious downtown address, and by acquiring the latest in computer equipment. The decor varies from ultramodern chrome and smoked glass to Ye Olde New England antique, but in every case it proclaims Money. The internal structures of the firms are also similar. Administration is ordered by a series of committees and a system of ranks, each with distinctive obligations and privileges. The already specialized services of each firm are further subdivided internally by substantive areas of the law. The structure of the law firm thus has evolved into a complex web of departments, committees, and ranks.

The single most significant distinction is that of rank. Partners own the firm and therefore divide its considerable profits at the end of the year. Associates, who do not share in the profits of the firm, are its employees, working for a generous but nevertheless fixed salary. At the time this study began, new associates fresh from law school were earning annual salaries of approximately $35,000, and associates just before partnership about twice that amount. Partners are sometimes differentiated into junior and senior levels, as in three of the firms reported in the present study. Senior partners make capital contributions to the firm and decide among themselves how its profits are to be apportioned. Junior partners share in the firm's profits, but they have no voice in devising the formula by which profit sharing is accomplished.[7] In most other matters, the distinction between junior and senior partners is insignificant.

Firms with a junior partner rank consider associates for junior partnership after five or six years and for full partnership three to five years later. Firms with only one class of partners admit associates to

<hr />

5. This trend toward increasing specialization is nationwide in scope. See, e.g., Springfield Morning Union, 1983.

6. Nelson (1983) maintains that Chicago area law firms recently have broadened their definition of acceptable law school credentials for new associates.

7. For a detailed account of the economics of the Boston law firm, see Higgins, 1985.

partnership after seven to ten years of service to the firm. In all firms, the timetable for full partnership is similar: after a decade, attorneys expect to be full and permanent members of the partnership. Under the current system, then, salaried employment (associateship) is a temporary status designed to lead into either partnership (owner-ship) or exit from the firm. The possibility of a partnership secures the associate's loyalty, although the probability of being made part-ner, discussed below, is almost certainly declining.

Firms vary somewhat in their treatment of associates. Two have a policy of formal rotation. New associates work in a number of differ-ent departments during their first two years before a final assignment is made. A third firm has no formal rotation but treats all its first–and second–year associates as a pool of talent to be assigned to any department as fluctuating work loads require. A fourth organiza-tion rotates the summer associates, many of whom later become its newest recruits. The remaining partnership has no formal rotation provision; incoming associates are assigned directly to the depart-ments in which they are tentatively expected to remain. However, this firm is relatively tolerant of requests by associatets to change their assignments during their first two years. In short, whatever their formal rotation policies, all firms recognize that new associates present distinctive administrative problems. They need both close supervision and varied assignments to develop their talents and in-terests. The more senior the associates, the more like junior partners they should be, and the less supervision they should need.

Seniority, of course, is closely linked to substantive competence, which in turn is won through specialization—concretized by the di-vision of the law firm into subject area departments. Every firm dis-tinguishes litigation from business law and, within the business field, further distinguishes highly specialized fields such as tax law from a more general business practice. Some firms also provide services such as domestic relations and estate planning for their clients. Oth-ers do not. Some firms define department specialties narrowly, oth-ers broadly. Some cluster related departments into groups or sec-tions; others have only departments. In all cases, however, the large law firm rewards the specialist. Generalists are tolerated only among the newest associates who have not yet picked a specialty or among the most senior partners who function as rainmakers rather than as working lawyers.

Two lawyers' comments reflect the pressure to specialize. A junior partner insists that, despite pressures from senior partners, he continues to be "the last person that does it all." He adds that in comparison with the job of a small-town lawyer his work is "incredibly specialized, [but] for this sort of environment, I'm diversified . . . I do commercial leasing, bank loans, securities work, and bankruptcy." A second-year associate is less able to resist the pressure to specialize, in spite of the fact that his mentor is one of the last old-school generalists: "I started out in more than one area. I started out working for a man who himself is in the litigation department and the business department, he's in the estate planning department, he also does labor work, he does everything. That's basically what I wanted to do when I came." But, he adds, "I knew when I started that after a year and a half, two years, not too much longer than that, I would be encouraged, or forced, to specialize. What I'd hoped when I started is that I would have liked something, one thing, more, enough, to the exclusion of others . . . but that hasn't happened." Wistfully, he concludes, "If someone wants to be more of a general practitioner, well, maybe, working in a firm such as this may not be the place for them."

Whereas the substantive work of the firm is structured in departments, the administrative work of the firm is performed by committees. The broadest parameters of policy are decided in partnership meetings held annually, semiannually, or quarterly. Usually the partnership as a whole decides such questions as areas of substantive coverage, management systems, and firm size and shape (for example, whether or not to establish branch offices or seek mergers). In its deliberations, the partnership is guided by reports prepared by the executive committee, which in turn implements the partnership decisions. The executive committee, consisting of five to ten senior partners, meets monthly or weekly. Its members are almost always the principal money-makers and consequently those who are more equal than others in formulating policy. Much of the day-to-day administration is delegated by the executive committee to a managing partner, who may be assisted by several associate managing partners and a nonlawyer business manager. Each of the lawyers involved in administration also maintains an active professional practice.

In addition to the executive committee there is a compensation committee, which allocates to partners their share of the firm's profits. Positions on these two most significant committees are reserved exclusively for partners. A myriad of other committees—to oversee office space, library development, associate relations, and so on—may be staffed by both partners and associates. Recruitment and interviewing committees consistently rely on the contributions of associates.

Although all firms are similar in their committee structure, they differ in the locus of real power. In the traditional firms, patriarchs may reserve the dominant positions on the executive committee for themselves and their allies. The more collegial firms often insist on short terms of office and forbid successive terms on key committees, thus spreading participation in firm governance widely among the partners. In some cases, the executive committee runs the firm. In others, the span of the executive committee's control is limited by the policy-making function of the partnership above it and the daily administrative activities of the managing partner below it.

Partners, of course, are aware of the costs of doing their own administrative work. But, unlike New York organizations, the New England regional partnerships have resisted the complete separation of administration from professional practice. Their thinking is summed up by the comment "From time to time we wonder whether we shouldn't get one [an office manager], but we've always come back to the theory [that] you really have to be in the trenches to a considerable extent to really know what the choices are." Another executive committee partner sounds a somewhat more jaundiced note: "Lawyers are very egocentric people," he explains. "Everybody who's a partner in this firm and, I think, in the city thinks he's absolutely top-flight and thinks that he can do it better than anybody else, and aren't you foolish for not wanting me to participate in the decision-making process. That's because if I don't help you, you'll make a terrible mistake."

The lawyers' insistence on maintaining control over their own firms produces varying results: disgruntled subordination, amiable chaos, bureaucratic systematization. Nowhere, however, has it produced outright revolt among associates.

PARTNERS AND ASSOCIATES: THE SORCERER'S APPRENTICE

For the most part, the law firm secures the loyalty of associates with the simplest of incentives — monetary reward. Generous salaries are made possible by enormous profits. These profits, however, do not simply flow into the firm's coffers. They must be secured by careful attention to all aspects of the productive process: recruitment, training, evaluation, formal and informal incentives. In effect, partners have evolved a highly effective series of technical and social controls to shape the behavior of associates and, ultimately, of individual partners as well. Although they do not explicitly invoke the vocabulary of social control, the partner's accounts that follow clearly show how such control is achieved.

Concern for productivity begins with the recruitment of people who have been preprogrammed to work hard and to compete with one another for the rewards that management offers. One young associate explains: "You're dealing with a group of people that are highly, highly motivated. If you take the young associates, you are looking at a collection of people who, every one of them, graduated summa cum laude, they've been valedictorian in every class they've ever been in, and they are by nature competitive people. People compete because they're used to competing." The firm does everything to encourage these proclivities, to reinforce the pattern of a self-generated need to work hard. "You take an aggressive young lawyer," comments a particularly astute managing partner, "and you say to him, 'You work hard for us and you'll make a lot of money and you'll be successful and you'll get a lot of respect from your colleagues.' And then, he starts doing that because he wants to get to that goal. Pretty soon, he gets so that it becomes a way of life for him."

The firm also structures its activities so that habits of hard work acquired elsewhere are reinforced by the incentive system in the workplace. For associates, the principal goal of work is admission to partnership. "No one works hard here for the money, for the difference of what you'd get if you didn't work hard and what you get if you do. The reason you work hard is you want to be a partner. And the only way you're going to be a partner is if you work hard and you work well." Is the hope of a favorable partnership decision half a decade or more away really enough to motivate people on a daily basis? "I think it is," adds the same associate. "It doesn't sound like it ought to be, but I think it is."

For partners, the incentives to keep working are largely financial. "We have no involuntary servitude," says one senior partner. But the basis for profit sharing is known to all partners. Though it is less forthrightly expressed in Boston, it does not depart much from the Houston standard: "You eat only what you kill" (Aric Press et al., 1984, p. 66).

Nevertheless, the firm needs a number of chores performed and so must reward a variety of talents. For example, one firm has a system that designates a partner as "client attorney" for each of the office's clients. Every time a client brings a piece of work to the law office, the client attorney is given an origination credit for the project, even if he or she does no work on it. The attorney who actually does the work is designated as the matter attorney and is given credit both for his or her own work, such as negotiating, and for supervising associates who do the project's support work, such as research and drafting. At the end of the year, when profits are apportioned among the partners, the firm's interest in productivity is expressed by awarding about 60 percent of the partner's profit share on the basis of the sheer number of hours he or she billed. An additional 15 percent each is awarded for the partner's contributions in the roles of matter and client attorney.[8] Thus, partners are rewarded primarily for their own work but also for coordinating and supervising the work of others.

8. The remaining 10 percent of the profit formula is used to take into account such "intangibles" as extraordinary contributions or hardships.

Such a system produces certain tensions. For example, in the more entrepreneurial firms, the profit share apportioned to the client attorney serves as an incentive to the aggressive pursuit of clients. In the more established firms, the designation of a client attorney for clients of long standing may become a source of friction between younger and older attorneys, as older attorneys use their origination credits to maintain their incomes even as their billable hours diminish.

Whatever the tensions in the ranks, however, the law firm safeguards its interests in productivity throughout the career cycle. Associates work toward partnership; partners work toward a bigger profit share. Elderly partners are phased out with mandatory retirement plans. One of the entrepreneurial firms even goes so far as to rescind partnership from aging partners with flagging productivity.

But partners do not live by bread alone. The status that attaches to members of a prestigious law firm also provides an incentive to work hard—to promote oneself by promoting the firm. Few working lawyers are recognized outside their firms by their own individual contributions. Business lawyers' reputations, in large measure, derive from the reputation of their firms. A senior attorney who sits on the board of directors of a number of civic institutions explains his appointments. "These things never happen all by themselves. It's not just because you work at [a prestigious law firm] that you get into something. But it's usually not just because you're *you*, either, that it happens."

Nor are money, security, and status the only incentives that compel attorneys in large firms to work long hours. They also respond to the pressures generated by their clients. Inevitably, business clients pursue deals that have timetables and deadlines. "I've had the experience when I've had two deals that had to be done by Friday, and even if I stay here 'round the clock, I can only get to so much of each of these deals. You could work at this firm every night and every weekend and never run out of work" was the way one attorney described client pressure. "You can always stay another hour," adds another. "You're balancing the self-compulsions versus your burn-out point." "I sense that most people who are here work more than they would like to," concludes a third, "but there's a commitment to the needs [of] our clients."

One obvious solution to the problem of client pressure would be to take on more associates. But the partners reject this option as long as they can; they want to keep profits high and production costs low. Yet, while they know that they can count on associates to work as many hours as it takes to get the job done, the solution of overburdening associates has a point of diminishing returns. Besides, partners too are constrained by client demands. Ultimately they, not the associates, will satisfy or disappoint the client. Hence, when the pressures are great enough, partners cave in—they agree to do more hiring. Each of the firms participating in this study has done so on occasion to alleviate the crush of work.

But in these circumstances, new law school graduates may not represent the most desirable recruits. They do not know enough; they need too much supervision. All partners agree on this point: a novice creates almost as much work as he or she discharges.

This, then, is the situation in which the old Cravath edict against lateral hiring—recruiting already experienced attorneys who began their careers with other law firms—is set aside. Fully one-third of our respondents came to occupy their present positions through a process of lateral entry. Sometimes such transfers bring their clients with them to their new firm—the more experienced they are, the more likely this is to happen. Always they have already learned at least some of the ropes at someone else's expense. "What we want to hire, when we hire laterally," explains a senior partner, "is somebody whose supervisor at the firm swears to get even with me for hiring him away."

However, lateral recruitment also has some disadvantages. Transferees may cost less in supervision, but they also expect more than a beginner's salary. The new firm is not yet familiar with their strengths and weaknesses and so cannot use them to maximum effect. And the associates already in the firm become fearful as they see their promotion opportunities shifting in unanticipated ways.

In short, large law firms cannot grow easily. They are constrained in part by the partners' desire to hold down production costs and maintain high profit levels. But they are constrained also by the intrinsic difficulties of rapidly absorbing new lawyers of unknown capacities into an ongoing work load.

Moreover, careful recruitment, lavish material and status incentives, and the press of daily routines are not sufficient to secure good work. Even the most motivated workers must be taught how to do what both they and their bosses want them to do.[9] In every organization, newcomers must be shown the standard operating procedures, the local way of handling things. According to law firm partners, new lawyers face this problem in especially severe form because they need to unlearn many of their law school habits before they can begin to absorb their firm's way of doing law. One hiring partner says, "We hire fifteen people a year, all law review [editors], super academic performers. They come out and are confronted with the banalities, the peccadillos of clients in the 'real world.' It re-orders their priorities. In law school, you only need to raise issues and discuss them intelligently." And that stance of disinterested scrutiny, says another hiring partner, is precisely what will "drive a client up a wall. Because what a client wants you to be, first and foremost, is an advocate. He's in an adversary situation. And he wants you to represent him, and he wants to feel that you're just in his corner."

New lawyers must learn not only to be partisan but also to be economical. They cannot pursue the intellectual history and byways of a problem "for pure intellectual delight." They must remember that the practice of law is "first and foremost" a business. In that business they "must learn to get a deal done even if it isn't absolutely perfect. When you first come here you think you have to have every answer down to the last [detail.] You don't need that in the practice of law. You need to know a yes or no answer a lot of times, or you need to know only the parts of the law that apply to particular facts. You don't need to know everything." In short, the joys of legal prac-

9. The classical statement of the difficulties encountered by the well-intentioned recruit is provided in a study of medical students by Becker et al., 1961.

tice are "more concrete and discrete" than the joys of legal scholar-
ship. And, it would seem, the taste for the concrete and discrete pleasures of practice is an acquired taste.

In the law firm, the transformation of a promising law student
into an accomplished attorney is secured by emphasing skill development rather than work simplification. The heart of this process is the
ever more loosely structured supervision of an associate by a senior
partner—a strategy that firms describe as "mentoring." While skill
development includes training in the use of office routines and standard forms, there is little or no attempt in mentoring to simplify
work or to de-skill workers. Mentoring therefore is the opposite of
the many forms of technical control over industrial labor that seek
precisely these ends. On the contrary, successful mentorships produce autonomous craftsmen.

The process begins with an intensive period of supervision. As
associates enter the firm, they are assigned work on specific matters
by supervising senior partners. First assignments are typically in research, requiring work very similar to that already undertaken in law
school: the partner wants a memorandum on a particular point of
law or a particular fact situation. He outlines his problem and, in the
process, points the associate in the direction of an answer:

> When I assign a memo, I try to block out what I think is the right
> approach. To begin with I'll say, "Yesterday [a public utility] had
> this moratorium whereby it has refused to grant service to anybody
> who's not already a customer of the office." We had a lot of prob-
> lems in real estate with [the utility] taking this position that "they
> ain't gonna do nothin' for nobody." I had a two person team in here
> and I told them basically that I wanted them to be exactly sure of
> what their own [the utility's] regulations said, and how does this re-
> late them to the statute under which those regulations were promul-
> gated? I want to know whether they can, in fact, be as highhanded as
> they are. I give them all that. I don't sit there and do the research
> with them. My contact on an average situation will be that for every
> five hours of work a lawyer does in researching a statute and writing
> a memorandum and rewriting it, I will get the memorandum. I will
> make four corrections and I will comment with respect to the rele-
> vance of the client's problem, to the appearance of the memo-

randum, to the innuendoes that might arise from it, and my own thoughts as to how to do it better.

Inevitably, of course, a certain number of mistakes will be made by younger attorneys. But even mistakes have their uses: they become opportunities for further teaching. Thus, one partner reports:

> The way I handle mistakes is to talk to the lawyer, to discuss how the mistake may have been avoided or might be corrected. [I] really look at it as a learning experience. If the mistake is made another time then I might note that to myself. You shouldn't be making the same mistake twice, but anybody can make mistakes. You also try and find the source of the mistake. Is it that someone is not alert? Was it not a definitive enough assignment? Did four or five things happen that one day and they were trying to do their best on all of them and just couldn't do it? Really, there are an awful lot of reasons behind mistakes. I think you owe it to someone professionally to talk to them about mistakes. They should be able to understand it themselves and figure out what happened there, so that it doesn't happen again.

Eventually, the associate will be producing satisfactory memoranda and will then go on to other tasks. A senior associate recalls his first rotation assignment:

> I was assigned to a very senior partner here and I was basically his boy for that six months. And I carried his bags and I followed him around and I went to all of his meetings with him and I did a lot of his work. And he was very good about it. He took his training job very seriously. At first he had me doing some very minor inconsequential things, sort of useful, but he certainly could have gotten by without having [them] done. Then if he was satisfied with that, he expanded what I did, and he expanded it and expanded it, and eventually he basically gave me a couple of matters to just handle on my own and he was just available for supervision on those. It was very exciting, of course. I sort of had my own clients then to deal with, but it was a very gradual process.

The pace at which this apprenticeship progresses is largely controlled by the mentor, as one of them points out:

> If we do anything we overdelegate. We push a person beyond their capacity and let them come up to it, rather than the other way

around. The speed with which that person comes along is in many respects a direct result of how you delegate and how they're supervised. You have to let the associate feel the buck ends with him, it's his client, his case and he's going to rise and fall with it. It's time consuming. It's a hell of a lot easier to just do it yourself than to teach somebody. So you have to swallow right then, make the time commitment up front. Otherwise you're not going to have time for anything else in your life.

At the end of a successful apprenticeship, the mentor has developed a reliable colleague. "Depending upon my confidence and the level of familiarity with the lawyer I give the job to, I might send somebody a four inch file with a memo, only half in jest, [which] says, 'Please do the necessary.'" Associates, in turn, have developed sponsors who know their work and will speak on their behalf. The better associates have also begun to make their way into broader exposure within the firm by virtue of the approval of their individual mentors. "People talk about the new people in town, the new kids on the block. How are they doing? Around this time of year [December], I think those questions start getting asked. There'll be general chats and someone will say, 'Geez, X is just doing a terrific job for me on these five matters.' Well, that word gets around and suddenly people are knocking on your door and its because they've heard you're good; they want you on their project."

Once associates have passed through the apprenticeship stage, supervision is converted into consultation. Associates begin to work with increased autonomy. First they are encouraged to handle small matters on their own. Soon associates may even be allowed their own less important clients. Then they join in the recruitment activities of the firm and in the training of younger associates. Eventually, they become members of the teams handling the largest and most sophisticated deals and cases in the office. When this happens in an orderly progression, associates can expect to be made partners.

The autonomy of a partner, of course, is greater than that of an associate. As long as partners continue to bring money into the firm, they enjoy enormous freedom in almost all aspects of work: client selection, case staffing, scheduling, billing, travel, continuing legal education.

Client selection usually poses no problem: by joining the law firm, both partners and associates signal their willingness to serve the interests of big business. Thereafter, the principal issue at stake in client selection is the avoidance of conflict of interest. In the rare instances where philosophical or ideological issues alienate specific attorneys from particular clients, the firm allows individuals to decline assignments so long as the work remains within the office. Among the 33 law firm attorneys interviewed, one had once declined to work for a weapons manufacturer, and another, who was married to a kindergarten teacher, refused to represent a school board engaged in massive teacher layoffs. More typical by far, however, is the attorney who never raises such issues "because once you step down that road, once you eliminate people who own real estate and people who manufacture anything but toys, you don't have much left. You can't have banks because banks make loans to all kinds of godawful people."

A more common scenario for losing a client is one in which the client persistently engages in activities that seem highly dubious or overtly illegal to the law firm. This loss is hardly ever occasioned by lawyers' assuming the role of the corporate conscience. On the contrary, partners and associates regard most of their clients' projects as "doable, one way or another." Nor do business clients appear to fear whistle-blowing on the part of law firm attorneys, for the obligation to report client wrongdoing falls far more heavily on the corporate in-house lawyer (discussed in chapter 3). Rather, it seems that lawyers and clients part company when clients find their lawyer's strictures too cautious and decide to seek more accommodating advice.

Frequently, attorneys are forced to decline work because of the inability of their firm to staff a case or to cover a particular specialty. Not all firms, for example, do labor or bankruptcy work. And one firm has an explicit policy of maintaining a diverse client base: no client should be allowed to generate more than 5 percent of the firm's revenues lest the firm be "captured" by a client.

Firms vary, too, in their interpretation of conflict of interest problems, just as they do in their view of client conduct. Some firms allow partners to proceed in a conflict situation as long as full disclosure has been made. Others hold themselves to a "Calpurnian" standard: like Caesar's wife, they wish to be above reproach and so will withdraw from situations in which there is even the appearance of a conflict. Here again, ethical concerns are linked to pragmatic business concerns. Particularly in litigation, firms may reject one type of client to maintain their standing with another. "You know, you're interpreting statutes and regulations in cases. And you're trying often to argue for one way of interpreting it, or one particular emphasis. And you don't want to be establishing a precedent and then turning around to try to argue the other way."

On all these issues of firm-client relations, partners are the final arbiters. They interpret policy as it applies to their individual situations and accept or reject clients almost at will. Once a client, or a particular case or matter, has been accepted, the partner managing the work is also free to staff the project as he or she sees fit, subject only to the availability of individual associates. This autonomy extends to fee setting, for the partner in charge is free to bill for the firm's time at exactly the number of hours logged; at a discount if a young associate was trained on the project or if an error was made; or at a premium if the client concluded a very lucrative transaction or if extraordinary efforts ("all night at the printer's") were required.

Furthermore, partners enjoy autonomy in many other areas less directly related to their productivity. They are free, so long as they are available to clients, to work in the office or at home, during business hours or at all hours of the night and weekend. Short of riotous living, they will be reimbursed for any reasonable work, travel, or continuing educational expense.

Law firm attorneys thus enjoy a great deal of latitude in arranging their work. To assist them in this enterprise, they have developed routines and forms called "boilerplate," which standardize some aspects of their written work. Each law firm in this study has developed an elaborate menu of forms and documents that attorneys consult to organize deals and business matters. There are "bibles" that contain all the documentation associated with particular deals, banks of briefs and pleadings for litigators, and drafts of "opinion letters" for business lawyers. There are standard forms available through word processing for buyer-seller agreements, for corporate minutes, for condominium conversions, and for estate plans. "We never do anything from scratch" is the universal consensus. Every deal starts with a form and is modified by negotiations between the parties, by changes in regulatory and reporting requirements, and by the idiosyncratic drafting practices of individual attorneys.

The essential point to remember in assessing the impact of boilerplate is the guild-like quality of life in the law firm and the craft character of its product. Like mentoring, the use of boilerplate is carefully harnessed to the development of skills, not to their destruction. Indeed, associates tend to be more enthusiastic about the labor-saving potential, the shortcut quality of boilerplate than the partners are. An executive committee partner relates:

> The tendency you observe, which I deplore, you give something to a young associate and the next thing you know, you hear him inquiring all over "Do you have a precedent to this?" I don't want him to find a precedent. I want him to do it, even if he does it poorly than just to take a crutch from somebody without knowing what it means. Every word means something, it's there for a purpose. Use of precedent is not bad per se, but not as a substitute for knowing what you are doing. You can always test what's going on if you've got a fairly complex document by picking out some particular sentence and you say, "What's the background of this? Why did you say that?" You have to remember, by and large, the form books are bad forms because they are forms that have been just good enough to withstand court challenge. Most of the forms in the form book, you will find, cite a case: "This form has been upheld in this case." It should never have been in court at all if it had been properly drafted in the first instance.

In constrast to this attitude, a young attorney enthuses: "I can imagine coming in and saying, 'Here is the form file, it's going to be your best friend. You would be well advised to have a look in here every time you need to draft a document.'"

At first glance, it seems strange that senior partners, who look to the firm for profit, are less enthusiastic about a labor-saving device than are younger men and women on fixed salaries. This apparent inconsistency is resolved, however, when one considers the structural position of associates and partners in the firm. Associates normally have only one desire: to make partner. To this end, they welcome anything that enhances their efficiency. Partners, on the other hand, face not only inward toward the staff and the firm but also outward toward the market in which the firm offers its services to clients. Frequently senior partners explain their market philosophy, the position of their firm, with an analogy. Their work, they say, is like the work of a fine custom tailor: highly individualized and with exquisite fit to a particular situation. Custom tailoring may, indeed, be only a tiny percentage of the garment trade, but it is a highly lucrative niche for those who occupy it successfully. And so, while senior partners are concerned with efficiency and with cost containment, they are also concerned with developing a labor force skilled enough to supply custom-crafted services. Hence their somewhat cautious enthusiasm for boilerplate and their lack of ambition to control their subordinates through technical devices that standardize work.

If the partners' concern for custom-made services leads them to lavish attention and resources on the training of associates, the same cannot be said for their treatment of support staff. In general, support staff are paid the lowest possible salaries and given only the least interesting tasks. Paralegals are used for file maintenance and documents work; for example, they compile the bible after a deal is complete. Almost universally, attorneys in the regional law firm admit that they do not use paralegals extensively or well. Of secretaries they say: "She's terrific but she's not paid enough and we lose secretaries for the sake of $5 or $10 a week. That's absolutely insane. There's such a disruption when you lose a secretary. We can lose damn near that person's salary in billing time by just not having a good secretary." And another adds: "The firm encourages secretaries [to form personal attachments to their bosses] because it's a substitute for pay. You give somebody status and you don't have to give them that much money."

Apparently the support staff are not impressed with the trade-off of status for money because they have begun to organize unions to express their grievances over pay, promotion, job security, and due process issues. Paul Hoffman (1982, pp. 336–337) chronicles the spread of unionization among law firm staffs. At present, the unionization movement is still being heavily contested and, in the large firms at least, has been limited to the the nonprofessional staff. (This same limitation does not apply, however, in other settings that employ attorneys. Legal Services offices, discussed in chapter 5, are unionized in both the professional and nonprofessional ranks.) In opposing unionization, management not only issues legal challenges but also attempts to coopt the union initiative with wage increases. Hence the winning issues for nonprofessional unions in law firms have become due process issues, with unions pressing management for such reforms as formalized promotion rules, job postings, and established and publicized grievance procedures. Suffice it to say here that unionization drives are no longer unknown among the support staffs of the regional law firms. And, if the fate of unionization efforts in such firms parallels the history of unions in the New York law firms, it seems likely that they will serve as a further incentive to systematize firm management.

At present, firm management is bureaucratic in the folk sense of that term. It is impersonal and cumbersome; committees exist where once people discussed policy matters over lunch; senior members of the firm no longer know all the junior people; lawyers are increasingly specialized in their work. Nonetheless, law firms are not fully bureaucratized in the sociological sense of that word: that is, the hierarchies within them to not order the entire life of the firm, and the rules do not seek to specify systematically all aspects of behavior. Indeed, some lawyers, in lamenting the confusion of the firm and the lack of consistent attention to administrative matters, complain that their firm is not bureaucratic enough.

Whatever their administrative style, all law firms have some rules that order the essentials of work. Every office, for example, has a clearly established procedure for screening incoming cases for conflict of interest with already established cases. Likewise, every firm has a process for reviewing documents, such as opinion letters that

commit the firm as a whole to a position it may later be called upon
to defend.

Yet many of the formal rules arise not strictly from the professional side of the practice but from the need to rationalize the business aspects of firm operations and to safeguard the partners' financial interests. First among these imperatives is the rule to keep track
of one's time. Ideally, every minute attorneys spend working on firm
business, in the office or away from their desks, should be billed to
an account—either to the client's account, when the attorney is engaged on the client's business, or to the office account, when he or
she is working for the firm itself on administrative matters.

Firms generally ask attorneys to keep records of their time in
15-minute segments, and some are contemplating a time diary arranged in 6-minute intervals. When attorneys are dilatory about this
chore, they become diary delinquents, and firms devise various penalties to enforce record keeping. One firm compiles and circulates a
diary delinquency list of lawyers who are three weeks or more behind in their record keeping in the hope of embarrassing them into
compliance. Another withholds pay from associates and even partners who are more than a week behind in their diaries. One new
partner explains that late billing "is really very unfair to people who
do bill, because they get in the money and then the partnership has
to borrow and pay 20 percent interest rates to cover bills that haven't
come in from others. If you've got three or four partners who don't
bill then basically the partnership is carrying them and it's coming
out of everyone's hide." In any given year, adds another partner, the
firm's inventory of uncollected bills may run into millions of dollars;
therefore each attorney, whether partner or associate, must do everything possible to shorten the elapsed time between doing work and
the firm's being paid for it.

Time diaries are kept for the purposes of billing the client and accounting for administrative overhead. There are also rules in most
firms that direct associates toward the total number of hours they are
expected to work. For example, in three of the five firms in this
study, partners had decided that 1,700–1,800 hours of billable time
per year constitutes a satisfactory amount of work from associates,

with the understanding that time billable to clients will constitute about two-thirds of the total number of hours worked. This quota is usually made explicit in the interest of clarity, sometimes at the behest of associates themselves. Once the number is announced, however, many associates come to view it not as an average figure but as the miniumum acceptable performance, which they would do well to exceed. "For me, I sense a difference in my thinking," says an associate in response to a newly proclaimed 1,800-hour quota. "I've been keeping time sheets for six years. I've worked harder than that for the past several years without having a number to shoot at. That's not a problem. But having a tangible yearly goal concretely in mind, that's different. The number in the back of my head makes me start thinking quotas during the week and keeping up with myself so I can take a vacation. By stating the expectation, the minimum has been raised. Now, in order to [make a good impression] you've got to get above it."

By working the requisite number of hours and more and by keeping detailed records of the work they have done, associates compile a profile of their performance that they hope will favorably impress the partners. The latter, in turn, seek to systematize their impression of associates in an ongoing process of formal evaluation.

During the first two years that associates spend with the firm, they are evaluated twice yearly. The evaluation process begins with a work load report that new associates compile on a weekly basis. In these reports, the associates identify all the projects on which they have worked during the week. On the basis of the associates' accounts of their work, the evaluation committee identifies the partners who supervised them and solicits their opinions of the associates' work. The opinions are collated and finally transmitted back to the associates. But communication is not just a one-way process. An associate also has the opportunity to guide the development of his or her career. In discussing the semiannual evaluations, in filling out the weekly work load reports, and in dealing with mentors on a daily basis, the associate can identify areas of work to which he or she would like to be exposed.

At the end of two years, a more comprehensive review is often performed in which the evaluation committee interviews all the partners in depth about the performance of the entire second-year group. This evaluation is focused primarily on the following questions: Have the associates made an adequate transition from law student to lawyer? Can they identify the essential issues and separate relevant from irrelevant facts? Do they merely raise issues or can they come to conclusions?

With or without a formal review, most attrition seems to occur in the first two years. No one has precise figures on attrition by cohort, but partners in all five of the study's respondent firms estimate that about half of any entering class will become partners. Associates often concur in that estimate as a summary statement even when the anecdotes they recount about their own peers suggest a much higher attrition rate. It would seem that, whatever the real rate, the perceived rate of attrition is acceptable and relatively nonthreatening. This perception arises in part because many variants of leave-taking from the firm seem, in some sense, not to count as failure. Anyone who leaves in the first two years "just didn't work out." For those beyond the early trial period, this form of attrition is not a source of anxiety. People who leave because they prefer a less hectic or more intellectual life style also do not raise the specter of failure among the remaining associates, although the degree to which such "preference" for other work may be induced by unenthusiastic evaluations is not clear. What is clear is the regional law firms' adherence to the old Cravath standard that "nobody starves." Associates who are pressed to leave the firm are helped to find other jobs. In all the interviews, we heard of only one decision to withhold partnership after many years of service that was described as a "bloodbath."

After the second year, evaluations are done annually. At about the fifth year, another thorough review is conducted. In firms that have the junior partner rank, this review takes the form of candidacy for promotion to junior partner; in firms without such a rank, it constitutes a dress rehearsal for partnership. After five or six years, everyone agrees, there should be no surprises.

The general bottom line sense of the partnering process is that regional law firms, unlike most New York firms, still "hire only partners": that is, in principle they have no fixed size and will admit to partnership all who prove themselves qualified over the probationary period. There is as yet no sense that the New England partnerships have placed an upper limit on growth which would force an indefinite number of fifth-, sixth-, and seventh-year associates to compete for a fixed number of openings. Nor is there yet a sense that the regional firms are willing to reevaluate the old Cravath interdiction against keeping permanent associates.

However, the process by which associates make partner is changing. Firms are increasing the number of years required to become eligible for partnership review. Lateral transferees now wait for four years rather than three; new law school graduates wait eight or nine years rather than seven. In part, this occurs because, as the partnership expands, it takes longer for partners to know associates and for associates to know partners. In part, extending the probationary period is a relatively painless way to control explosive firm growth. But, most important, it enhances the firm's profitability, since associates are the partners' source of profit: "From a crass and selfish economic point of view, everybody's aware that you make money on associates. You pay them X dollars a year, obviously, and you bill some factor times X, and so you make money on them. It's called leverage," explains an executive committee partner.

One final comment is in order about possible changes in the partnering process. To date, all the rule changes being devised in the New England law firms favor the interests of the partnership by requiring more work from associates. But, however manipulative these rules appear to be, they are being instituted in the face of even more ominous developments in the trend-setting Wall Street firms. Recently, several New York firms have announced their willingness to countenance the previously unthinkable step of limiting the size of their partnerships. This freeze, in turn, is being used as the occasion to create a caste of "permanent associates"—a group of professional employees forever ineligible for partnership review (Lewin, 1984). The New England firms, smaller in size and more conservative in culture, are not yet in a position to introduce this innovation. Nevertheless, if traditional patterns hold, it is only a matter of time until

the permanent associate program makes its appearance in the regional law firms as well. The conditions that might lend themselves
to such a drastic step are discussed further below.

Suffice it to say here that in spite of (or, perhaps, in some measure, because of) all the formal rules that partners have devised, associates are anxious about their prospects. As in most human settings,
formal rules never fully prescribe or control behavior. Partners therefore are concerned not only to develop explicit guidelines but also to
manage the informal social life of the firm so as to enhance productivity. At present, most of the firms are quite social, not in the old-
fashioned sense of demanding that associates lead a particular kind of
private life, but in the sense of consistently financing after-hours,
Friday afternoon, and luncheon functions. Most of them also have
softball and basketball teams that play rival teams in a law firm
league. Are the teams sponsored deliberately to foster office loyalties? "I don't think so," replies a new partner. "I used to play some
softball," he continues. "It was a lot of fun and I enjoyed it, but I
don't think it was cementing any loyalty to [the firm]." But another
new partner says of his softball playing, "I think, really, the incentive
you get not to let so-and-so down is just from having worked or
played with so-and-so." An executive committee partner is even
more explicit: "We certainly use some [social incentives]. I think we
take some steps to make it a reasonably happy place to work. There's
a softball team. There are regularly, in here, departmental lunches.
That is, of course, pretty much professional, but, still, everybody's
eating together. There are some efforts at organizing parties in people's homes. The idea is to have [the host] get a smattering of people
at different age levels in that department."

Associates rely on the informal atmosphere of the firm to accomplish their ends as much as partners do. Specifically, associates find
that after the first few years the official evaluations become somewhat pro forma. Just when the partnering decision begins to loom
large, the official reports by which associates gauge their progress
become uninformative. Under these conditions, associates, like the
early Calvinists, begin to search for signs of their election and, as

with the early Calvinists, the signs are embedded in the fabric of daily life. "Repeat business," says one, is a good sign. "The partner's attitude toward whether or not we do the same deal again together later tells me something." In the repeat business, freedom from supervision is also a good sign. "Afterwards, if you have to do something like that again, you do it, send it out, [that's a vote of confidence]." Another big vote of confidence from the partners is the appointment of an associate to a firm committee. An associate one year before the partnership vote recounts: "The operations committee appointment was a significant appointment because it seems indicative of the fact that I'm perceived to be a comer."

Sometimes associates read the signs correctly, but at times they do not. For instance, in one of the established firms, an associate boasted of his progress: "I guess I'm a little unusual in that I'm generating a number of my own clients at the associate level. Frankly, I can't envision that being detrimental, keeping in mind that the partnership is a partnership organized for profit. The more business I bring in, it seems to me, the more I enhance the potential of the firm." In that very same firm, however, an executive committee partner commented: "You've got to start from the premise that this is a big law firm and has a really strong client base, and although one is always interested in new business, there is plenty of business here. A large part of growth comes not from the introduction of new clients but from the growth of existing clients. There's really no need for younger people to bring in clients. We let 'em bring it in if it's good for their ego, it makes them feel important because, by God, they've got their own clients, but I think it can be an impediment. If he just stuck to his knitting and attended to the good work already here, [the associate] would do better."

In the final analysis, however, associates gauge their success on the same scale that partners use: "The amount of one's bonus certainly can be taken as a signal of how you're doing and what people think of your past contribution." In the world of the large law firm, success equals money.

LAW FIRMS AND BUSINESS CLIENTS: THE LIMITS
TO GROWTH

Money is valued not only in its own right but also for its association with the other rewards of law firm life. In general, business lawyers feel that they can exercise their craft most satisfyingly on behalf of wealthy corporate clients. "Interestingly enough it's the size [of the deal]. Not because I have a real snobbery [that] everything has to be the size of a huge acquisition or heavyweight but simply, when you have a good sized deal, you can really get your teeth into it, spend a lot of time, go through ten drafts if that's what it takes. I can't afford to do a good job on a little deal. The clock is running. I tend to try to dash through it. I don't do a good job on that basis." In short, big clients command big resources.

Business people also tend to fascinate business lawyers who have no qualms about promoting their interests. "I like the corporate world," confides one attorney. "You're dealing with businessmen, bankers, lawyers. Let's face it, those are the guys who make the day-to-day world go round. They are capable, intelligent, basically interesting people." Association with business clients gives lawyers a mosaic-like picture of the financial life of the community: how a symphony orchestra relates to its members, under what conditions poured concrete loses viability, how municipalities organize bond issues, how shopping mall managers handle trade shows, how major companies reorganize under bankruptcy law, how publishers process manuscripts—the list is endless. So too is the challenge of combining the technical requirements of good law with its business features. "I suppose I enjoy in a pure technical sense, the drafting of a very, very complicated instrument, the correct use of language to express clearly and without ambiguity a very complex thought" shades into "I enjoy drafting to embody the intent of the parties."

Attorneys are pleased not only with the variety of business matters they handle but also with the diversity of their own skills. Says one:

One reason I like [real estate law] is that it really calls for a very wide variety of lawyering skills. You would expect a lawyer to be an advocate . . . which is true . . . where I often do public hearings before zoning boards, things of that nature. But in addition I'm also doing a lot of business negotiating, negotiating a transaction, a sales contract, a document of some kind. In addition, you have to write well. You're trying to draft something that is unambiguous and clear, so that 20 years from now, if someone picks up a deed or an easement or some other real estate document, they're going to know what it means so you don't create litigation by being unclear about something. Then there's also the analytical part of it, the conceptual analysis: analyzing a transaction, either from the technical real estate point of view of what documents are needed or from a straegic point of view, the political side of the practice. So, I like the variety.

And, in the end, there is the satisfaction of concluding the deal. "I guess I [particularly like] transactional type work like mergers, acquisitions, things that get to a closing where everything comes together and money is passed and the deal is made. Deal making—I like that."

While partners enjoy their work and their success, associates live in the hope of becoming partners. Everything else flows from that. If the firm makes its profits on associates, that is acceptable to those who are paying their dues because they expect someday to join in the profit-sharing system. If influence and standing in firm management accrue to the rainmakers, the finders, then that is as it should be since the management oversees the business rather than the professional aspects of the partnership. Associates, in sum, are much like apprentices and journeymen in the old guild system—they do not occupy the most comfortable positions, but they are making their way by a series of clearly demarcated steps through a structure whose basic legitimacy they endorse. And if they chose to enter this particular system in the first place, they are unlikely to encounter anything thereafter that would make them question its legitimacy. The practice is prestigious and lucrative. Clients provide the resources to do the work well. If, in the long run, the whole of the attorney's work is given over to "saving money for people who already have a lot of money," if they never in their work life encounter the issues that in their student days made them "pound their fists on the table and argue all night," they are apt to dismiss these earlier concerns as "youthful naiveté."

There are, of course, anxieties and pressures in the law firm. Just as associates must come to terms with the partners who are their employers, so too the partners must come to terms with the clients who retain their services. Partners, explains one, "come up to bat every day." There is no "golden retirement" in the practice of law, says another. In this environment, the partner's concern to maintain or enhance the firm's market position leads them to dominate associates and to woo clients. How manipulative is this courtship? The relationship of the law firm with its corporate clients is an interesting one on which to test the idea that "knowledge is power." Are lawyers able to redefine their clients' goals? Are they able to subvert plans of which they disapprove? Does their professional identity confer upon lawyers goals of their own that they might wish to substitute for the clients' purposes? If so, are they able to do so, overtly or covertly?

Some attorneys do, in fact, claim that they control their clients by virtue of their knowledge. "The sad fact is," says one, "I can essentially make it [a business decision] myself by presenting the choices in a sufficiently slanted way." Most lawyers, however, are somewhat more modest in assessing their impact. The client selects the goals, but the attorney demands some latitude in translating these goals into the technicalities of legal procedure. The strongest proponent of lawyer independence put it this way: "If someone came to you and said, 'Look, I have a big contract problem where I want to sue because I think that he broke this contract with me'—that's a layman's conclusion as to what his legal problem is. You get the facts from him and find out [that] what he really has is a major anti-trust problem with unfair and deceptive practice limitations, with violations of various franchise laws, with a whole host of other things that never occurred to him. An individual may come in and say, 'Look, I didn't get paid and I just want to sue, because I understand you can sue to get back wages by going to the state.' And you may find that he works in interstate commerce and he really has a Fair Labor Standards Act case, which means treble damages, attorneys' fees; it's an entirely different thing."

Several things are implied in such comments. First, the attorney, even in the more modest persona of diagnostician, does have a significant impact on the client's course of action. By virtue of the lawyer's definition of the problem, the client will be able to consider many more options and remedies than most lay people can devise on the basis of common sense reasoning.

Second, the elaboration of legal strategies works to the lawyer's benefit as well as to the client's. Antitrust suits, for example, certainly involve more work and hence higher fees than simple breach-of-contract suits. Lawyers, it seems, benefit from other people's troubles—not only in litigation but in business matters as well. Whether clients win or lose, the lawyer wins so long as clients pay their bills. Lawyers believe that they do well even when the economy as a whole falters.[10] "It doesn't matter what the economy is doing," says an associate; "lawyers win because people are always doing deals. They're just doing different kinds of deals, depending on the economy. When economic times are bad, maybe you don't do as many deals, but you do more bankruptcies. So lawyers can't lose." No wonder so many popular commentaries on the legal profession begin with Shakespeare's exhortation: "First we kill all the lawyers."

It is important to bear in mind, however, that even as lawyers advance their own interests, they seldom subvert the corporate client's goals. Typically, the lawyer's contribution to the conduct of business is the ability to stave off potential legal difficulties through good diagnostics and careful drafting. It may be that an exaggerated concern with uncertainty and ambiguity is an occupational hazard which follows from the exercise of the lawyer's craft. Lawyers themselves recognize that they occasionally impair their client's best interests by being too cautious. "I think that certainly a lot of things happen dif-

---

10. This is a widely held but seemingly incorrect perception. For a detailed account of the determinants of lawyer's incomes, see Pashigian, 1978. Pashigian argues that the financial well-being of lawyers is tied to general prosperity. However, his analysis deals with all lawyers as an aggregate and does not differentiate between business and individual service attorneys.

ferently because lawyers are involved. Sometimes lawyers tend to over-lawyer a transaction and I think that's a negative—what I identify as risk aversion." But, by and large, if lawyers know themselves to be risk-averse, they respect the risk-taking capacity of the entrepreneur. The lawyer cited earlier who feels that business executives are "intelligent, capable, basically interesting people" is not alone in his opinion. Another recounts:

> I can recall one situation where I was working with a client who was trying to get a big government-subsidized loan and he was really sort of a dumb guy—not an idiot, but he was not terribly bright. And, at one point, there were three or four of us sitting in the room, running up the clock at $400 an hour, and somebody said, "How come we're so smart and he's so rich?" And somebody else said, "You know why. It's because we don't have the kind of investment that he does." When that company was at a turning point, he signed his own name, he signed his wife's name, he had every asset they had tied up in that business. If it had gone down he would have been out searching for a job at an hourly wage. You know, that's a commitment we have never been asked to make.

Lawyers differ greatly in the extent to which they will let themselves be drawn into giving their clients business advice. Several lawyers with business training were not at all averse to doing so. Others insisted on having the client make the business decision while they confined themselves to legal counsel. But all agreed that the essential task of an attorney is to "think like a lawyer."

One lawyer elaborated:

> The thing that I'm trained to do, which may help in some of these situations, is to ask the flip-side question. I'll give you an example. This is what happens fairly frequently; it's kind of fun. You get two or three guys and they want to start a company. One of them, typically our client, has some dollars. Another one has some operational expertise and a third one maybe is the world's greatest salesman. And they want to form a corporation. Well, that's fine. How are we going to have stock ownership set up? Well, in thirds. OK. What is somebody dies? Well, they hadn't thought about that. What if someone wants to quit? They hadn't thought about that. Different criteria for different people too. The money man presumably is not going to contribute to the company anyway, other than his money. If

he dies, you might as well just let his wife or kids keep the stock in the company and the benefits. If the operational guy dies, you got to get the stock back, 'cause you're going to need it to give to the new operational guy. You're going to bring in different criteria for each of them, really. What are you going to do when you just get your high-speed printer on line and this guy, the salesman, decides he's going to go to work for [another company] and takes your customer list? They all say, "Oh, Joe would never do that." And I say, "Oh yeah? Well, what if he does?" So what you're doing is asking them the question about "What if it doesn't go the way you think its going to go?" And I think that's really specifically what business lawyers are trained to do. If you've ever seen a settlement agreement written by litigators, it's hysterical. It assumes that everything is going to happen. There's never any provision in it for what happens if the contingencies don't happen. Business lawyers, that's exactly what they want to know. That's what we're trained to do. I think in terms of analyzing social situations and business situations that probably carries over, that [habit of] always looking on the down side.

Prolonged and systematic contemplation of the down side is one of the lawyer's unique contributions to the conduct of business. It may have the intended effect of making business persons more orderly, more farsighted, more cautious. Or it may have the unintended effect of making them so hesitant as to be impotent. In either case, however, it does not change the locus of control in the lawyer-client relationship, for it is still the intent and interest of the client that define that bond. Moreover, the lawyer's role, after he or she has pointed out the hazards from which a client should seek protection, is to devise a way to attain the client's ends in spite of the difficulties. "The clients don't want to be told they can't do something. They want to be told how they *can* do it. Part of our job is to be ingenious," says an attorney of 40 years' experience. He tells clients, "It may be that you can't do *that*, but if you do it *this* way you may be able to come out at the same place. That's one of the lawyer's big jobs—supply imagination—because most things are doable one way or another."

It is also important to note that the lawyer's skill is only one element in determining whether or not clients attain their goals. More important is the client's command of financial resources. "What makes the world go 'round in our system is capital," says a senior partner. "The best deals I've negotiated are probably less attributable to my skills as a lawyer than [to] the strength of my client's bargaining position. Because there isn't anything [more] calculated to let you make that deal on your terms than your client's willingness to say, 'Hey, I can get up from this table and go home, I don't need the deal.' Lawyers probably will not be thrilled to hear this [but the outcome of a negotiation] doesn't reflect their expertise, it reflects the depth of their [client's] pocketbook."

The depth of the client's pocketbook is not only a significant factor in determining the outcome of litigation and negotiation, it is also a significant factor in structuring the lawyer-client relationship. The United States, as remarked earlier, graduates more lawyers every year than are needed in the entire economy of Japan (Bok, 1983, p. 41). To some degree, therefore, lawyers are selling their services in a buyer's market. They are in no position to challenge or subvert their clients' goals, even if they have a clear agenda that motivates them to do so. One attorney, formerly active on behalf of the Civil Liberties Union and in the Legal Services program, explained: "I think Legal Services people see an issue, want to represent that *issue*. On the other hand, when you're involved in this type of practice, you are a tool of your client. You're part of *his* team—you're there to advise the client, structure the deal, whatever, but you're still doing it within what his goals are." A client who has any question about his firm's loyalties replaces the firm. A firm that has any question about an associate's loyalties replaces the associate. "A firm like this hires half a dozen people, maybe eight or nine, a year. And that's out of 50 interviews, out of 1,500 submitted resumes." This, clearly, is not a climate in which attorneys are likely to substitute causes of their own choosing for the aims of their clients.

CONCLUSION: THE RULES OF THE GAME

The form and texture of life in the large law firm derive from its market position as counselor to big business. The law firm offers highly specialized, finely crafted advice. To do so it has marshaled a large professional work force, more than half of whom are employees. Thus, to the problems of maintaining a market for their own work, law firm partners have added the difficulties of managing the labor of others, often as highly skilled as themselves.

This they do mostly through financial and status incentives. Law firm associates earn the largest salaries of all lawyers in staff positions; they work in settings that are highly regarded by other lawyers; they bear none of the burdens of starting up a practice. Associates interpret the inevitable tensions and anxieties in their work as no more than "paying their dues." This they are eager to do because they identify with the partnership and wish only to join its ranks.

The job market is the mechanism that guarantees this kind of ideological kinship. Obviously, lawyers do not go to work for Wall Street-type firms if their primary professional goal is to protect Indian land claims, endangered species' breeding grounds, or the rights of workers to compensation from runaway factory owners. Lawyers who choose to work for large law firms may devote themselves to civic, religious, or charitable activities after hours, but they do not seriously challenge the preeminence of big business in American life. They are not bothered by the fact that big businesses devour small ones. They sometimes believe that they may be a moderating influence on corporate behavior, but that is not their major concern. Ultimately, they are comfortable with the position that everyone, corporations included, deserves representation and that their role in the division of labor is to aid business clients.

Financial and status incentives, however, are better guarantors of enthusiasm than of efficiency. Even highly motivated associates must learn how to accomplish effective work. To this end they look to the partnership for guidance. The partnership, in turn, reserves for itself the right to make all the rules that impinge on the associates. Partners determine which law schools provide acceptable credentials to potential recruits; they decide how hard associates are expected to work and how long they must expect to wait before being considered for partnership; they decide (under pressure from other firms) how well associates are to be paid; they decide how large the firm should be, what services it should offer, what clients it should court (or, more rarely, reject). In short, the partners maintain decisive power over every aspect of operations, and in so doing they turn the bureaucratic features of their environment deftly to their own advantage.

Associates may occasionally pressure the partnership to raise their salaries or to lower their demands or to be more explicit about their expectations, but they never challenge the partnership's basic prerogatives; they are great respecters of the rights of property. The net result of having associates voice their anxieties is to speed up the process of bureaucratization that partners have begun for their own reasons. The more associates push for the articulation of rules and the codification of standards, the more they contribute to standardizing administration. To the extent that the articulation and orderly application of rules replace the seemingly capricious demands of patriarchal partners, associates believe that they have gained more control over their work lives. Moreover, they are apt to feel that justice is served when even individual partners are subjected to the impersonal, automatically operating rules that have been developed to order firm affairs. Yet this semblance of impersonality is deceptive. An examination of the rules would show that, however cumbersome they may sometimes seem to partners, they serve the interests of the partnership far better than the interests of the associates.

Associates seem to be blinded to the manipulative quality of bureaucratic rule-making in part because the rules enshrine domination by fellow professionals rather than by business people, and in part because their daily experiences depend less upon the rules than upon their relationships with mentors and sponsors. Much of the actual labor of the law firm, as of any small office, is still accomplished through a system of teamwork in which older, more experienced persons (in this case, partners) supervise and train younger ones. In this respect, the law firm represents a modern variant of the old guild system, in which master craftsmen supervised and developed the skills of apprentices and journeymen. The law firm's commitment to developing the skills of its associates is, of course, a direct reflection of its basic market position. If its advice is to be sought by corporations, it must have a staff capable of crafting expert advice. Given the firm's ability to recruit loyal associates, its interests are better served by building up than by breaking down their skills.[11] And, by a circular process, the associate's sense of growing mastery cements his or her loyalties to the firm. The mentoring system thus preserves standards of professionalism in an otherwise increasingly bureaucratic environment.

If the law firm's reputation for custom-made legal advice helps to safeguard the skills and autonomy of its associates, other forces are at work to diminish them. For the first time in recent history, law firms are, in net terms, losing business to corporate in-house counsel (Lewin, 1983e).[12] Although the market for custom quality legal advice may not be shrinking in the aggregate, the law firms' portion of this market is declining. They are pushed in two directions by this trend. First, it puts them under tremendous pressure to keep costs down. Second, it accelerates their tendency to do increasingly specialized work.

The pressure for cost containment is reflected in a number of ways: in the firm's decision to increase the number of years that associates must work before they can be considered for partnership; in its insistence that individual billings be kept up to date; and, not least, in most firms' mandatory retirement rules and in one firm's decision to revoke partnership from individual partners who are not billing enough hours. All these decisions illustrate, too, the way in which even formalized rules can be used to the advantage of the partnership and the disadvantage of staff.

Specialization is another response to economic concerns. Because corporations are giving more and more of their legal work to their own in-house law departments, the law firm must offer increasingly specialized services to survive. The pressure is also reflected within the firm. Associates are urged to cut down on their rotations and to

---

11. On this point see Derber (1982, p. 201): "Where workers strongly identify with the firm or its goals, however, or are characterized by strong internal discipline, their continuing possession of technical knowledge and skill may serve management's interests more than it threatens them."

12. A less widely used but nonetheless stark threat to the law firm's business is posed by relatively inexpensive private mediation services (see Homer, 1984).

pick a permanent assignment quickly; partners are discouraged from handling all aspects of their client's work—in the name of efficiency, they are urged to call in colleagues from other departments when consultation is necessary.

In the past, specialization has been used largely to achieve greater efficiency. But it also has another, more alienating potential. Ultimately, New England law firms may choose to safeguard their profits, as the New York firms are doing, by limiting the size of the partnership. This innovation would require a substantial change in current practices. Specifically, it would mean the creation of a class of permanent associates: young men and women who would work for the firm without ever expecting to be considered for partnership. At present this is not done in New England, because the partnership relies on the loyalty of its associates and so cannot afford to disappoint the reasonable expectations of reasonable people. But were a group of associates to be assigned only highly routinized or minutely specialized work, the legitimacy of their claims to partnership would be diminished. Seen in this light, the trend in large firms toward increasing specialization takes on a threatening hue. And, indeed, the "senior attorney" and "corporate counsel" programs recently announced in the Wall Street firms confirm this very scenario: lawyers who have a narrow, highly specialized field of expertise are the very ones being shunted into the permanant associate programs (Lewin, 1984).[13]

The creation of a permanent associate program signifies the abandonment of a key guild-like feature of the law firm in favor of a corporate model. Currently the possibility of a partnership works in tandem with generous salaries, high status, and mentoring to make associates identify their interests with those of the firm. The permanent associate program does not threaten associates with poverty; it almost certainly will leave intact many of the benefits now available.

13. There is also evidence, as yet only anecdotal but still plausible, that law firms identify women as the typical permanent associate. During recruitment interviews partners steer female candidates toward permanent associate positions, touting their advantages for reconciling career and family demands. Gladys Topkis, private communication.

Perhaps it will even enable some men and women to achieve a better balance between work and family commitments than associates in the partnership track are able to do. Nevertheless, it does diminish the degree to which associates can realistically identify their interests with those of their employer.

For the moment, two other trends hold center stage. The first is a move to protect the interests of the firm by making its management more businesslike. The second is to keep a sharp eye on the activities of the corporate general counsel, whose experiences in a much more fully bureaucratized setting are the subject of the next chapter.

CHAPTER 3

COMPANY MEN THROUGH AND THROUGH
Corporate Staff Counsel

The principal competitor of the law firm, the in-house law department, is of relatively recent origin. In the early years of this century, corporations hardly ever included a group of attorneys among their administrative staff, and those rare lawyers who were in-house counselors answered directly to the business executives who retained them. The work that such attorneys did was universally regarded as routine, not to say boring, in quality. All the significant, challenging, and lucrative legal work of the corporation was conducted by an independent law firm.

In the past two decades, however, this division of labor between staff counsel and privately retained legal talent has undergone a dramatic change. Corporate legal staffs now constitute the most rapidly growing sector of the burgeoning legal profession (Businessweek, 1984, p. 66). One authority estimates that the number of staff attorneys has increased by 400 percent in the past 25 years (Gallucio, 1978, p. 169). Another reports that, currently, in-house law departments are growing twice as fast as law firms (Galanter, 1983, p. 167).[1] And a third commentator, extrapolating this trend into the future, remarks, only half-jokingly, that "by 1990, all corporate lawyers will work in-house—except for 80 holdouts who will be charging $5,500 an hour for their time (Lancaster, 1982).

---

1. Only a single writer has voiced the opposite opinion—that the growth in the corporate law department is already leveling off (see Lewin, 1983b).

Perhaps the single most significant spur to the growth of the in-house law department is the cost of privately retained legal counsel. In general, it is estimated that the cost of legal work done in-house is 35 to 50 percent less than the cost of comparable work referred out (Banks, 1983; Bernstein, 1978; Chayes et al., 1983). Nevertheless, the trend toward establishing in-house law departments is fueled by more than considerations of cost containment. It is also a response to pronounced changes in the legal and economic environment of the corporation.

In the legal sphere, increasing government regulation has changed the character of private business transactions. The board chairman of IC Industries says:

> Years ago, legal activity was remedial, not preventive; it was sporadic, not so continuous; less demanding as to deadlines, more controllable by counsel's ingenuity. Today the old kind of work is still there, but it doesn't predominate. The corporation lawyer is more likely to be relating to a federal, state or local government agency rather than a contesting private party. And his text is more likely to be a big book of agency regulations than the statutes, judicial decisions, or Rules of Practice. Thus most active companies now require—or are best served by—the constant availability of counsel who is informed on a day-to-day basis of the company's activities and directions. (American Business Lawyer, 1978, p. 827)

The chairman of Bell and Howell adds that if a corporation wants lawyers who know their business, it also wants officers to know their lawyers. "The law is rather frequently a matter of interpretation and judgment and you depend heavily upon knowing the quality . . . the cast of mind of the lawyer with which you are dealing (ibid., p. 818). To the extent that corporations want lawyers who are both knowledgeable and known, they want an in-house law department.

Changes in the legal context of business are matched by changes in the economic organization of the corporation. Increasingly among large businesses, corporate growth is accomplished by a process of vertical integration; a development that enables the corporation to absorb into a single administrative superstructure as many stages as possible in the production and distribution of its products. (For example, in the petroleum industry, vertical integration is described as extending "from the well-head to the pump.") Essentially, vertical integration is a flight from the market. It reduces the frequency with which the corporation is subjected to the disorderly and unpredictable relations of buyers and sellers; it substitutes for market relations the more calculable relation of parent corporation to subsidiary or headquarters to divisions. The development of in-house legal staffs is consistent with the general pattern of vertical integration—it is one more instance in which the corporation becomes an employer rather than a buyer of some element necessary to its production process, with all the enhanced control that such a move implies.

CORPORATE LAW DEPARTMENTS: FINANCE AND INDUSTRY

Corporations differ in their histories, and these differences are often reflected in the corporate law department. Some corporations grew directly by expanding their own operations; others grew through a merger and acquisition process, adding subsidiaries and product lines to achieve their present size. In general, large firms that have grown by the relatively simple process of expansion also have a unified, centralized law department housed in the corporate headquarters. Work within the law department in such corporations is often based on the development of substantive specialties, as it is in a large law firm. By contrast, corporations that have grown by a merger process tend to have divisionalized law departments. Attorneys are dispersed among the business divisions, and their work is structured by the business project served rather than by substantive fields of legal specialization. Thus, for example, a bank might have a law department divided into a real estate section, a tax section, and so forth, whereas the conglomerate would be more likely to assign staff attorneys to subsidiaries: the food products division, the home entertainment division, and so forth. In short, as one general counsel explains, "The law department that functions efficiently reflects the philosophies and the attitude of the company."

This restriction goes beyond the official structure of the law department to include organizational culture. Consistency of management style throughout the company prevents the grass from seeming greener in some department than in others. "If the rest of the company [had] management by delegation and management by objectives and I ran a bureaucratic, dictatorial, non-involved department, I would fail. I'd lose my people, because they interact with all these other people. And they're going to say, 'Hey, wait a minute, how come we're different?'" Similarly, business managers interpret the parallels between their own operations and the law department as indicating that the lawyers are part of the team, not intruders to be viewed with suspicion.

Corporate history determines not only the formal and informal structure of the law department but also its age. All five corporate law departments in this study number at least 30 staff attorneys, but they differ greatly in the recency of law department growth and, therefore, in the degree to which law department administration has been systematized.[2] In one setting, the expansion of the law department has been so recent that comprehensive evaluations of staff counsel are being conducted for the first time, and the results have not yet been tied to salary expectations. In another setting, a large number of attorneys have already reached the limits of their advancement within a well-defined corporate structure and are lamenting the fact that they are "burdened by the personnel department . . . structured in a job grade . . . under the strictures of personnel policies."

Perhaps the most significant differences among corporate law departments lie in the type of industry they serve: among the five firms hosting this study, two are financial service corporations (a bank and an insurance company), one is a manufacturer of consumer goods, another produces industrial goods, and the last is a mixed corporation serving both industrial and consumer markets. All but one of

2. The data on law department administration confirm the suggestion of Wright and Singelmann (1982) that the more experience an industry or corporation has with staff professionals, the more subordinated those professionals are likely to be.

these firms do a significant volume of business abroad. Each is confronted with considerable government regulation. The financial service corporations are regulated by the Securities and Exchange Commission and other government agencies as to the kinds of products they can offer the public and the structure of their internal financial practices. The manufacturing companies must comply with workplace safety standards. The consumer goods company must also establish the safety of its products for the public. The industrial companies sell a significant portion of their product directly to the government and are thus constrained by the demands of an extremely powerful and bureaucratic customer. And all the companies operating directly in the consumer market must satisfy Federal Trade Commission and Federal Communications Commission standards about their advertising claims and practices. In short, every corporation is confronted by a complex legal environment that provides many occasions for the use of lawyers. For staff attorneys, however, the financial service corporations offer a significant opportunity lacking in manufacturing companies. When the conduct of business requires scientific knowledge, lawyers' careers are limited to the confines of the general counsel's office; when business is based on financial rather than technical knowledge, lawyers often can look forward to business careers beyond the law department.

Yet while corporate law departments differ in economic base and history, they are remarkably similar in the structure of their internal operations. In each of the settings we have studied, the law department is a fully independent entity headed by a general counsel who is also an officer, usually a vice-president, of the corporation. Typically, the loyalties of the general counsel are to the company. "I always feel I have one hat, and this is: I am a corporate officer who is a lawyer" is the way one general counsel described the balance he maintains between business and professional commitments.

Because the development of corporate law departments is a relatively recent phenomenon, the philosophy, loyalties, and managerial style of the general counsel are extremely important in determining the quality of life in the department. Within their own domains, general counsel are often like patriarchal partners in the Cravath mold.

"What we have here," declares the general counsel of a mixed industrial corporation, "I call a benevolent dictatorship. Clearly a law department reflects the personality of the vice president or the general
counsel more so than a law firm." To the extent that general counsel
have near-dictatorial powers, committees and other vehicles for staff
participation have little importance in law department governance.

The general counsel unanimously agree that the mandate of the
law department is to facilitate the business person's tasks. They express this commitment with varying emphases, however. An aggressive young deputy general counsel of a financial services corporation
says the mission of his department is to "take business initiatives,
shake them, twist them, turn them around to see if you can make
them go forward without legal risks." The general counsel of an industrial firm puts it more circumspectly: "My standard of success is
that if the company can design, manufacture, sell, and service [the]
products it wants in the way it wants, without knowing the law department exists, then I've succeeded. It's just that simple." This difference in emphasis between the two men is more than idiosyncratic.
It reflects the nature of the lawyer-client relationship in different industries. In the manufacturing industries, lawyers perform a necessary but peripheral function, and accordingly they are forced to be
modest about about their own role. In financial service corporations,
lawyers play a more central role and can therefore be more aggressive in the exercise of their craft. "We create our own products, but
these products are legal contracts that have actuarial structure, so the
actuaries and the lawyers are an integral part of the creation of the
product and the sale of the product and the administration of the
product," explains the general counsel of another financial service
company.

The centrality of legal expertise to financial endeavors is significant for another reason as well. As we shall see in more detail below,
corporate lawyers face the distinctive problem of career ceilings (one
man described it as being "burdened by the personnel department"),
which limit the promotions and raises available to staff professionals.
In the financial service companies, lawyers often try to surmount this
career ceiling problem by transferring to the business side of the cor-

poration. This pattern, in which success rests on abandoning one's career rather than advancing within it, has previously existed only among engineers (Meiksins, 1985; Perucci and Gerstl, 1969). Now it seems to be emerging among corporate staff attorneys too. Perhaps the general counsels' insistence that they are corporate officers first and lawyers second should be seen as creating an atmosphere that facilitates this transition.

Beneath the general counsel in a large law department are a series of deputy of associate administrators. At the bottom of the professional pyramid are a number of staff attorneys distributed throughout the ranking system established by corporate personnel policies. The entire department is aided by a small support staff consisting of miscellaneous paralegals and one secretary for every two or three attorneys. The general counsel and his deputies are responsible for overseeing both the work within the department and the relationship of the department to its corporate host. Annual budgetary requests, for example, are transmitted from the general counsel to the corporation. Budget allocations—typically amounting to several million dollars per year—in turn are funneled through the general counsel to the department.

Routing the budgetary process through the general counsel is less a constraint than a source of autonomy for the corporate law department. It creates a situation in which attorneys are directly responsible to their superiors in the law department rather than to the executives they serve. Thus the law department is a self-contained entity for purposes of evaluation and reward even when its members are physically dispersed among divisions or subsidiaries of the company.

This arrangement is designed to protect not only the autonomy of the law department but, more important, the corporation's long-term interests in having its executives' business practices adequately monitored. As one lawyer puts it: "You work with people, you become close associates, you like them. And it becomes very difficult if they want to push into something that you feel they shouldn't and they do it anyway. What you're concerned about is working for the client in a direct sense and having your client totally in control of whether you have a job or don't have a job. The fear is that it will interfere with your ability to exercise independent legal judgments." Hence the preference for keeping the evaluation of house counsel within the confines of the law department.

Yet the insulation of the law department from business pressures can never be complete, because the law department as a whole exists exclusively at the pleasure of corporate management. It therefore faces an entirely different set of opportunities and constraints than does the independent law firm. The law firm must attract a multiplicity of clients, each of whom provides only a part of the firm's revenues. The law department has only one ultimate client. The law firm attracts its clients by offering a highly specialized, highly individualized legal service. By contrast, the law department's basic responsibility is to discharge the routine legal business of the corporation as economically as possible.

In general, the corporation views the expenses of the law department as part of overhead costs. Staff attorneys are quick to point out that their departments are not "profit centers." The tendency to view lawyers as a drain on the corporation's revenues is further exacerbated by two pieces of conventional wisdom. First, lawyers, whether inside or outside the corporation, are often viewed by business people as as deal killers. In this spirit, the law department is sometimes referred to snidely as the "Department of Profit Prevention." One staff attorney describes his client's frustration and his own:

> They may be good credit analysts and good business getters, maybe good customer relations guys, [but] when the customer says, "Here, I'll give you a mortgage on the house," to the businessman that means, "He's willing to give me additional security which I can rely on in the event the loans go bad." To the lawyer that means: What entity is going to give the mortgage? The guy or his corporation? What's it going to secure? What is the legal description of the property? What additional covenant do you want in the mortgage? Do you want a title examination? So, in other words, to get the security that's any good, you've got to know certain things. And he may say, "Well, Jesus . . . !"

In addition to the general suspicion that business people harbor about lawyers, corporate managers also view their staff attorneys as having an easy assignment. They have only a single client—the corporation—and that limits the size of their work load. Staff attorneys, too, cite this as one of the distinctive features of their work. A young woman compares her schedule to that of law firm associates: "The market dictates your time schedule. So I pull all-nighters periodically but the reasons why I don't do it all the time is that it is project-specific. I represent one issuer. It's a very active bank, but there's only so much one issuer can do in a twelve month period."

The conventional wisdom about the limited demands on the staff attorney's time is not entirely correct, however. True, each corporation conducts only a limited amount of business in any given time span, and some of this business does not require the participation of lawyers. Further, not all the legal work that is needed is performed by staff counsel. Outside firms are typically retained for litigation, for example. But, conversely, corporate officers finance a law department not simply to substitute less expensive legal services for more expensive ones. The staff attorney's position exists also so that business people can have the benefit of legal advice long before it would be economical to call in outside talent. Corporate staff attorneys pride themselves on doing preventive law by advising on the structure of a business deal as it evolves.

Firms differ in the degree of their insistence that staff lawyers be consulted early in the development of a business project. In one firm, the general counsel tells his staff: "There's no requirement in the company in the day-to-day operation of the business [for managers to] come to us. They don't have to." He warns his attorneys that they cannot rest on their professional laurels; they must establish their usefulness if they wish to be consulted. "You will not be respected [simply] for being a lawyer. You will be respected for being the person who performs a legal function." More commonly, however, firms require project managers to seek legal clearance routinely in almost all business matters. The real work of the general counsel's department is to review the legal implications of every deal in light of the environmental, product safety, SEC, labor, antitrust, and fair trade standards the government uses to scrutinize private economic activity. A typical account by a staff attorney specializing in contract review is: "All contracts have to have a legal review. Contracts and important documents have what's called the 'green sheet,' where the vice president in charge will sign, the legal person will sign, the procurement person will sign, so they make sure that everybody involved knows what's going on."

The lawyer's involvement in giving clearance to business deals that commit the corporation to a particular line of action shades by imperceptible degrees into availability as a sounding board for the business person's ideas before they evolve into specific proposals. Additionally, a business manager who is used to having a lawyer's ear for company business may also turn to that lawyer for personal advice. For example, one staff attorney recounts: "Oftentimes we do things like notarization. Some bosses send people down here, some guy, sitting at his desk, staring at the ceiling and not knowing what to do, because he signed up for a swimming pool last night at 12:00 with some salesman who showed up at his doorstep . . . so he's in a cold sweat, and he's no good to the company at all." Frequently the staff attorney is called upon to resolve such problems in the interest of retaining the goodwill and trust of managers. Given this expanded definition of the staff attorney's mandate, it is not entirely accurate to say that he or she has a limited, narrowly defined work load.

GENERAL COUNSEL AND THEIR STAFFS: PROFESSIONALS AS BUSINESS EXECUTIVES

In fact, the corporate law department's mission is complex: to provide legal commentary on developing business ventures, to transact all the routine legal business of the corporation, and to do as much of the corporation's more specialized legal work as circumstances permit. The law department does all this from the position of the poor cousin of the lawyer family. Both the relatively low status of the house counsel and the use of the law firm as a point of reference are reflected in the very offices of the law department. Among corporations that treat in-house lawyers particularly well—in this study, the two financial service companies—staff attorneys work in offices almost as lavish as those of law firm associates, with panoramic views of a harbor or a mountain valley or a bustling downtown scene, carpeted floors, and good quality prints on the walls. But these offices are also small, and quite a few of them have no doors to close against hovering supervisors, overanxious clients, and the noise of nearby office machines. In corporations that are less enamored of their law departments, many of the legal staff occupy back offices that have a view of a parking lot or no windows at all, tired office furnishings and equipment, and a generally harried atmosphere.

House counsel are acutely aware of their disparagement by other lawyers. One staff attorney describes his leaving a law firm to join a corporate staff. "Once we got through the initial interviews, the question for me was: could I bring myself to work for a corporation when all through law school that was second rate. And I knew the attitude of the lawyers I was working with, that generally in-house counsel are the bottom of the barrel. So it was a big stigma that I had to overcome." Another staff attorney admits that the "job doesn't really use half of [my] talents." But, he quickly appends, "I feel myself that that is true of most people."

The heads of corporate law departments are also aware of this problem. Despite their growing share of the law job market, virtually all of them have abandoned the attempt to recruit new law school graduates. Explains one general counsel:

> People who are in the higher part of the class are more oriented to go into firms and government and into the Justice Department or the Federal Trade Commission. Consequently, if you hire directly out of law schools, you're inherently relegated to the lower parts of the class in terms of optimizing your possibilities. The way a company should do it is to hire people that have gone to a good firm because there the talent you're dealing with tend to be at the higher level. The firm has screened them once. The firm has trained them, and that kind of training you can't get in a company. And then you go through the second screening. The people that you're talking to are people that have somehow come to grips with the fact that they don't really like working in a law firm for one reason or another.

Typically, then, the corporate law department recruits its members from the ranks of lawyers seeking to leave law firms and government work.

When they arrive in their corporate work settings, lawyers are confronted with a set of controls that are similar to but not identical with those used in law firms. As in the firm, ideological issues are deemphasized by the assumption that the job-seeking process has eliminated those who have any objections to the kind of business conducted by the company. Only one attorney (a Jewish man who was asked if he would mind working for a company doing business in the Arab world) recalls an ideologically colored question during the job interview. Nor do corporate staff attorneys mention ideological issues that arise later in their employment. The remarkable similarity in outlook between these lawyers and the business executives with whom they work is discussed at greater length in the section dealing with lawyer-client relations.

In technical matters—in the day-to-day office routines by which work is accomplished—the corporate law department is also very similar to the law firm. It is in bureaucratic matters that the two branches of the business bar seem furthest apart. The elaboration and systematization of rules governing such matters as recruitment, training, and advancement are far more pronounced in the corporation than in the law firm.

The difference in tone and emphasis is nowhere more clearly illustrated than in the ranking system. As noted, law firms have partners, sometimes junior partners, and associates. For associates, the year of entry into the firm fixes the earliest date at which they can be considered for partnership. But in all other matters year of entry is insignificant; the firm's profits and hence the individual's bonuses are more responsive to the number of hours he or she bills than to accumulated seniority. Not so in the general counsel's office, where rank in a corporation-wide system of personnel grades and lockstep promotion by seniority are paramount facts of life.

As new attorneys enter the corporate law department, they are immediately positioned on the corporation's ranking system, normally in the most junior grade available to the professional staff. Persons in this rank are subjected to a six-month or year-long probationary period despite previous experience in other settings. During the probationary period, the newcomer is expected to learn the corporation's particular way of transacting legal business. A more senior attorney will normally review the newcomer's work. But occasionally supervisors rely on the entrant's prior experience in making assignments. One new staff attorney, quoted also in chapter 1, describes her first day at work. Her full account is:

> When I first came [we had a] closing on a financial deal at 11:00 in the morning, and I was asked to attend. Now, I kid you not, I knew not the meaning of the word "closing," and I thought "Hm, I'm going to learn this by jumping in, but I don't think I should do this." And I went to about three attorneys and said, "Could you just give me a clue as to what happens in a closing? Do I light candles and wear black robes? I have a feeling it's a special event!" And they laughed and said, "You will do fine, just go." [My client] thought it was so wonderful that he was protected by his attorney. And I thought, "what a team we make!" I mean, in a way, it's been frightening.

This is what one law firm partner called overdelegation with a vengeance!

Once staff attorneys have passed through their probationary period, they can expect to be promoted through the ranks at about four- or five-year intervals until they reach the highest staff positions. The entire process usually takes them twelve to fifteen years. Thereafter, the attorney is at a kind of career ceiling; to continue the climb up the corporate ladder, he or she must secure one of a very limited number of supervisory positions. Their paucity is one of the most significant differences from the corporate law department, where a very high percentage of associates will ultimately become partners.

Even when supervisory positions are available, there is relatively little that staff attorneys can do to secure these positions for themselves. A widely shared perception holds that promotion through the ranks occurs principally on the basis of seniority. One general counsel says tactfully that "experience is a big factor but young people that are hot shots can move up fairly fast now." His staff is less sanguine. A woman just past her first promotion describes the advancement process in these words: "It's a very lockstep arrangement. I knew after I'd been here four years I would get promoted. And it didn't matter that I did well or poorly as long as I didn't kill someone and/or lose the company a billion dollars, I would get promoted.

There is no reward for talent." Another attorney, close to the ceiling of his promotion possibilities, reports:

> I'm at the third level at this point and I've probably gotten here quicker than a lot of other people have, so that's nice. But now everything narrows down. The hierarchy isn't that broad up at the top. I remember there was a lawyer who had a perfect flow chart that he used to carry around—which senior people were going to be retiring in what years, when they came in, and when they were leaving. It was fun for him to figure out who would be moving where and when. I think everyone does that, at least mentally. I'm trying to figure out now, [my boss] is 56, he'll be here nine more years or less, perhaps, with encouraged early retirement. And who will take over? Are they going to pick someone in their 50s at that point, or are they going to pick me?

The more senior attorneys are well aware of the propensity of juniors to carry around mental charts of their probable retirement dates. In the older departments that already have a substantial number of people at their career ceiling, veteran staff attorneys are beginning to fear being forced into early retirement.

The negative effects of career ceilings on the advancement of staff attorneys are augmented by the budgeting practices of the corporation. The law department operates on a fixed annual budget that allots certain moneys for salaries, equipment, fees to outside counsel, and the like. This means that individual attorneys can receive better than average raises only to the extent that others receive less than average increments. The law department is hardly ever in the position of being able to hold onto an attorney by matching an offer he or she may have secured from another corporation. A staff attorney recalls discussing a rival firm's offer with his boss: "I didn't want him to be surprised. And I think I also wanted to see whether he would talk about the future at all. He did a good job of keeping a poker face. I know that he was really glad I didn't leave, but I don't think he really felt he could do much about it."

Within such a framework, the question of salary tends to become an increasingly sensitive issue as years go by. Each year, the salary levels of entering attorneys rise to keep pace with the market. During the first five or six years, the staff attorney's salary is almost as high as the associate's salary in the law firm. But the staff attorney's earning power gradually diminishes, not only in comparison to that of the associate, then partner, in the law firm, but also in comparison to that of younger attorneys entering the law department. "You go to college, you go to graduate school, then you start off in a job with a good salary [but] they peak early. Starting salaries go up fast and if you've been at it for ten or twenty years, you're not making that much more than the people just starting out," explains a staff attorney in his fifties.

The rigid hierarchical structure that surrounds the staff attorney's career does not preclude the development of office politics, but it does mean that political infighting is usually futile. On rare occasions an individual may advance faster than his or her peers by virtue of behind-the-scenes maneuvering. But normally such politicking has little impact on the salaries associated with particular positions, the number of promotions available, or the seniority of those eligible for promotion. The only leeway in this generally predetermined picture consists of the money set aside by the general counsel for merit bonuses. In principle, the general counsel can evaluate and reward the individual staff attorney's work more or less as he sees fit. In practice, he usually seeks advice from lower echelon supervisors. The assumption underlying salary adjustments is that everyone who is doing satisfactory work should get much the same raise. People who do not quite come up to expectations may receive a smaller raise or none. People who have done consistently excellent work might win a substantial increment. And, finally, those who have done heroic work on significant projects might be given a one-time bonus as an expression of appreciation. For example, one woman recalls: "After I'd been here not quite two years my mentor had to go to a management school. He weas gone for ten weeks. I did all of his work and all of my work for those ten weeks. I nearly died, I was here twenty hours a day. And what they did, the following spring, was to give [me] a bonus." The bonus in this case took the form of a single cash award. In other companies, bonuses are distributed through stock-option plans and profit-sharing systems, both at the discretion of the general counsel. Stock-option plans are particularly valuable, first because they allow lawyers to acquire bonuses that are sometimes (cumulatively) in the six-figure range, and second because the recipients can defer the realization of these benefits over a period of years, using them at times of maximum financial need—for example, when sending children to college.

The arbitrary power of the general counsel to reward individual effort is becoming somewhat curtailed as the law department matures. All the companies participating in this study now have in place some form of routinized annual evaluations tailored specifically to attorneys. In one company, the assessment is so pro forma that attorneys write up their own evaluations and have their bosses initial them. But in another company, evaluations pinpoint criticisms that, it is hoped, will lead attorneys to alter specific behaviors. "There are a few things that I have been trying to get to, rather than leave slide, because I'm concerned about having a quicker response time. That was a valid criticism that was made," says one attorney. Ruefully, she adds, "I think I have too much work, but I also tend to take what I find to be more interesting, and I leave the more boring things at the bottom, and I shouldn't do that."

In still another company, the evaluation process becomes a means of organizing career development. Supervisors and their staffs take seriously the opportunity to identify weaknesses, to laud strengths, to discuss future plans. An attorney who evaluates lawyer-interns and paralegals and is herself subject to evaluation in turn says of the process: "I think, overall, it does give you, if you use it well, the opportunity to focus in on the important things that you want to identify for a person. I believe very strongly in an evaluation process that really helps someone move along."

In business, moving along ultimately means moving up or moving out. Opportunities for moving up are limited by the very nature of an organizational pyramid that has fewer positions for chiefs than for Indians, and also by the conventional wisdom that law department costs are corporate overhead, to be kept to an absolute minimum. Attrition does in fact often result from an individual's perception that his or her mobility is blocked. Just as a law firm associate who fears an unfavorable decision on partnership may join a corporate law department, so an in-house lawyer from a large staff may leave to become the general counsel or deputy general counsel at a smaller company or may try to move into a business career.

To forestall attrition, one corporation has recently begun an experimental system of distinguishing two separate promotion ladders: one for managers, who have supervisory responsibilities, and one for the professional-technical staff, who have no such role to play. The purpose of this two-tiered system is to allow for the continued promotion of professional people who, in the nature of their work, will not be be managing ever larger numbers of subordinates. Studies of other corporations that have tried such a two-tiered system suggest that only the managerial track leads individuals to positions of real power in the host corporation (Ritti, 1971). However, within the general counsel's office, any system that breaks through the ceiling on nonmanagerial promotions has some value to professional employees. At the very least, it permits continued step increases in salaries. At most, continued promotions have the advantage for staff counsel of enhancing their authority vis-à-vis business clients. "I suppose part of the theory behind it is that people who are working with senior management of the company should be of a fairly equivalent level," muses one staff attorney about the impact of the company's system of job grades.

To maintain the possibilities of promotion, other companies have developed executive training programs that enroll selected senior attorneys who are nearing their career ceilings. Such programs groom executives for positions in the business divisions of the corporation. As mentioned earlier, a transition from the law department to the business side of the corporation happens most readily in banking and insurance companies, where the lawyer's skills are absolutely central to product development. In industries based on chemical or engineering expertise, lawyers have almost nowhere to go. They can normally leave the law department only for personnel, planning, or tax work. Finally, the executive training program has little value for those business lawyers who prefer not to abandon their own profession, although such reluctance was not very evident among this study's respondents. On the contrary, in the financial service companies four lawyers at their career ceilings already were planning to move into business, and even in the corporation producing consumer goods two lawyers were contemplating similar moves. Certainly the seedbed for career change is visible: the general counsel themselves urge upon staff attorneys an identification with corporate values, a number of lawyers already have business training at the MBA level, and there is pervasive concern about the career ceilings (and, to a lesser degree, the financial limitations) of the law department.

But the fundamental limit on opportunity for in-house lawyers arises not from corporate personnel and pay policies, but from the corporate stricture against billing the business people who use the services of the law department. Were house counsel allowed to bill their clients as law firms do, they could generate more than enough income to run their own departments, with higher pay scales and an expanded number of positions. Some companies, in fact, tolerate a hybrid arrangement in which the general counsel is reimbursed for litigation costs by the division whose interests are represented. But in all other matters—negotiation, advisement, contract review— the law department logs the number of hours it devotes to each project but does not bill those hours to the business division that generates the work. Business people are informed of the time spent on their concerns so that they can estimate the administrative overhead associated with each product line, but the law department itself lives on a fixed income. For readily understandable reasons, corporate management favors the interests of the production departments over those of the administrative sections. Given a choice between the financial ambitions of the law department and the willingness of business people to seek preventive counsel, corporate management chooses to encourage the business people to consult lawyers at no cost to themselves.

Lawyers, of course, resent this arrangement, which they regard as an injustice. They maintain that what management views as preventive law is often a waste of their professional time. "One of the frustrating things here is that you deal with a lot of people who don't know how to use lawyers. Now, let me tell you, if you come into my office [in] private practice and I'm billing you a hundred bucks an hour, you're not going to waste my time. But a lot of these people never get charged, and a lot of them probably never used lawyers personally, and so they don't know how to use one in a corporate way because they never see the actual expense. There's no discipline." In some instances, the justice of this remark is acknowledged in business circles by rules that specify that only project managers or business people above a certain rank can refer work directly to the law department.

If the corporate law department differs fundamentally from the law firm in its economic rewards, it makes every effort to resemble the law firm in the day-to-day structure of its work. For example, a staff attorney describes the mentoring process in much the same terms that law firm associates use:

> I was assigned to work with a senior attorney, and he progressively gave me increasingly responsibility and guided me to where to find the answers to issues. What you learn in law school is just a threshold: corporate housekeeping issues, creating corporations, dealing with shareholder issues are a very minor part of corporate practice. It's virtually a new learning experience when you get here.

The corporate law department is distinctive only in that its mentoring relies on the recruit's prior experience and therefore moves more quickly than in the firm. The speed with which new attorneys expect to be accepted as full-fledged members of the law department is reflected in the definition of bad supervisors as those who "will very actively keep their people in a hole in the ground and never let them out." Good supervisors recognize that delegation is not only a way to protect themselves from being overburdened but also a way to signal their confidence in subordinates.

The system of mentoring is bolstered by the fact that staff attorneys do most of their work in their own offices, within earshot of their superiors. "We're a home office law department," explains one, and "most of our work is transancted on the phone or by letter or by sending documents back and forth." The ability of law department supervisors literally to see who is busy and who is not is enhanced in some offices by a "scrutiny file" or "letter pack"—a compilation of all the major documents drafted by attorneys in the course of a month that is circulated about the office. "There are times when I agonize over something because I know it's going to go in the letter pack and we know everything is going to be seen by the senior people."

In fact, the scrutiny file that brings peer pressure to bear on attorneys is probably a much more effective way to control their work than is the use of fixed forms of various sorts. Even in the settings where the routine legal work of the corporation is conducted, lawyers' work can be standardized only up to a point. As one attorney explains, "Today's marketplace makes all deals more negotiable. [For example] the balance shifts between the lender and the borrower depending on the availability of money." Adds another: "The customer wants a contract in which he gets unlimited warranties, pays when he gets around to it, and has delivery tomorrow. We always want very limited warranties, immediate payment, an advance if we can get it. There's a lot of negotiation that goes into that. Resolution of disputes takes up a surprising amount of our time."

Like law firm lawyers, then, in-house attorneys may devote a substantial portion of their work to delicate and complex legal tasks in a context of loosely structured supervision. The staff attorney's work differs from the law firm associate's principally in that it is less highly paid and less prestigious. Even without the incentive of money and prestige, however, the corporate law department is able to elicit high levels of productivity from its staff by using a variety of lures and prods.

Chief among these is the attraction of challenging work. Given a choice between controlling staff by de-skilling them and controlling them by motivating them, law department supervisors clearly have chosen the latter strategy. One general counsel speaks of supervising professionals: "They want challenging work and we can afford them that. They can take on great responsibility because a company this size has a lot of responsible transactions for lawyers to work on, and a lot of difficult problems for lawyers to resolve." Another general counsel adds, "You have to have more than a financial incentive to keep a professional interested in you. If the professional is worth anything, you have to give him a challenge. You have to make sure the professional is not doing a lot of routine, repetitive work."

Staff attorneys agree wholeheartedly. They find, often to their surprise, that the reputation for routine work that attaches to the corporate law department is only partially correct. The attorney who feared the stigma of transferring to an in-house staff recounts: "When I first came on, we were doing all commercial [real estate transactions], no small residential stuff. And the biggest surprise to me was that [when] I used to work [at my old firm] on a bank loan for 120,000 bucks, that was a lot of money. I came here and I did not touch anything for less than two million." In part these comments reflect a kind of professional machismo—just as doctors derive more satisfaction from successful intervention in critical than in routine cases, so lawyers prefer those cases in which the financial stakes are highest. But this comment also reflects the understanding, similarly prevalent in the law firm, that when the financial stakes are highest, attorneys can exercise their craftsmanship with the least pressure to compromise or economize on the quality of their work. In another office, a young woman who recently moved from a government job was also pleasantly surprised by the quality of corporate work: "Here, they do not make their money on you through repetition. You get to do different kinds of things: mergers and acquisitions, corporate financing, research and development, new products. . . . The areas you can get into are more interesting." To delay the day when work becomes repetitive, one company even has a rotation program similar to those in the law firms. The head of this program remarks, "One way to help [maintain motivation] is to give people interesting things to do that they haven't done before."

A general counsel expresses the policy of motivating professionals with challenging work in almost pure form:

> There's a buy-in. This whole concept of high performance [is] predicated upon ownership. If you have an assembly line and everyone does one piece, no one owns that thing that comes out at the end, so the guy in the beginning doesn't care what that thing looks like. Well, in the law department we try not to segment a problem. The problem is someone's problem, and if he doesn't have the specialty

to solve it, he brings in help from within the department, but he never loses the problem.

Professionals in corporate law departments are also lured by material incentives. Although their salaries compare unfavorably to those available in law firms, corporations large enough to have a sizable law department typically provide excellent fringe benefits in addition to stock-option and profit-sharing plans of substantial value. For example, one law department has "a very liberal sick leave policy. For every day you work here, you're entitled to a day of sick leave." Job security is high, and when on rare occasions people are asked to leave, parting takes the form of "a golden handshake," which provides tailored recommendations and allows time for the departing attorney to find another job.

For the vast majority of lawyers who stay with a large corporate staff, the atmosphere is relatively relaxed. Says one general counsel of his staff, "They're not lazy people, but they just want to get their life regulated. They want to be able to go home to dinner at night most nights. We have the stability of a normal working life." A normal working life for the staff attorney is generally 50 hours a week: 9 to 5 in the office, with work taken home or reading done several nights a week. The expectation is that the necessary work will be done even when this requires extra effort.

The pressure for productivity is also reinforced by a policy of deliberate understaffing. One general counsel says, "Well, one [work incentive] is to keep a very small group, compared to the quantum of work so they're always under a little bit of pressure." The policy of deliberate understaffing produces the desired results for management, as the following remarks indicate: "For a year," says a young woman, "I have been saying I have too much work. We really need to get a new person because [the clients] are having to wait too long to get an opinion. [The boss's] reply is, 'I have to think about it.' Then I can either disappoint my clients or work longer hours. I choose to work longer hours. At some point I'm going to go over and say 'I just can't do it. Something is going to go really wrong very soon unless you get somebody.'" She concludes: "I think we have to do it that way." Another attorney summarizes the consequences of understaffing: "The last year or so, my major hope in life is to stay afloat."

Despite the occasional feeling of being in over one's head, the position of staff counsel in a large corporate law department is a relatively sheltered one. In fact, it is probably the most attractive option in the law job market for those who cannot or do not wish to become law firm partners. The corporate employer shoulders all the burdens of overhead, equipping and staffing an office, leaving staff counsel free to get on with their professional work. The work itself is becoming more varied and stimulating. Working conditions appear to be acceptable. There are, of course, pressures, some of them created deliberately by pitting a policy of understaffing against an ethic of responsiveness to clients. These pressures, in turn, are one of the many forces that shape the lawyer-client relationship in the corporate setting.

THE LAW DEPARTMENT AND ITS CORPORATE HOST: INFORMATION AND CONTROL

The first determinant of the lawyer-client relationship is the lawyer's mandate to exercise professional judgment in order to keep the corporation out of legal trouble. To this end, in-house lawyers typically perform a kind of legal triage on the problems brought to them by business people. They distinguish problems that require only a sounding board from problems that call upon the lawyer to explain the "risk profile" of a deal. Generally, such risks are business risks that the executive is free to accept or reject. For example, one insurance company attorney says: "My observation after fifteen years here [is that] if I said to a claims person, 'As a legal matter you can raise the defense that you want to raise. But as a practical matter, if you go before a jury with that technical type defense [against] a poor disabled guy, out of work, with a family to support, they're not going to listen. You're going to lose. It's probably going to cost you penalties. It might cost you punitive damages. It's also going to cost about

$50,000 to try the damn thing.' If I say that to them, I have never in my life seen an instance where they pursued the legal [claim]."

More typically, the lawyer's advice is not to abandon a course of action but to alter it in the company's favor. For example, an attorney may be called upon to remind a salesman that it goes against company policy to accept a penalty clause for late delivery.

> They [the buyers] say, "If you are late in delivery, for each day you are late, [you] will pay, as liquidated damages, X dollars." Now there is nothing illegal about that [but], normally, we have a policy that says we don't accept those. Now, there are exceptions to that policy and through a method of counseling we say, "Well, look, we think that if you put a cap on that so that those liquidated damages in no event exceed, say, 5 per cent of the contract price," now you present a package to management that [they] can approve. If he thinks he is only gambling his expected profit, then that's a natural business decision. But if you took something like [liquidated damages] that could go on ad infinitum, you could really pull the plug on the company.

The influence of an attorney in suggesting an alternative course of action depends mainly on the business person's prior experience with that attorney. "You attain a lot of credibility in the company," says one lawyer, "because of your aptitude with business issues, your apparent willingness to really dig in and examine issues closely and develop a solution and not take the easy way out and say you can't do something." In short, the job of the lawyer confronted with a risky business deal is to find a way to minimize the risks so that business can proceed.

In certain cases, however, the lawyer may feel that a business person's proposed course of action goes beyond financial risk, raising the specter of criminality or other major corporate liability. In distinguishing the legally unacceptable from the economically precarious, the lawyer completes the third leg of the triage system. By all accounts, staff lawyers are very rarely confronted with circumstances that call for them to flatly veto a suggested course of action. Even more rarely does the business client ignore the attorney's estimate of legal risk. When such a situation does arise—depending on "how adamantly the business people are inclined to want to do something and how adamantly we think they shouldn't"—the lawyer's major recourse is clear: he or she refers the decision to higher management levels, both within the law department and within the business divisions. "The lawyer says to the manager, 'I am bumping your decision up one level, so that my manager goes to your manager.' And that continues all the way up to [the general counsel] talking to the president if the issue is strong enough."

The foregoing presents a fairly clear-cut account of the steps a staff attorney takes in responding to business questions and in restraining individual executives when the larger interests of the corporation require that this be done. Yet this account is incomplete in one significant respect: given almost daily accounts in the media of corporate misdeeds, how can it be that staff attorneys so seldom encounter situations that call for whistle-blowing?

In part, the answer to this question hinges on the real incidence of corporate lawlessness,[3] a topic outside the scope of the present study. In part, the answer lies in the legal profession's ideology that "everyone deserves representation; the truth shall emerge from the clash of interests." The degree to which this view justifies unthinking partisanship is greatly enhanced in the corporate law department by the general counsel's stance of "being first a corporate officer and second a lawyer." The offsetting stricture—that lawyers are also officers of the court who may sometimes be obligated to disclose client wrongdoing to protect the public interest—is simply given less support and attention in the general counsel's staff despite efforts in the bar, documented by Jeffrey Slovak (1981), to emphasize this obligation. In part, the answer lies in the fact that business lawyers have been trained to think of breaches of professional ethics as occurring in other segments of the bar.[4] The oft-heard disclaimer "We don't repossess washing machines from little old ladies" deftly admits that

3. For a discussion of the complexities of assessing corporate lawlessness, see Clinard and Yeager, 1980.

4. Carlin's work (1962, 1966) has shown clearly how certain breaches of professional ethics occur more often among solo practitioners and those who serve poor clients.

lawyers who serve small, fly-by-night businesses may engage in dubious conduct while deflecting attention from those who serve established interests.

Business attorneys also fail to perceive potential ethical issues because their attention is focused elsewhere. A number of corporate attorneys maintain that their chief problem in dealing with clients is not recalcitrance in accepting legal advice but overconformity. Especially in dealing with middle-level managers, lawyers fear that their opinions will be taken as directives instead of as advice. Says one attorney: "The lower echelon business people would be very reluctant to do something that a lawyer says shouldn't be done, because they don't know what kind of impact that could have on their careers." "Business people feel [that if] they disregard law department advice and they get burned, their careers will suffer," concurs another. Moreover, adds still another, if business people were inclined to be "swingers," they would soon run afoul of the accounting department's checks as well as the law department's review procedures. Even in the largest corporations the upper echelon managerial ranks are thin, and few secrets can be maintained at that level. An executive who departed too far from company policy would be subject to a variety of constraints; the law department, according to its members, is not the only corporate watchdog.

Finally, as John Donnell (1970) has documented, conflicts between lawyers and business executives are rare because the two have so many traits in common. They share a decision-making style—one that stresses identifying the essential components of a situation, weighing costs against benefits, and arriving at practical solutions in an imperfect world. According to Donnell, they also share a fairly high tolerance for ambiguity, which allows them to leave problematic situations unresolved as long as no one complains.[5]

5. On this point, Donnell (1970, pp. 99–100) writes: "Legal principles and standards are not clearly defined. Examples of some of the rubber yardsticks that courts apply are 'due process,' the 'reasonable and prudent man,' and 'due care,'. . . . [A]pplied to a given dispute [they] can lead to conflicting conclusions. . . . [I]t is the ambiguity of the law that makes it possible for each of the opposing lawyers to argue that his client has the law on his side. To the lawyer, then, ambiguity becomes an opportunity rather than a threat." This interpretation would seem to contradict some of the

If lawyers and executives do indeed share these paradoxical traits of tolerating ambiguity while avoiding or displacing risks, then the question arises: Who ultimately controls corporate behavior? On the whole, the foregoing discussion suggests that staff attorneys act primarily as facilitators for business executives. Rarely do they exercise the veto power implicit in their mandate to make the corporation's business "proceed without legal risk." Moreover, the structural incentives that make lower level managers reluctant to ignore a lawyer's advice apply with much less force to higher level managers, whose reputations depend upon successfully completing business projects.

Perhaps the chief factor that keeps lawyers from encroaching on business prerogatives is the practice of understaffing the law department. Simply put: "Everyone here has a little bit more work than they can comfortably get done in a day, so nobody's chasing for more work or to try to expand their work." Again, this statement confirms Donnell's earlier findings: the pressures of work are such that everyone is trying to do less, not more. Because of this, the staff attorney would like the business client to take responsibility for as many tasks as possible. Such tasks include the burden of reviewing contracts. "Now let's see what kind of things you're giving us and maybe you can review things in greater detail so we have less to review," a general counsel tells the people who consult him. Another attorney wants business people to use their own resources to verify the facts that bear on impending litigation. When he hears something like, "I've got this case. Here's the facts I have, here's a letter from the attorney saying thus and so," he replies: "Well, my advice to you is, you better go find out if thus and so is really the case." This, he acknowledges, "calls for further investigation, further expense. [But] I don't have to worry about their expense budget for investigation. I'm just telling them what they need to have." The net

---

comments made by law firm associates about learning to draft documents to support a client's claim without ambiguity. Yet it is consistent with criticisms that lawyers sometimes direct at themselves about "over-lawyering" a deal—that is, resolving ambiguities at great expense and without affording the client commensurate gains in protecting their interests.

effect of this pattern is to allow business people nearly complete freedom to marshal the facts that the lawyer scrutinizes. To the extent that they are permitted to establish the fact base from which legal work proceeds, they are likely to retain control over the course of events.

The foregoing discussion once again confirms John Donnell's observations of more than a decade ago: if there is to be a "professional revolution," it is one that is awaited with some eagerness by business executives, while staff attorneys are dragging their feet about getting on with it. On the whole, Donnell's business respondents expressed much more interest in having their staff attorneys play the role of the corporate conscience than did the lawyers themselves. Upon closer examination, this difference turned out to be a disagreement about costs. When business people said they wanted lawyers to be aggressive, they meant that they wanted the lawyers to use the law department's time and effort to keep abreast of potential legal issues in the corporation. Similarly, lawyers wanted business clients to incur many of the costs of discovery. Thus, far from usurping managerial prerogatives, lawyers were often seen by executives as shunning responsibilities that were properly theirs.

Office politics also serve to restrain any ambitions lawyers may harbor to usurp managerial prerogatives. Nominally, of course, house counsel are protected from the demands of business executives by the structural autonomy of their department. In reality it is less this buffer and more the limited number of benefits to be distributed that makes office politics somewhat futile. Nevertheless, few staff attorneys are willing to forgo what little gain might accrue to them from the approval of corporate officers. "I make it a point to be as personable and as lovely as I can to a lot of people in this [corporation]," says an attorney who perceives that her general counsel got his promotion through school ties with the chief executive officer of the corporation.

Individual attorneys vary in their accounts of who really controls the attorney-client relationship. At one extreme is the woman who believes that lawyers have a great deal of power. She says, "Sometimes we get a little bit too moral. We forget that the ultimate is the bottom line dollar product." At the other extreme is the man who feels completely powerless. He laments, "You're just a piece of meat; they buy you and sell you just like anything else at the market." All, however, agree that assignment to high visibility projects and the goodwill of business executives are valuable resources and virtually the only way to beat the seniority system of promotion. As long as this belief prevails, business people have a great deal of power over the attorney despite the formal autonomy of the law department.

THE COMPETITORS: LAW FIRMS
AND LAW DEPARTMENTS

Just as individual staff attorneys depend in some measure on business executives' approval for their own promotions, so the law department as a whole depends for its very existence on corporate philosophy. Corporate management is always free to choose between the legal services provided by its own law department and those available from an outside law firm. A significant element that bears on this choice is the independence of the law firm and the dependency of the law department.

In any comparison of in-house and outside legal services, law firms maintain that their independence is their single most significant asset. One law firm partner explains:

> It is not uncommon for us to tell the president that he's a turkey. You know, "You're a goddamn fool, and you've got an environmental problem right now and you've got to spend a million dollars to fix it even though it will lose you money this year, or you're going to go to jail. That's the magnitude of your problem." I'd like to hear an in-house lawyer say that to a president who just had a stockholders meeting where he's promised them the world. I'd like to see an in-house lawyer tell his board of directors that his president is violating the Foreign Corporate Practices Act. The fact is, there's just no room for willful blindness at that level. If you have both loyalties and accountability to the superior, you can't be independent.

This stance is in sharp contrast to that of the in-house lawyers who say, "I am first a corporate officer and second I happen to be a lawyer," or, again, "I'm pretty much [a company man] through and through."

In fact, staff attorneys do worry about conditions that compromise their independence.[6] They recognize that the autonomy of the law department does not wholly insulate them from unwelcome pressures, especially in circumstances that call upon the lawyer to act as whistle-blower. It is not sufficient to say, as one does, "My job should be to see that the [corporation] is adequately protected. I don't represent the guy downstairs, I represent the [corporation]." The option of bumping the problem up a level, however much it is mandated by corporate policy, is not without costs for the attorney who uses it. Says one, "If the business people refuse to accept [my advice], then my role is to go up in the legal organization with the problem. And my experience has been that when I do that, the problem goes away. The risk and the problem that's created by that is that then the business people whom you have just gotten into trouble by squealing on them find it very difficult to deal with you from then on. So you've got to balance that problem against how you're going to relate with those people after you've brought the world down on their heads."

Nonetheless, on balance, in-house counsel maintain that situations seldom arise in which they are pressured to compromise their professional judgment. As one put it: "Am I always to take the American Constitution with me or am I to take the company by-laws with me wherever I go? I don't think we're asked to make that choice." Indeed, several lawyers argue that in the world of big business, the clash between the lawyer's ethic of risk prevention and the entrepreneurial ethic of risk-taking is greatly exaggerated. "You

6. Slovak (1981) has detailed the structural arrangements most conducive to staff lawyer independence. All these conditions—the administrative autonomy of the law department, and the encouragement of individuals to participate in bar association and other professional activities—are met by the corporations in this study. And yet staff attorneys remain diffident.

know," says one staff attorney about his business clients, "we don't have many mavericks in the company. As a matter of fact, there's probably hardly any."

In practice, it seems that house counsel discharge their obligation to give ethical advice by urging executives to favor long-term over short-term interests. Once this equation is made, lawyers feel perfectly comfortable in asserting that they routinely advise their clients to follow the ethical course. And if such advice is not often accepted, that fact, they feel, is an aspect of American business culture; it can hardly be blamed on the staff attorney.

Moreover, some attorneys assert that the vaunted independence of the law firm is more apparent than real. Outside firms are rarely retained directly by the business projects they serve. Typically, the judgment of when to call in outside counsel and which firm to retain is left to the general counsel. Sometimes firms are retained on a matter-by-matter basis. Sometimes they are placed on retainer to preclude their "accepting legal work from [the firm's] competitiors." But in all instances, the conduct of the outside counsel is closely monitored by his or her counterpart in the corporate law department. General counsel are unanimous in saying that they do not hesitate to replace outside counsel if they are dissatisfied with either the financial or the substantive aspects of the work they have commissioned. Law firms may "still think they're alchemists. No one understands what they do, so they should just do what they want." But general counsel disagree. Specifically, general counsel expect to retain veto power over the strategy of a case or deal that is being conducted by an independent law firm, and to have some say about the law firm's staffing of the case. Moreover, disagreements about hours and fees are common. "If a law firm will not give me a breakout by who does the work, how many hours, their hourly rate, I will not give them legal work," reports one general counsel. Another adds, "The case is managed by us. And if the local firm is, for instance, putting too many hours into the case, I want to know about it. We challenge them all the time. We get a firm that costs too much, we use another firm."

The foregoing suggests that the choice between using in-house and outside legal talent is often not a choice between loyalty and independence; between the "company man through and through" and the one who speaks truth to power. Frequently the choice is made on a more mundane basis: the cost of in-house lawyers is substantially lower than that of the independent law firm. "The reason why economics generally favor in-house is because you have people that understand the products and who understand the company and can work the matters more efficiently than an outside counselor can. You get more productive hours on the problem inside than outside." With the exception of litigation, discussed below, the only limits on the economies of inside work seem to be the corporation's willingness to spend money in order to save money. One corporate lawyer explains: "When times are difficult you will have anywhere from one to 15,000 suggestions as to how to spend money to save money. And if you'd [heeded them all] you'd probably go down the drain."

The independent law firms do not dispute the economies of staff counsel. Nevertheless, they do assert that "it's fair to say that the best lawyers are not in the corporate structure." Law firm lawyers, says one staff attorney with private practice experience, are treated like "thoroughbreds. You snap your fingers, you get whatever you want, when you want it, with very little questions asked." The excellence of their work is supported not only by the resources at their command but also by the nature of the work itself. They see the results of their efforts, and that sustains them. "One of the main things that I would say about private practice as I saw it versus corporate practice is that if you are going to be motivated [in a staff position], you have to be a self-starter because in private practice you are more apt to see the immediate result of what you are doing. In corporate law you don't always see that kind of result, because it's part of a big picture."

The law firm's most significant claim to excellence, however, hinges not on resources or motivation but on the exposure of its attorneys to all aspects of a complex legal environment. "If you have a [business] firm in waste management, for example, [their in-house lawyers can] build up an expertise in environment law [but] there is one dimension that they lose that we have. They tend to measure everything in their own universe. They think that every environmental case is the same, because that's all they ever see, the environmental cases that that particular firm generates, while we see it generated by seven different firms. Even if they see, in sheer volume, the same number, they're seeing a particular character, while we see the total universe," explains a law firm partner.

House counsel agree that their diverse client base gives private practice attorneys an edge in their overall knowledge of the law. However, staff counsel point out that, beyond a certain threshold of competence, knowledge of the business of the corporation is more germane to the satisfactory completion of legal matters than knowledge of the law. A general counsel explains his decision to increase his in-house staff: "It turns out to be more efficient to have people who are familiar with the company's problems, already know the background of the company's operation, don't have to be educated on the whole legal background every time a legal question comes up." Repeatedly, staff attorneys asserted that the undivided attention they can give to the business person's problem is more useful than the expert but minimal attention the private attorney devotes to any one deal. "For example," reports a young woman, "somebody called me yesterday about an OSHA problem and finally ended up saying to me, 'You know an awful lot more than the outside lawyer does who's supposed to be an expert.' Well, they're so diversified out there that they can't hone in on subjects [the way] we do."

In this morass of claims and counterclaims, one fact stands out: even as individual law firms continue to grow and prosper, law firms en masse are beginning to lose money to corporate law departments (Lewin, 1983e). The loss of revenue by the firm does not mean that they are being shut out altogether, but it does mean that their largest clients are using their services more selectively. Typically, outside counsel are now retained only for work that is unique or intermittent in character. A one-shot appearance before any of the government's administrative agencies or a one-time business deal such as an acquisition may lead the company to hire a law firm in order to save the costs of training attorneys in fields that they will not put to much use later.

Outside representation is also essential for deals in which the financial stakes are so high that the corporation is willing to pay both in-house and outsider fees to protect its interests. For this reason, a bank or an insurance company whose capital is financing the construction of a major office complex or sports arena will have both in-house and local real estate counsel working on its behalf.

The most common use of outside counsel, however, is for litigation because litigation is a highly decentralized activity. If a company is sued, either by a consumer, another business entity, or the government, the litigation that follows is normally conducted in the plaintiff's jurisdiction far from corporate headquarters. Local counsel are therefore retained to conduct the trial. In-house counsel will usually select the local attorney and work with him or her on the case. The corporate attorney expects to control case strategy, to conduct most aspects of discovery (framing and answering interrogatories, preparing witnesses for depositions), and to find and coach in-house expert witnesses. The outside counsel, in turn, expects to conduct the trial itself and to be the respected authority on the vagaries of local civil procedure. A staff attorney illustrates the division of labor between in-house and local counsel:

> I had a product liability case. I picked up the file from another lawyer and, reviewing the state of the law in New York, I said, "Gee, this looks to me like it's ripe for a summary judgment motion." I went back through the file, trying to see why one had never been filed, and called up the lawyer. I said to him, "You know, just out of curiosity, it looks like the law's on our side, why haven't we ever filed a summary judgment motion?" He said, "Well, we did talk about that way back. But it's our feeling that the injuries suffered in this case—there's malpractice involved, the hospital's a co-defendent—knowing the court as we do in this jurisdiction, we think the judge is going to let this go to a jury no matter what the state of the law is, and our only chance is going to be on appeal." But [she continues], after our employees are deposed and we read the plaintiff's depositions, once we have more discovery done, then we might in-

sist that he take a shot at it, because we don't want to have to try it because of the expense involved.

This account of the litigation process clearly evokes the widely repeated comment made at an American Bar Association meeting that "the average litigant is overdiscovered, overinterrogatoried and overdeposed. As a result, he's overcharaged, overexposed and overwrought" (American Business Lawyer, 1978, p. 834). It also illustrates how unlikely it is that the shift from private to staff counsel will curb this trend to any significant degree. Yet the legal maneuverings of staff attorneys and private counsel, although certainly self-interested, still seem pretty well subordinated to business goals. If lawyers are making work for themselves, they are doing so in ways that are consistent with the aims of their employers. Moreover, lawyers are quick to point out that the basic impetus for their work comes not from their own self-promotion but from the regulatory activity of government. "We have not changed the course of business. Washington, D.C. has changed the course of business, and that's why we're here. We're strictly a service organization" is a common refrain.

Regulatory activity is also a primary occasion for the joint use of in-house and outside legal talent on the same deal. If a corporation chooses to pursue a line of action for which it anticipates governmental challenge, corporate counsel will often ask a private law firm for a second opinion. This seems to be done only in part because the actual substance of the second opinion is valued — the whole "opining process" also maintains appearances. The presence of "the outside law firm may make a decision appear at least prudent if not correct," explains an insurance company lawyer. Another attorney is even more candid: "Anything we want someone else on the hook for, liability-wise, goes outside. In an antitrust question, for example, if we're thinking of setting something up and we're not sure if we're going to run afoul of anti-trust law, we get an outside opinion and then they're on the hook for that." In some instances, then, the corporation is protected against business losses by its right to sue an outside law firm for any incorrect advice the firm may give. By retaining outside counsel, corporate management has someone other than its own employees "on the hook, liability-wise." More commonly, however, the corporation does not intend to sue anyone. Rather, it wants to create the appearance of probity by soliciting the opinion of a prestigious law firm.

CONCLUSION: THE CONVERGENCE OF BUSINESS AND LAW

The foregoing discussion suggests that the general counsel's office is a hybrid creature, having some characteristics in common with the free-standing law firm and some with other corporate departments.

As much as possible the general counsel runs his domain like a mini-law-firm. He recruits lawyers who have no qualms about serving business interests, who need little supervision beyond the apprenticeship stage, and who will cede to management without much struggle the right to establish the substantive and personnel policies that organize the life of the workplace. House counsel and law firm members differ principally in their ambitiousness. Attorneys in the law firm will work longer hours for more money and status. Staff counsel will settle for less money in return for a more routinized work life. If they do not look particularly proletarianized by their experiences as employees, neither do they resemble an emerging new class of technocrats bent on replacing their employers' interests with their own. On the contrary, it is their hope of becoming partners or executives—joining the owners, not beating them—that cements their attention and their loyalty.

The threat to this modus vivendi arises not from employee demands but from competition between law firms and in-house legal departments that exerts financial pressure on both. In response to such pressure, the in-house law department has adopted many of the features found in other corporate operations. The deliberate use of understaffing and of scrutiny files, the policy of rendering service to business projects without billing them, and the problem of career ceilings are all features that the law department shares with other service divisions in the parent corporation.

The hybrid character of the corporate law department is signifi-

106

cant because it is more than a purely economic phenomenon; it also reveals a substantial lessening of the distance (perhaps never great in the first place) between professional and business values. In the firm, efforts are made to be more business-like,[7] but in the general counsel's office this telescoping has proceeded even further: corporate career ladders are now coming to define success as the ability to leave one's profession in order to become a business person. Nor has this development met with outraged cries from the bar. On the contrary, leading law professors (for example, Fried, 1984) are encouraging their students to learn from business people, to become more sensitive to the discipline of the bottom line and less concerned with exploring all the legal issues implicit in their work.

Only a small force operates to stem this drift toward making law a branch of business rather than a discipline in its own right. Change in the law itself, wrought by government action, requires business lawyers to remain attuned to new legislation, emerging legal theories, and changing regulatory practices. Of necessity, then, the business lawyers's point of reference includes not only corporate executives but also other lawyers—especially those in government work, whose activities are the subject of the next chapter.

7. Jenkins (1984) reports a further step in blurring the distinction between business and professional organizations: a number of law firms outside the area of this study are now establishing a variety of business corporations as wholly owned subsidiaries of the law firm itself.

CHAPTER 4

GOOD SOLDIERS
Civil Service Attorneys

While law firms and in-house legal departments compete with each other for the legal work of corporations, much of the market they seek to control is being created by government action. The significance of government regulation for business and society has been a matter of debate since its inception in the late nineteenth century. But one outcome is clear: regulatory activities produce employment for lawyers, both in the private enterprises being regulated and in the government agencies doing the regulating. Indeed, along with in-house legal staffs, government positions until recently have been the most rapidly growing sources of employment for lawyers.

This chapter examines the work life of the civil service attorney in the federal government. State and local government offices are not considered, because they are often too small for the purposes of the present study and sometimes too politicized to admit a research team. The consequences of this choice should be noted: to focus on the federal civil servant and not on the local district attorney is to limit the results of this research to the experiences of lawyers in elaborate bureaucracies—albeit bureaucracies molded by both impersonal, organizational forces and explicitly political-ideological pressures.

THE LEGAL ARM OF THE GOVERNMENT:
REGULATION AND REFORM

At present the federal government engages in a wide variety of activities. It provides certain essential services directly to the public: for example, it controls the national currency. On other occasions the government furnishes money to the private sector to create services that the market cannot sustain on its own, such as medical and legal services to the indigent. Third, the federal government monitors activities undertaken through purely private initiative. To this end, the Federal Trade Commission, the Securities and Exchange Commission, the Department of Labor, and a host of other agencies have a voice in regualting the behavior of corporations. Most important for our purposes, all government programs, whether of the service-providing or the regulatory variety, have legal dimensions that require the participation of lawyers.

The particular lawyers whose work is described here are employed in the regional offices of three cabinet departments and one independent subcabinet agency of the federal government. Their offices typify the civil service setting that C. Wright Mills (1951, p. 189) once described as "the enormous file." The building where they work is one of the less imaginative elements on the city's skyline, and the offices themselves are uniformly small and drab. Everywhere one sees evidence of penury: unwashed, streaked windows, old and outmoded typewriters, frayed carpets, bent and rusty file cabinets, squeaky chairs. Even the plants, clearly the personal property of those who work in these offices, seem to droop dispiritedly under the fluorescent lights. The work life that develops within these confines is shaped in part by this generic civil service atmosphere. But, more important, it is shaped also by the division of labor specific to government lawyers: the distinctions they draw between the home office in Washington and the regional offices around the country, and between the Department of Justice and the law divisions of the other cabinet departments.

Within the federal government, every cabinet department has its own specialized legal branch, analogous to the office of the general counsel in the private corporation. The autonomy of this legal branch is jealously guarded in both settings; just as, in industry, the general counsel reports only to the company president or vice-president, so, in government, the general counsel is answerable only to the cabinet secretary or undersecretary. Staff attorneys in both cases report to departmental superiors and keep their clients at arm's length for purposes of evaluation and reward.

The federal government also resembles the private corporation in distributing its legal work over several different providers. At headquarters in Washington national policy is formulated, the functions of the regional offices are coordinated, and appellate work is undertaken. The job of the regional office, in turn, is to provide direct legal services to the field programs of its host cabinet department. For example, a Department of Agriculture inspector who had trouble getting access to a grain storage site would be directed to seek help from an attorney in the nearest regional solicitor's office of the Agriculture Department.

The balance between the home office and its branches is a fluctuating one because regional programs demand some latitude in adapting national policy to local situations. The regional solicitor who was most insistent on local autonomy put it this way:

> It may be perceived that something like a regional must, in all cases, defer to a central office and there's some kind of almost a funnel approach. But in this agency, there's a sufficient independence. There are lawyers out on the scene where the action is who have an expertise: the kinds of judges; aspects, perhaps, of state or local laws; knowledge of the particular U.S. attorneys; plus familiarity that may cut across program lines. I just don't want to create the impression that we don't have a great deal of individual responsibility and discretion. But, at the same time I view as a primary responsibility, in the absence of true formalized structures like the ten commandments, that a regional person just has to work out a set of appropriate ways of keeping the necessary people advised.

In another agency, a chief attorney places somewhat more emphasis on conforming to Washington policy: "We're given a considerable amount of discretion [but] I mean, of course, we know what their policy is." Staff attorneys, whose work is scrutinized by both regional and national officials, are even blunter: "The agencies get the message from Washington, what to do, what to lay off and so forth." Adds another, "If you were way out of line for a period of time, you would get reined in pretty hard."

Activities in the regional solicitor's office are circumscribed not only by national policy but also by the distinction—as in the British legal system—between negotiation and litigation. Normally, the regional solicitor's office pursues only those problems arising between the federal government and the citizen, corporation, or service provider that can be resolved by negotiation or by administrative hearing.

Once litigation is invoked, cases move from the regional solicitor's office to the U.S. Attorney, the regional representative of the Department of Justice. With rare exceptions, the U.S. Attorney acts as the barrister, the trial arm of the government's legal capacity. By law, the U.S. Attorney's office is authorized to proceed entirely on its own when it takes over cases from the regional solicitor. In fact, however, the U.S. Attorney's staff works with varying degrees of intimacy with the lawyers from the referring agency. "You have to talk to the U.S. Attorney's office," explains a regional solicitor. "Some agencies just simply dump everything on the U.S. Attorney's office and say, 'Here, you do it and let us know what happens.' I have been told my agency is one of the most active in terms of providing support." Usually such support takes the form of a brief that the U.S. Attorney can use to prosecute the case. Somewhat less frequently, members of the regional solicitor's office are invited to act as co-counsel on the case. Thus, despite the official monopoly on litigation enjoyed by the Department of Justice, opportunities for cooperation between the regional solicitor and the U.S. Attorney are numerous. Indeed, so common is the chance to go to court that one significant source of job satisfaction in the regional solicitor's office derives from the frequency of exposure to trial work.

On occasion, cooperation between the two sets of lawyers breaks down. This is most likely to occur when an overloaded U.S. Attorney's staff defers work sent to it by one cabinet department while pursuing the work of another. In such circumstances, regional solicitors do much the same thing that corporate staff attorneys do with recalcitrant clients: they ask their superiors in the general counsel's office to put pressure on their opposite numbers' boss in the Department of Justice.

Regional solicitors' offices vary greatly in the extent to which they depend on the cooperation of the U.S. Attorney. The programs of certain cabinet departments generate notably more litigation than others. This variation results from historic differences between regulatory agencies (for example, the FTC or the SEC) and reform programs such as those mandated by recent environmental protection and workplace safety legislation. Regulatory programs are the oldest attempts of the government to order business behavior. Two of the offices participating in this study derive their mandates from the reform efforts of the Progressive Era. In these agencies a relatively mature, routinized, stable relationship has been developed over time between the regulatory agency and the private sector. Regulatory work typically focuses on fact-finding and investigation in its initial phases and on negotiation thereafter. Litigation is rare to the extent that both parties have clear, realistic, and convergent expectations of each other and of the administrative and judicial boards that might be called upon to resolve differences between them.

Clear understanding between regulatory agencies and regulated industries is greatly enhanced by the number of attorneys who have moved from government agency to private industry. Historians (for example, Kolko, 1963) and political scientists (for example, Quirk, 1981) have scrutinized this traffic with a jaundiced eye: watchdogs do not normally join the ranks of those whom they should be watching. Lawyers in the regulatory agencies report no such reservations. Good lawyers, they say, are craftsmen. They have no purposes of their own; they take their marching orders from their clients. "I do admire attorneys who are courageous leaders of one cause or another," says an attorney in a regulatory agency. "I think it more professional; however, I have a higher regard for a person's capabilities as an attorney, when I see that they are are able, in effect, to argue either side of any question." Another elaborates on this ambidextrous view of professionalism: "I have no qualms about changing sides. Will I be comfortable defending [businesses] in front of the [agency]? I can hardly wait! Certainly there are two sides to every story. In fact, I haven't entertained the thought in a long time, 'Would I be promoting justice to be on the other side?' . . . [That] is really not a concept I'm thinking about. I don't even think about it on this side."

However, as willing as lawyers may be to switch sides, they cannot always do so. Sociologist Malcolm Spector (1972, 1973) has shown that the flow of employees from government to industry has a distinctive structure. The government's capacity to initiate and to reorganize regulatory activity begins the process. As a consequence of government initiative, civil service lawyers develop expertise in newly defined regulatory areas more quickly than their counterparts in the private bar. As the government's regulatory policies change, so those civil servants with the most experience in new fields become attractive to private employers. They are courted and often recruited. But, in the aggregate, movement from regulatory agency to regulated industry turns out to be a sporadic and shifting pattern, not a steady, continuous stream.

Far from deploring this pattern of movement, regional solicitors positively endorse it. One agency head believes that former civil servants often retain the values and commitments of their old agencies. "There is a great deal of loyalty, even on the part of private law, to the [agency]," he claims. Another explains how these loyalties manifest themselves: "I've talked to attorneys that have left the agency. One of the things that bothers them most when they go outside is not that anybody is asking them to do anything illegal or improper, but the business person is interested more in the bottom line. They're coming to their attorney [demanding services] some of which are very gray areas in which the attorney is not comfortable. They are not happy with that type of pressure."

In addition to carrying loyalties to government programs and perhaps a restraining influence with them into the private bar, former government employees also take their network with them. "You tend to know the person you're dealing with and he tends to know you," says the regional administrator of an independent regulatory agency. "You can reasonably rely on the fact that he knows what you are talking about, which is a great problem when you are dealing with lawyers who don't have a [government] background."

Finally, the commerce between the regulatory agencies and the private bar is thought to keep government attorneys on their toes. Given the economic advantages of the corporate staff counsel's position, the lure of such jobs serves as an incentive to the civil servant. In the words of a regional administrator, "I think it's healthy for them to want to get out. It makes them better lawyers here, even if they never get out. As long as they have that ambition, they keep upgrading themselves, and they are more aggressive and they deal with the law better."

Despite the advantages that accrue to a long-standing and intimate relationship between regulators and regulated, litigation still occurs between them because both parties see the relationship, no matter how routinized, as essentially adversarial. The real meaning of changes in the regulatory mandate is often established only through litigation. And finally, a certain number of businesses will always try to defeat even a clearly understood regulatory system. Still, litigation amounts to only a small percentage of the caseload of the older regulatory agencies.

The same cannot be said of the work of those government reform programs that owe their existence to the legislation of the New Deal, the Great Society, and more recent social programs. Two agencies participating in this study derive the bulk of their cases from relatively new reform legislation. Because the agencies operate in areas without generations of precedent to give shape to their work, litigation is relatively more common in these two settings. Litigiousness is also augmented by the fact that often industry still is engaged in a wholesale effort to delegitimate the most recent reform efforts.

The substance of the work in reform agencies also lends itself to strong adversarial feelings, if not to actual litigation. Social reform efforts are often mounted by agencies that deal directly with disadvantaged members of the public. Face-to-face encounters with the dependent, the old, and the needy tend to enhance government attorneys' zeal for their work. Moreover, attorneys who enter these programs frequently bring with them a reformist desire to improve public life through government action. Typically, attorneys in the social reform agencies initially choose government work not as a springboard to the private sector but as an end in itself. One lawyer who made an unusual, against-the-stream move *from* business *into* government points out, "I was making a lot of money for people who I wasn't really interested in, and I wasn't really interested in helping them accumulate more of that cash." So saying, this lawyer echoes the refrain of the law firm associate who explained that the real object of business law is "saving money for people who already have a lot of money." Still another government attorney affirms the distinction between public and private work: he chose his present job "for reasons other than practicing business-related, profit-oriented law. At that time, law as an instrument of social change was not only probable, but it was very much happening." A third attorney reflects on the satisfactions of government work: "I feel good about [my job]. In that respect, I'm really lucky because, generally speaking, in the legal profession, a lot of times you end up being a hired gun. I know people who have ended up representing causes I wouldn't feel particularly comfortable doing. To some extent, being here for three years and not having done anything that I don't feel good about is a real luxury."

REGIONAL ADMINISTRATORS AND THEIR STAFFS: PROFESSIONALS AS CIVIL SERVANTS

Despite these differences between the business-regulating and social reform agencies, all government law offices have a number of significant features in common. First and most important is the fact that the government law office owes its existence to legislation rather than to market demand. Both its charter and its economic base are wholly political in character: offices and programs exist by virtue of the congressional appropriations process. Indeed, during the time it took to complete our interviews with government attorneys, two of the offices participating in this study were threatened with federal budget cuts that made no provision for them, a third was faced with the dismantling of its entire client base, and the fourth found that everyone on its staff was periodically issued 30-day Reduction in Force (RIF) layoff notices that constitute the first step toward dismissal. Thus, the shelter from market forces that civil service employment is said to provide seems, in these times, to be a fragile protection at best. It would probably be more accurate to say that government employees and private legal staffs are at the mercy of different sets of pressures, but that neither has ultimate control over the development and disappearance of their jobs.

The vagaries of political funding have a number of consequences. Primarily, government managers complain that both the penury and the uncertainty of their budgets deprive them of the tools that are ordinarily available in the private sector to motivate workers. Regional solicitors concur that "Congress is ultimately the employer, and they react according to a variety of situations which aren't based on any real managerial theories; it's based purely in politics." As a result of this dependence on congressional largesse, "You can't reward. It is ridiculous. I remember a few years ago, they established the Senior Executive Service. They had all these great promises! If you do good work, you'll get bonuses, you'll get rewards. The private industry consultants came in and said, 'We give bonuses to 75 percent of our executives.' [Here they] said, 'Well, we'll cut that to 50.' They implemented the plan and they cut it to 25 and then dropped it down to 20. In my agency last year, only 7 bonuses were awarded to 65 executives. And I think this is true throughout the government."

If managers do not feel capable of rewarding good work because of budgetary constraints, they are equally reluctant to penalize unsatisfactory work because of the protections that accrue to civil servants with tenure. "You can't fire anybody" is a frequently reiterated theme. It is supplemented by another: despite some lip service to the idea of merit evaluations, few managers are willing to penalize a staffer with smaller than average annual increments for fear of having a disgruntled employee on their hands. "You still have to keep the mediocre guy," says one manager, "and cutting his pay [increase] by

2 percent isn't going to hurt him at all. [But] the heartache it results in can impact on the effectiveness of other aspects of the office, create more harm than is worthwhile."

On this issue, staff attorneys and their managers see the world in much the same terms. "What happens," says a staff attorney, "is that most managers take the course of least resistance because they've got more important things to worry about, and they give the person a minimum which will not cause fuss." Another adds, concerning merit pay,

> There was a kernel of an idea [but] it doesn't actually work in fact. One of the reasons, the people you're in competition with are not in this part of the country at all. They're in other regions. By the time you get to the decision, the people who make the decision have so little appreciation of what the problems of the person's work [are] that they can't make sensible decisions. So what they do is mush everybody together in the middle and they end up distributing the pot pretty equally. And also the amount of money involved, particularly when government salaries are as stagnant as they are, it's a couple of hundred dollars a year. So you don't actually base your performance week-to-week and month-to-month on the hopes of merit pay.

The lack of pay differentials is, of course, significant to government attorneys in and of itself. But it is interesting too because of the sharp contrast it provides with the private sector. In law firms, good work can yield more profits for partners and can be rewarded with larger bonuses for associates. In corporations, bonuses, although less routine, are also a real financial incentive, as are fringe benefits like stock-option plans. In government, however, good work has be to be rewarded by nonpecuniary means.

Recent management literature (for example, Kanter, 1977) has speculated about the hidden significance of financial incentives. According to this research, bosses who motivate their workers with carrots—opportunities to earn bonuses and win promotions—are much better liked than bosses who use sticks to elicit compliance from their staffs. The choice of stick or carrot, however, seems to be only partly a matter of personal preference. In large measure, management style is a reflection of the boss's own position. Executives on their way up the corporate ladder take their teams with them, thereby creating carrots to be distributed. Bosses at their own career ceilings can offer their subordinates fewer opportunities and are often perceived to be unduly preoccupied with issues of deference. Accordingly, such managers are unpopular.

The foregoing suggests that the difference between effective and ineffective management results in large part from a manager's structural position rather than from his or her personal characteristics. In government, unfortunately, most managers seem to be in the position of bad bosses: the seniority-based civil service promotion system allows them to hold out little hope of access to a fast track, and the nature of their funding gives them few monetary rewards to dispense. This pattern, it seems, contributes to the widespread complaints about civil service administration.

Nevertheless, individual offices vary in their morale. The more troubled ones are generally the business-regulating offices, whose staff see no promise of private sector jobs when they are threatened by cutbacks. The happier offices seem to be reform agencies whose staffs are ideologically committed to their work. In such agencies, lawyers will pull together to protect their programs even in the face of adversity. In one such office the regional solicitor recounts with pride: "The national office put through a conference call shortly before Thanksgiving and they said a RIF program was in the offing and it should take effect shortly after the first of the year unless we received a certain number of applications for a voluntary RIF—in other words, take two weeks of leave without pay. Well, the exact figures I don't have, but something like 450 people volunteered to take a reduction of up to two weeks in pay, and we had more than our share in this particular office. People agreed to take two weeks off, a day here and a day there, without pay, so that other people would not be RIFed."

But the team spirit of this office is a rarity. More typically, government bosses, with little latitude in their own careers, are more insistent on the prerogatives of their rank than are private sector managers and hence are less likely to inspire this kind of esprit de corps. For example, law firms and corporate law departments encourage, indeed rely on, the informal social bonds that develop among their staffs to enhance productivity and commitment to the workplace. In contrast, the regional solicitor is much more likely to insist on controlling communications among his staff and between his staff and their clients. All four of the men who headed the government offices in which we interviewed retained the assignment of cases as their exclusive prerogative. All wanted to be consulted by their staffs for advice, even when they typically responded by referring the staff person to another colleague for further consultation. Only in the highly motivated office described above could the regional solicitor boast that "every attorney in this office has an opportunity to handle the whole spectrum of the laws that we handle." More common was a pattern in which each attorney served a limited number of programs within the agency. As a result, individuals become familiar with only a small segment of the work done in their department. Such specialization further serves to orient staffers away from their peers who are unfamiliar with their work and toward their bosses, who assign cases and specialty areas.

At present, government attorneys reject the notion that specialization could be carried further—that, one day, attorneys might not handle whole cases but only single functions such as discovery, trial work, or negotiations. Yet this very pattern is already established in other levels of government; in public defender offices, for example, attorneys are often assigned to stations (arraignments, jury trials, bench trials, sentencing appearances, and so forth) rather than to cases (Sudnow, 1965). As we have already seen, law firm associates also underestimate the potential for control implicit in specialization; when they bemoan the narrowing of their assignments, they do so out of fear of boredom rather than fear of being controlled. Government attorneys similarly deny that their offices could ever structure work as public defender programs do, with the resultant increase in repetitiveness and decrease in the span of assignments. In general it seems that staff attorneys are somewhat naive about the organization of their work: they are apt to see its present features as immutable even as precedents for its drastic alteration are being constructed in other offices.

The incentives that spur regional solicitors to maintain tight control over the life of the office arise not only from the paucity of rewards they have to offer but also from their own feelings of being very much subject to the scrutiny of the home office. "I read everything that goes out," says a regional solicitor. "I see everything that comes in. It is a reflection of the extent to which my central office is counting on me to know everything that's going on. It somewhat goes against the grain of my philosophy. But almost more than the substantive aspects, what I want to check out is the coordination aspect. In other words I just feel that my accumulated knowledge and background may bring some aspect, even if it's nothing more than the internal politics of it, that I just would like to lend to the situation."

The distastefulness of having someone constantly looking over one's shoulder is underscored for government attorneys by the fact that they continue to use private law firm experience as the measure of a good work life. Unlike corporate staff attorneys, however, government lawyers are unable even to pretend that their positions compares favorably to the private business bar. First of all, civil servants earn less than private business attorneys. "In this country, measurement of success by economic definition is very ingrained. The general public, using that yardstick, will evaluate that the private corporate lawyer is far superior in all respects to the public lawyer, because they make more money. Lawyers themselves, I think, tend to feel that way also; that the job, because it pays half as much as what you would earn in a private law firm immediately, from the economic point of view, takes on second class status."

Not only the pay but also the quality of daily work life is thought to be less bureaucratic, therefore better, in the law firm than in the government. One regional attorney compares his experience in law firm work to his current managerial responsibilities: "Half a generation ago the practice of law in a law firm was a kind of a loose association of people who worked at their own capability. You didn't have any kind of structured approach to it, assembling troops and passing out assignments and marching all in the same direction. I really want to run this office as if it was a small office, where people work because they care about it and where there isn't any need to have rigid rules." Unfortunately, this man finds himself implementing both substantive and personnel policies with which he disagrees. Even though it is generally recognized that private firms are now coming to be more systematically administered, the government law office has always been highly bureaucratized and remains a much less glamorous workplace.

Nevertheless, the advantages of law firm and corporate life are offset to some degree by the dark side of the private bar. For example, the economic advantages accruing to private attorneys are thought to give life in the law firm its peculiarity cut-throat character. One agency head explains: "If you're [an] associate in a private law firm you're in competition with five or more other associates. The associate knows that they're not going to keep all these people, and obviously they're [all] trying to make the partnership, so there's less of a sharing of knowledge and ideas within that type of setting, [whereas here], if somebody is competently doing the job, we're permitted to promote them."

Perhaps more convincingly, government lawyers claim that members of the private bar often devote their professional lives to intrinsically trivial matters. "It doesn't necessarily follow [from their earnings] that the more interesting work and the weightier legal issues are being handled by attorneys in a corporate law firm. For example, one of my friends works in a large law firm. About four years out of law school he's earning what an attorney in the government would earn maybe ten years out of law school, and is doing such cases as a person wishes to sue their architect for faulty design of the swimming pool, or two old spinster sisters are fighting over a piece of property—and either in the social utility or the legal complexity one could not equate with that amount of remuneration." By contrast, government attorneys report with pride that they have "a real awesome client: the people of the United States!"

Not only do government attorneys feel themselves to be addressing significant issues of law and justice. Often their access to important work comes more quickly than it would in private practice. Just as the relative wealth of the private bar has a dark side, so the penury of the public bar has its advantages. Government work often is encrusted with layers of supervision, but it is also commonly understaffed. In this environment, young civil service attorneys are given significant work almost from the day they arrive in the office. One young woman notes: "The one advantage of government law is that at the beginning you get to do a lot of things yourself, so that whereas in a firm you would be under someone's direction, in [the] government office, you walk in and suddenly you're given cases and you handle them." The chief administrator in an agency that does some of its own litigation stresses the special value of courtroom experience for litigators.

> The person who came here just recently from a big law firm took a pay cut to come here. Especially in the big firms they're not allowed to do things. I said, "What have you done?" [because] you hear the rumor, people can be five years in the firm and they haven't even done a deposition. And she said, "Oh, I've done a deposition." With a straight face! [They are] not allowed to go to court, because the partners go to court. We are in with heavies on the other side because we're dealing with large projects. There's a lot of money. And, you know, usually when we go to court, it's the tough leagues. There are some sleazes that come against us, but a lot of times, three lawyers come in from Ropes and Gray—Winken, Blinken, and Nod—and the older one gets to say something. The other ones just say, "Yes, sir," and it's really kind of funny. And then you get one of our guys out of law school and we win them just as much as we lose them.

Indeed, ready access to significant and stimulating work is probably the single biggest attraction that motivates the government lawyer. Says one regional administrator, "The biggest payoff for someone working in a government agency like this, because there are definite limitations as to promotions and remuneration that you can't overcome, the most I can give people is responsibility." "On a macroscopic level," says another attorney, "the things that motivate me are the fact that I love our legal system. I want the government to work, I'm concerned [to get] the clients up to an effective level of functioning so that I can feel, as a taxpayer, that I'm not being robbed to pay for such an operation." Another speaks in more personal terms; "You know, you get a case where there is a life-threatening situation, something that could really impair people for the rest of their lives. Those cases you look at with relish, and you enjoy doing everything that you have to do. And you do a lot of extra work."

The promise of interesting and significant work thus motivates both those attorneys who plan to stay in government and those who look forward to leaving it. For the latter, ready access to important cases enhances the value of their apprenticeship; for the former it is an end in itself.

Yet, as we have seen, motivation alone is not enough. Just as law firm associates must learn to translate enthusiasm into effective effort, so too government staffers, often fresh from law school, must learn to apply themselves to the tasks at hand. However, associates and the junior grade civil servants are taught the ropes differently. Associates may be confined to writing memoranda on minor points of law longer than they would like. Yet, paradoxically, they eventually emerge from their apprenticeships with a strong sense of their own efficacy and craftsmanship. Civil servants, on the other hand, are given whole cases almost at once, yet are not always able to realize the sense of autonomy and effectiveness such experiences could provide. For, in addition to getting significant case assignments, new government attorneys are also "given" the full weight of civil service supervision: someone is always looking over their shoulders, and, indeed, their boss's shoulder. "It goes through enough here," says a second-in-command. "It starts at the attorney, then it goes to the branch chief, then it goes to me [deputy regional administrator], then it goes to the regional administrator, and then it goes to [two rounds of supervision in Washington]. So there are enough layers." Nor is the scrutiny of the successive ranks of bureaucrats merely pro forma. An attorney with strong reformist motives of his own says, "Supervision is not a rubber stamp. My recommendations are gone over carefully and fairly frequently amended, occasionally overruled."

The local supervisory structure, extending from the practicing attorney upward through a project manager, a deputy regional solicitor, and a regional solicitor, is tied to a national civil service ranking system. Most attorneys enter the civil service at the rank of GS11, with a salary range that in 1981 began at $23,566. Newcomers are rapidly and routinely promoted from entry level positions through the GS12 and GS13 rungs. Provided that satisfactory work is done, it normally takes three to five years to reach the GS13 level. Thereafter, promotions become somewhat more uncertain. In some branches of government, GS14 positions are reserved for staffers who carry administrative responsibilities. In other branches, supervisory work is not required, and GS14 status is accorded on the basis of seniority. In still other offices, administrative projects are created to make senior staff attorneys eligible for promotion.

Whatever the means of entering the GS14 positions, however, leaving them is still more problematic. The GS15 rank (whose top salary in 1981 was $60,689) is reserved for people who hold positions of major administrative responsibility, and the total number of such positions is therefore limited. For many attorneys, the GS14 rank represents the ceiling of their careers. In this study, for example, well over half the respondents were stalled at the GS14 rank. This distribution in turn diminishes the promotion possibilities for younger attorneys. It bolsters the conventional wisdom, especially prevalent in the regulatory agencies, that government work is good for a three- to five-year hitch but no longer than that. "I happen to subscribe to the theory that the government has two classes of people," says a GS14 attorney in a regulatory agency: "the young and the very competent lawyers who are in the [government] for up to five years, to learn the law and to develop their skills and then go out and earn a living, and the people who have been around twenty years, who are here because they are lazy or incompetent." This sentiment is widely shared and, in fact, does motivate many experienced attorneys to leave government work. Ironically, then, the very system of supervision that is designed to guarantee good work at the individual level often serves to undermine it in the aggregate by contributing to a high attrition rate among experienced lawyers.

Perhaps the best way to address this paradoxical picture of significant work bogged down in intrusive supervision is to recognize frankly that two sets of forces are at work in the government law office. On a day-to-day basis, the government attorney works much as the business lawyer does—that is, a certain ethos of professionalism pervades even the stuffiest regional solicitor's office. The following account, given by a regional solicitor, could have come equally well from a law firm partner or a corporate general counsel: "As an attorney becomes more and more adept at doing what they are doing, more and more confident in what they are doing, I supervise them less and less. As far as I am concerned, they are my peers. I will just simply give them my work and say, 'Here, what do you think?'"

Staff attorneys respond favorably to such appeals to their professionalism. People will stay at their desks as long as necessary to get the work done because, as one man says, "I feel an obligation to the law." "We don't look at the clock when we know people are busy and working," adds another manager. "Sometimes they stay until quite late in the evening, sometimes they're in here on weekends. And if somebody is not getting into the office until ten because they just want to sack in a little bit, sure, that's ok. Basically, what I keep telling lawyers who say, 'You're telling me that I should be working more overtime,' I say, 'No, I don't care if you work overtime or not. I know how hard you're working because I see what you're doing. If you're sitting in your office at 6 P.M. simply because you're waiting for me to come by and then slip out the door, why, I'm not that silly.'" The manager's willingness to disregard petty rules in favor of self-regulation adds greatly to the office esprit.

Peer approval also is significant here, as it is in other settings, in motivating staff efforts. An attorney who writes a particularly cogent brief for a case going to the Justice Department will be recognized as co-counsel, his or her name will appear in the official pleading of the case and thereafter in all the reports and abstracts that keep track of such things. There are also tangible satisfactions at the trial level. Especially in the business-regulating agencies, government lawyers can test their mettle against the leading partners of the leading law firms. "I have enjoyed the experience of opposing truly hotshot attorneys, big, nationally known attorneys," says one such lawyer. "My adversarial counterparts are almost always high rankins senior partners in big town law firms." In his most recent co-counseling efforts, he continues, "opposing us were 33 nationally known defense counsel, including one of the two leading professors who really writes most of the treatises in [this] field." Can the government staffer win against such opponents? "Yeah," they say, "we do." "As a matter of fact, yes, we usually win." "Generally speaking, I'd say we're fairly effective."

The astute reader may be suspicious of these optimistic claims by government attorneys. If law firm lawyers are as well trained and in-house counsel are as seasoned as they say they are, how can government attorneys win so often? A rigorous assessment of the success of government lawyers would require an enormously complex historical evaluation of regulatory programs and so is outside the scope of this book. What can be said here about winning and losing is this: most people who are committed to a particular occupation or career manage to construct for themselves a definition of success that is within their grasp and that enhances the value of their work in their own eyes. So it is among lawyers—with the additional proviso that the definition of success and failure is particularly complex for them because it encompasses much more than the final verdict on cases. Lawyers can win cases they ostensibly lose by keeping information that would be especially damaging to their clients out of the trial or by obtaining better settlements or lighter sentences than might be expected. They can also lose a case that is officially won if the cost of the victory renders it Pyrrhic for the client. For the government attorney, we have already had a hint of how the victory-defining process operates. "We win them just as much as we lose them," says a satisfied administrator of his rookies' performance against lawyers from "the tough leagues." Winning, then, means winning half the time, or winning occasionally over formidable opponents, or winning more often than government attorneys would expect to, given the disparity in resources between themselves and their opponents.

But even this definition of success—the recognition of one's peers and the challenge of worthy opponents—does not fully describe the work life of the civil service lawyer. Also present on a daily basis are the most cumbersome features of state bureaucracies. At every point, supervision is more coercive and less supportive in government than in the private sector. For example, whereas the law firm partner watches with half-tolerant, half-exasperated amusement as young associates brings in their own cases, the government administrator flatly forbids such initiatives:

> Certainly if one goes back, the pattern of attorneys following their own noses, following the line of least resistance, or following their own interests in developing cases was prevalent. I used to say, in effect, the way this place is run is: we've got some pretty good attorneys who are energetic. They'll take some cases and go off in a corner and they'll do them, come back and they'll be pretty good cases. Other people will take cases off in a corner and hope nobody sees them. And, literally, when I became responsible for the initial phases of trying to manage this thing, the first thing I found was that nobody knew which attorneys were assigned to what cases. And when we finally gathered that information together, we found that there were some cases to which there were no lawyers assigned and there were some attorneys who had no cases. This had been going on for years. Now we do have this rather intensive evaluating system which was developed out of the morass that existed that's become highly formalized and bureaucratic in some respects, in that there's an awful lot of second guessing that goes on within the evaluation system. In effect, people are told: "Well, that kind of case, we don't want that kind of case any more."

Following upon the rationalization of case assignments is the development of the computerized docket, which allows the regional solicitor to keep track of both individual cases and individual staffers. On a monthly basis the regional solicitor receives an inventory showing the actions taken in the previous month on each case and the number of cases analyzed, negotiated, or closed by each attorney. The monthly report is supplemented by a semiannual review that "is supposed to be a physical look by each attorney at all the cases in [the] general litigation file and a short written report to the supervisor as to why the case is still around or what needs to be done to effect the closing of that particular case." Thus a review procedure has been established that is meant to ensure that no case becomes lost in a bureaucratic limbo.

The implementation of this system varies widely. In some offices it is almost invisible; but more often it is highly intrusive. In the most collegially administered office, the regional solicitor says: "We try to keep an open door policy with regard to case load because it's sometimes hard to monitor just by looking at numbers of cases, to really know the extent of activity or work that's necessary at that given time. So attorneys are encouraged to indicate to us if they feel that they are jammed up and they can't really handle what's being assigned to them." But in a more bureaucratic office, the record keeping has expanded into a set of weekly, monthly, quarterly, and semi-annual checks. An agency staffer spoke of her annoyance:

> We basically had to account for all of the time we spent. We kept track of, for instance, how many phone call requests, formal requests for advice. We have to report weekly to our central office on how many briefs were written, how many briefs were typed, how many briefs went out, how many hours each of our summer staff worked, and how many hours they spent writing briefs. Plus, we have a monthly report which includes information on each brief that went out, including the grade of the person who wrote the brief, how long it took to write the brief, how long it took to review the brief, how long it took to type, and also how long after the record was received the brief was sent out. All this information is compiled and average figures comparing region by region in each of these areas [are issued].

The computerized docket is not the only device by which managers try to exercise ever tighter control over the work they supervise. They also use a variant of what corporate staff attorneys call a scrutiny file or letter pack. Within a single office, consulting still tends to be done informally: each person knows what everyone else is working on, what cases have passed through the office recently, what issues have been researched in the not too distant past. But, additionally, the regional solicitor culls the most interesting briefs, memoranda, and pleadings produced by his staff. These are forwarded to the general counsel's office in Washington. The general counsel, in turn, compiles the best documents from around the nation and circulates packets of them to all the regional offices under his jurisdiction. Thus the peer pressure created by a "scrutiny file" in the corporate law firm is augmented in the government office by the fact of national exposure.

Moreover, for the individual attorney, work is also heavily structured by the use of government-issue boilerplate. Especially the drafting of complaints—a necessary first step for either negotiation or litigation—can be reduced to standard components. Says one regional solicitor, "A lot of this stuff now has been done time and again. We have word processing machines. So there isn't a heck of a lot of room for pride of authorship." In this very office a junior attorney offers another, more jaundiced view of his boss's impatience with "pride of authorship": "He knows what is in the book is legally sufficient. But if I dream up something else, then he really has to do some legal thinking instead of having it routine." This stands in sharp contrast to the law firm partner who insists both that his apprentices learn to draft documents from scratch and that even such carefully drafted documents be revised to fit the particulars of each new deal.

The degree to which boilerplate so prestructures a case that it obviates the need for thinking is described by a senior attorney:

> It would start off with coverage. How is this firm covered under the law? The next area would be the entire industry: How many had been investigated in the past and what was found? The next area would be exemptions: Who would be exempt? We call it the loophole situation—who's going to escape by the loophole; that would be discussed. The next area is what the investigator terms "standard compliance," and they would then hit the major areas that are violated . . . section 6, section 7. . . . Then there would be a disposition section: What happened at the close of the conference? Who said what to whom? What was the attitude? Then the investigator would have a witness evaluation. The next area would be introducing the written statements taken by the investigator. Then, if there is a fairly recent prior investigation, say in the last 6 or 7 years, that investigation would be attached. Then you would write what we call a legal analysis, which is almost analogous to the investigator's report, and it would follow pretty much the same procedure, outline, except for the recommendations section.

Yet although this elaboration of boilerplate narrows the scope of the staff attorney's discretion, many forces militate against standardization. First is the fact that the forms can be filled in only after someone has evaluated the basic materials and decided whether there is a case and, if so, what strategy should guide its development. "In a legal case, you have to have an overall view," explains the man who listed the fixed components of a complaint. "Someone's got to go through the case and know what it's about," says another, who continues, "even in this office, you'll see people take the same case and treat it very differently."

Negotiation is another area where there is room for individual attorneys to treat cases differently. "We're not just making documents," notes a staff attorney. "We are also doing a lot of negotiating. Once you [file your complaint to get into court] whether or not you want to do discovery, or enter into negotiations right away, whether you want to move for summary judgment, those are decisions I can make recommendations on."

The behavior of the private party whose conduct is being challenged also influences the course of events. Civil servants have considerable latitude in recommending remedies and penalties. Often such recommendations are influenced by their opponents. For example, a reform agency attorney representing an investigator who was refused entry during an inspection recounts: "We asked for $5,000 a day in fines until they let [us] in. And we got that. That's a very aggressive thing for us to have done and I, as an individual attorney, wanted to do it that way, and I was backed in this office. We might have considered trying to get the guy put in jail for not letting us in." Another attorney recalls: "I've had cases, serious citations, where the maximum penalty is $1,000, and I've amended the citation to make it a willful violation where the maximum penalty is $10,000."

The foregoing anecdotes preview a discussion, to be taken up below, about the extent to which government lawyers can pursue their own visions of justice at the expense of public policies promulgated by elected officials. Clearly there is at least some scope for an attorney's personal feelings to enter into his or her work. A business person whose conduct is deeply offensive to a government regulator may well face relentless scrutiny and severe penalties. Yet the civil servant's freedom is limited to the occasional incident. In general, policy is set by the home office and enforced by an elaborate supervisory structure.

Nevertheless, business behavior serves as a significant source of destandardization in the work of all government lawyers. Regulators, for example, are often investigating allegations of fraud. And, to the extent that fraud is unique, so too is the work of the investigator. "When you get into a fraud case, there's seventeen thousand different things that have happened," which make it impossible to reduce the attorney's work to the mechanics of filling in boilerplate.

Finally, the legal system itself tends to destandardize the lawyer's work. Different judicial bodies respond to different arguments, require different standards of proof, review cases differently. All this diminishes the utility of boilerplate for cases that develop beyond the negotiating stage. One woman who does some litigation speaks of using boilerplate less than in the past. "We do use it to the extent that we can [but] we've been finding, particularly in certain districts, that the courts have become more and more scrutinizing. You really have to individualize these cases."

Because technical devices such as boilerplate cannot completely control the civil service attorney, managers must rely on social strategies to secure the behavior they desire. Thus, despite managerial skepticism about an evaluation system that can neither reward nor punish, periodic attempts are made to tinker with that system in order to enhance productivity. The most recent round of "improving" the evaluation system has led to the development of a "management-by-objectives" program, now in place in all the regional solicitors' offices. This plan calls for bosses and staff to confer before any actual assessment of individual performance occurs. Negotiations should produce an agreement about the particular tasks associated with each job title and the standards that will be used to evaluate individual performance. Staffers are urged to construct annual career plans that will allow them to develop more and more job-related skills and to demonstrate their preparedness for promotion. At the end of the year, then, the areas of conflict between management and labor should have been greatly reduced. The only real business remaining in the evaluation process is the assessment of the staff attorney's actual performance in light of an already agreed upon set of criteria.

In general, the lawyers who participated in this study seem more impatient than hostile with this means of evaluation. They do not seem to fear that bosses will use the system to make substantively or ideologically unacceptable demands. The tasks they are expected to perform appear, on the whole, to be appropriate. One attorney describes the components of his evaluation: "In [our] cases we have to get a memorandum analyzing the case, conduct thorough legal research, review and analyze litigation files, recommend appropriate action, analyze and provide legal advice in non-litigation, participate [in] and conduct negotiations and conferences. These are all things I should be doing, that any lawyers in the office should be doing."

However, in its implementation, the management-by-objective system is universally described as reducing concern for performance to a trivial and misleading numbers game. One attorney explains: "If you are a GS9, you have to get 60 percent of your analyzing memoranda within 30 days. If you're an 11 you have to get 75, if you're a 12 you have to [complete] 90. You can meet the standards and be writing crummy analyses of your cases, or you can not meet the standard but be writing excellent memoranda. It's very hard, trying to make quantitative standards for lawyers. It's so hard to measure the quality of the work that's being done. One person might settle all her cases and be getting excellent settlements and somebody else might be trying all their cases and be getting crummy wins." Another lawyer notes, too, that the value of certain achievements (settlements versus trials, for example) varies tremendously with changes in political climate. As a reform-oriented lawyer, she pointed out that at present "part of the problem is that the courts are so business-oriented that, generally, you can do better with a settlement."

If the implementation of a management-by-objectives system often trivializes the staff attorney's work, its results can nevertheless be significant for individual careers. Many lawyers report some version of the following story: "We were all evaluated 'satisfactory.' Never

higher. Reason is because in order to do higher, it had to be justi-
fied. And the person who did them didn't want to go to the trouble
of justifying."

Administrators see this pattern somewhat differently—not as a
product of managerial laziness but as an element necessary to the system. In the words of one regional solicitor:

> I think private industry always pursues excellence. The government
> operates quite effectively on a median type competency basis. Now
> they got off into this merit crap. It was whistling Dixie. You apply a
> merit-type evaluation to what is essentially a median competency
> structure, and one you can't change no matter what type of evalua-
> tion you make, [it's] just a waste of time. The government cannot
> pursue excellence. It should adjust itself to the fact. The people don't
> want to pay for the best. The system is designed to do a fairly good
> job for everybody. They should acknowledge that fact, forget the
> bullshit.

POLITICIANS AND CIVIL SERVANTS:
THE PRIMACY OF PUBLIC POLICY

In sum, the median competency structure of the civil service holds
out few spectacular rewards or fearsome penalties to motivate its
members. Why, then, do lawyers seek government positions? For
some, civil service jobs represent a stepping stone to more lucrative
corporate employment. For others, the security of public work is
preferable to the hectic life of the business bar and the financial pre-
cariousness of solo practice. For still others, government law work is
a vehicle for accomplishing social reform. But whatever the reasons
that attorneys have for accepting government staff positions, regional solicitors have much less leverage over their work force than
do law firm partners or corporate general counsel. For this reason
the wise regional solicitor prefers to run the office by appealing to
his staff's professionalism, their political commitments, or other
internalized motivations to work. In large measure, this appeal
succeeds despite the onerous federal bureaucracy that threatens to
swamp it.

The single most destabilizing force in this modus vivendi is an abrupt and substantial shift in policy initiated by the politicians who set government goals from above. At the level of the individual agency, changed policies mean changed routines and altered bases for evaluation. Dramatic policy changes thus become occasions for civil servants to reevaluate their work commitments and for bosses to reassess their power. Much has been written about the capacity of career bureaucrats to resist, to sabotage, and to outlast unwelcome policies initiated by elected officials. These commentaries are usually made to criticize bureaucracies for rigidity, inefficiency, or insensitivity. However, this same controversy—about who is really running the show—is also another instance of the debate about the relationship of knowledge to power. How effectively can lawyers or other professionals use their unique knowledge to control their clients? To continue in their own possibly self-interested paths despite an ostensible commitment to serving their client's purposes? In the case of the civil service attorney, the immediate client is a program or an agent of the federal government. There is little question that most of these civil servants will rearrange their work to comply with counsel's advice about the legal adequacy of a projected course of action. The ultimate client, however, is "the people of the United States" in the persons of elected, policy-making officials. To the extent that most elected officials of either party are mainstream and centrist, elections are not likely to bring major policy changes that civil servants might wish to resist. But sometimes politicians with pronounced ideologically motivated agendas distinctively to the left or right of center do try to alter the business-as-usual stance of the government. The presidency of Ronald Reagan provides students of bureaucracy with just such a fascinating case study.

When the announced policies of the government change, how much impact do the new policies have on the behavior of salaried professionals? The civil service attorneys who participated in this study gave mixed answers to the question: Who is really in charge here? Certainly there is some leeway for attorneys who are unsympathetic to a particular administration's policies to ignore or resist them, as in the previously mentioned case of the attorney whose per-

sonal beliefs led him to recommend the more serious of two penalties in an ambiguous situation. Nevertheless, the general tenor of
staff attorney's remarks suggests that they can be subordinated to
policy dictates far more readily than the "intractable bureaucracy"
rhetoric would suggest. Most of the civil service attorneys in this
study would agree with the woman who said that "we definitely are
a conduit" through which policy changes are put into effect.

Top level, politically appointed administrators have available a
number of mechanisms for subordinating civil servants. First and
most obviously, the programs that the civil servant implements or
monitors can be overtly and publicly altered. "The law has been
changing," says a woman in a reform agency. "It's really changed
quite a bit in the past couple of years. Statute itself as well as regulation. And in many respects, it's more restrictive now than it ever has
been. For instance, the Congress has mandated that a certain percentage of [those who receive public moneys] be re-evaluated every
year." Another woman in the same agency tells of the programs she
once monitored. Typically, they had "twenty pages of regulations.
Now, the program has four regulations, takes up approximately one
eighth of a page, and it just says, 'You don't have to have a program.
If you choose to have a program, you have to file a state plan.' And
that's it! Before, we were the big overseers. Now we've got nothing
to oversee."

Overt program changes can be costly, however, if they stir up
public indignation. Often, politicians can achieve their purposes by
less controversial means: they simply change the behind-the-scenes
rules and procedures by which programs are implemented. In a reform agency where attorneys work directly with the public to monitor the behavior of private providers of services to the indigent, one
lawyer explains: "We used to be quite responsive to the public. Now
the word has come down, don't be so responsive to the public, because you might be setting yourself up for a lawsuit by saying, 'Oh
yes, I sympathize with you. This is wrong.' We're being removed
further and further from the ultimate public." In another case, a regulatory agency manager wishes to endorse his staffer's recommenda-

tion to bring suit against a company that refuses to comply with federal law. But now, the staffer points out, Washington is "threatening to send people out, [to] go through all of your evidence and make you show where every bit of evidence is, that it proves the statement in the memo." This policy is in direct contrast to previous practice, in which the home office was willing to back up the regional solicitor's judgment; if he said that the evidence was sufficient to support a suit, then litigation commenced. Today there is an extra layer of review. Whatever the administrative rationale for this additional step, it gives private business extra time to defy the regulations.

Procedural changes in the regulatory agencies are more than matched in the reform agencies, whose programs are particular targets of the Reagan administration. In one such office a staffer reports with shock that her regional solicitor was accused of "getting too much" in a *voluntary* settlement between his agency and a private service provider. The proposed settlement was turned down and had to be renegotiated along lines more favorable to private enterprise. The staffer is less concerned here with a single settlement than with the message that is being sent. "You just can't crucify yourself," she says. The effectiveness of the agency "depends on the willingness of the people here to go ahead and keep plugging away. What, of course, I fear is that they will anticipate changes and then make them themselves."

One way to induce such anticipation is to change the standards for evaluating agency personnel. In another reform agency, entrepreneurs whose places of business are inspected are asked to evaluate the inspector. This evaluation, in turn, becomes part of the inspector's own personnel file. Still another attorney describes further chilling effects: "A couple of months ago, they distributed a questionnaire to all the staff which was on legal issues in [a particularly controversial agency targeted by Reagan during his first campaign] and none of us could answer it. More than 50 percent of the questions were technical questions about the approach of the agency under Reagan and how they would view certain kinds of enforcement things. We couldn't answer it. It's pretty apparent that that was put out to make the [staff] aware that they didn't know what was expected of them by this administration. The implicit threat: 'You've got to play it very cool.'"

An emphasis on complying with admistration philosophy permeates the civil service law office even when no specific programmatic or procedural changes are contemplated. This tendency is especially pronounced in the regulatory agencies, which by and large have met with less outright hostility and more subtle attempts to curb their efforts than the reform agencies. "You have a sense of the degree of support you will receive if you were challenged" is a frequently heard comment. In particular, members of regulatory agencies report that "the agency has changed its focus. We focus on fraud violations more than some kind of regulatory requirement." "Let honest business get on with its business, and let's be more careful that we are going after the real crooks," says another regulator. "We're not taking on frontier issues with men who are otherwise reputable businessmen," he continues. "That change has occurred. The esoteric issues are out and the peripheral defendants are out. It has moved in a way I'm sure Reagan is very happy with."

When regulatory activity does occur, a more conciliatory stance on the part of government attorneys is rewarded. The new philosophy is captured by a politically astute regional solicitor: "When you are a regulator and an enforcer, you have to wear two hats. As long as you regulate people, I feel personally, you have an obligation to help them to the utmost capacity that you have available to you. On the other hand, when they step over the line, you've got to make the other judgment. Now you have got a big action here. So you really have a friend/enemy relationship constantly."

The preceding discussion of changing regulatory behavior seems to imply that government attorneys, left to their own devices, would be zealous regulators. In this view, only deliberate, ideologically motivated directives could swerve the regulator from his or her intended path. Some attorneys, however, suggest that the current policies are welcomed by lawyers—and more for professional than for ideological reasons. Truly aggressive regulation almost always requires attorneys to move beyond their own expertise and to rely on the knowledge of others. For example, certain kinds of price-fixing agreements between ostensible competitors are illegal when arrived at through a process of secret meetings and negotiations. But the very same behavior of price alignment, when orchestrated through a public medium like a press conference, is entirely legal.[1] Lawyers are comfortable with maintaining this distinction because their expertise directs them to view as significantly different behavior arising from the deliberate coordination of activities and behavior that is more subtly choreographed. Economists, on the other hand, might argue that the distinction between price fixing through clandestine meeting and price fixing through open announcement is negligible since the effect on the economy is the same. If lawyers typically are loathe to acknowledge this latter point, it is precisely because making the admission would put them in the position of relying on other experts to assess the significance of certain patterns of behavior. A regulatory agency staffer captures this distinction: lawyers, he says, are reluctant "even to go after something which is other than conduct-oriented. In other words, you can tell people that they can't *do* something, because what they're doing is a bad thing; but you can't tell them not to *be* something because what they're being is a bad thing."

This preference for conduct-oriented regulation is in fact a preference for not venturing beyond the confines of traditional legal expertise to make a case. Further, the government lawyer's reluctance to depend upon expert witnesses[2] is augmented by the client's reluctance to pay for them. All in all, then, the Reagan administration's preference for using regulatory agencies to prosecute fraud but not to regulate business is one that coincides with many lawyers' own professional impulses.

1. Exactly such a case was reported by Michael Kinsley. An attempt at price fixing between Braniff and American Airlines was deemed illegal because it was done secretively. Much the same behavior among American, TWA, Pan American, Delta, United, Continental, Eastern, Northwest, Republic, US Air, and Western airlines was acceptable because company executives confined their contact to reading one another's press releases. See Kinsley, 1983.

2. Nevertheless, in many instances, lawyers overcome their reluctance. See, e.g., Jenkins, 1983. Others are urging lawyers to acquire additional forms of expertise. See, e.g. Freed, 1983.

The focus on specific illegal activities rather than general industrial conduct is buttressed further by the budgetary practices of politicians. Ultimately, many civil servants argue, the conduct of an agency is determined less by ideology than by budgetary constraints. Insofar as politicians control an agency's budget, they control that agency. At present all the offices examined in this study are subject to severe financial restrictions. For example, they are allowed to replace staff only on a ratio of four to one; for every four people who leave the office, one replacement may be hired. Obviously, no agency that is severely understaffed can effectively implement its mandate. And many lawyers feel that this is precisely why hiring has been limited. "The most important tool in government is budget," says a business regulator. "To the extent that you increase or decrease budget, you've increased or decreased the ability of the agency to perform the functions that it's charged with doing. . . . This administration is somewhat more sophisticated than prior administrations in that respect." The impact of limited hiring is further augmented by a policy of denying pay raises whenever possible. "If you have low salaries, which, I think, is a factor in turnover, you're always going back," a reform agency lawyer stresses. "You're always back to that level of service which is comfortable to political forces, I think because it's a low level of sophistication, a low level of service, and a low level of threat."

Politicians, then, have a number of powerful tools at their command for subordinating civil servants. Programs, procedures, philosophies, and budgets can all be manipulated to reward friends, confound enemies, and attain certain political ends. In the face of this considerable clout arrayed against them, civil servants have relatively little choice but to "sway a little with the tide." Outright opposition is all but impossible. Our interview elicited not a single account of a staff attorney's refusal to obey orders on political, moral, or philosophical grounds. Common responses to unwelcome directives are expressed in the following observations: "I know the pendulum swings, and I'm thinking in terms of what I'd like to do the next time around"; "I work within [the system] and I will make it work for me"; and "I'm a good soldier as well as having my own views."

Civil service lawyers also have available more specific adaptations to abrupt, unwelcome policy changes. They can concentrate their attention on the intellectual rather than the political aspects of a case. Sociologist Charles Derber has called this process "ideological desensitization."[3] It is exemplified by the lawyer who dislikes the policies he is currently required to implement but who nevertheless says of his work: "They're good cases, cases that use people's talents, capabilities. I find that my intellectual interests are fully served by being a part of this [agency] even though I don't like what they're doing. I find the process fascinating."

Finally, government lawyers can respond to negative changes in their work situations by seeking employment elsewhere. In this, they are following a well-worn route: "Three to five years at the [agency] and bango, into a good firm."

If the foregoing discussion suggests that attempts to alter government regulation along ideologically prescribed lines can succeed, it also suggests that there can be unintended consequences that follow from such attempts. Although outright resistance and deliberate attempts at subversion are rare, civil servants must nevertheless make some accommodation to changes in the philosophy, the implementation procedures, the budgets, and the staffing of their agencies. The result is often a kind of dichotimization in which lawyers, aware of hostile scrutiny, abandon certain cases but put correspondingly more effort into their remaining work load. Consequently, government oversight indeed is removed from the "esoteric issues," the "peripheral defendants," the "frontier issues," and the "respectable businessmen." But where the more narrowly focused government challenge does occur, it is now very likely to succeed. Explains one attorney: "The pressure of the case load is no longer so pressing. We

3. Of "ideological desensitization," Derber (1982, pp. 180–182) says: "The simplest accommodation to loss of power is to deny that the area in which one has become powerless has any real value or significance. . . . Ideological desensitization is highly developed in the labor force as a whole. Workers are generally socialized to a non-ideological understanding of work, including the social purposes of work institutions and of products, and a broader disinterest in work as a vehicle for any purposes other than wage earning . . . the 'intrinsic' work values that professionals overwhelmingly adopt are primarily those concerning intellectual challenge and stimulation, rather than meaning and social 'usefulness.'"

spend more time, as much time as you want, on a case." Another adds: "We tend to do a lot more investigation before we get into a litigation environment." A third notes: "The only purpose in bringing a criminal case is for whatever deterrent effect it might have. And so we don't want to send forth cases that are going to end up losers. Before a case really goes forward, everyone has to be in agreement that this is one that should be prosecuted."

In other agencies, increased scrutiny leads not to more litigation but to better settlements. "We have an extraordinarily strong investigative tool," confides an attorney. "We can issue our own subpoena so, by the time we get to file a complaint, we have subpoenaed in fifty witnesses and taken testimonies under oath, and those witnesses have very few places to hide. More often than not—I mean, in the huge majority of cases, 90 per cent of the cases—the defendant knows he is pinned and he just consents."

The foregoing remarks complete the discussion, begun earlier, of the meaning of victory for government attorneys. Winning may mean handling very few cases, but handling them meticulously. This definition of victory allows both business and government lawyers to win—one wins because his clients often escape scrutiny, the other wins those few battles he is able to fight. Similarly, the lawyer who obtains a consent decree wins the acquiescence of a corporation to change its behavior, perhaps to pay small fines, after a mountain of evidence has been marshaled against it.

The cutbacks of the Reagan years have changed the definitions of winning and losing for civil service attorneys. The significance of this change cannot be assessed fully by the regulators themselves. Nevertheless, certain trends are discernible. It seems to government lawyers that, given their new selectivity, their opponents rarely challenge them directly on the merits of a case. More often, private parties defend their interests by using what Marc Galanter (1983) calls "mega-lawyering" techniques: the application of massive resources to defeat an opponent by inflating the costs, in time or money, of pursuing a claim. "Under the federal rules, you have this discovery procedure, and it's been whipped to death by many attorneys on the outside. You'd think they were being paid on the basis of papers filed, rather than work accomplished," one government lawyer comments about the behavior of his adversaries.

Businesses thus seem to be evolving new variants of old strategies. They try to thwart government regulation by exploiting the procedural safeguards of the American legal system. In doing so, they generate increasingly elaborate cases. Ironically, such megalawyering serves to increase the work of the government attorney even in an era of declining regulatory zeal.

CONCLUSION: THE DIFFICULTIES OF GOVERNMENT WORK

The government lawyer's work is shaped by both the policies of elected officials and the reactions of private interests. The interaction of these forces produces a work environment for the civil service attorney that is substantially different from that of the salaried attorney in the private sector.

For business lawyers, the job market provides a measure of control over the ideological aspects of professional work. Young lawyers choose to work for private firms and corporate law departments at least in part because they share their employer's view about the kind of work they want to do, the kinds of clients and purposes they want to serve. Government lawyers have no such control over the social purposes of their work. Elected officials are free to change the philosophies, the programs, the procedures, and the budgets that define the civil service mandate. Insofar as lawyers accept government employment merely as a stepping stone to corporate work or as a flight from the burdens of solo practice, these politically motivated policy changes do not matter. But many civil service lawyers see government work as an end in itself. They derive satisfaction from dealing with matters of social policy and representing the public interest. They hope to do well for themselves by doing good for others. For them, any rapid about-face in public policy is disconcerting. It threatens to undo the work they have devoted years of their lives to accomplishing. Ideological issues are therefore a particularly acute source of discomfort for many government lawyers (Taylor, 1984).

The fact that some government lawyers have a vision of justice that encompasses more than the ability to argue all sides of any issue lends support to one element of new class theories: experts may have their own agendas that differ from their employers' purposes. Yet attention to the political visions of staff professionals is incomplete unless we inquire also about their opportunities for realizing their visions. Once this second question is raised, the experiences of civil service attorneys suggest not only the strengths but also the weaknesses of new class theories: government attorneys seldom get to implement their ideological intentions. On the contrary, more often they are thoroughly controlled by their employers. Not only are they unable to prevent redefinitions of purpose and cutbacks in funding for the programs that command their loyalties, they are also subject to much more intrusive management practices than private lawyers in the technical dimensions of their work. To be sure, pressure for cost containment exists in virtually all settings that employ staff attorneys. But only in the civil service is there such a persistent attempt to measure productivity in sheer numbers and to subject each attorney's work to repeated rounds of scrutiny.

More generally, the private business bar holds out the promise that strenuous efforts will be closely tied to rewards in the form of profits, partnerships, raises, promotions, bonuses. None of this is true for the civil service lawyer. In the government, financial and career development rewards are modest and largely unresponsive to individual effort. Correlatively, heavy-handed management techniques predominate. For example, promotions can be held up to threaten someone, but the opposite is not true—very rarely can promotions be expedited in order to reward an attorney.

The balance of costs and benefits makes the government lawyer's position much less attractive than the job of the business lawyer. A great many civil service attorneys respond to the difficulties of their situation by leaving government work. But the number of lucrative staff positions in the private sector is not large enough to absorb all those who want to leave, and the burdens of a small private practice are, in many ways, more onerous than the costs of staying on in government positions. Thus a member of lawyers are trapped in government work. Their ranks are augmented by those attorneys who trap themselves; who harbor lifetime commitments to reform work that can be accomplished only by government agencies. For these groups, the difficulty of building a satisfying professional life in the civil service is a problem that cannot be ignored. A few express their dissatisfactions and aspirations by joining staff unions. But public sector unions are weak instruments at best and find only sporadic support among potential recruits. For a fuller understanding of the role of unions among staff attorneys, we must turn to the experiences of poverty lawyers in the federally funded but nominally private Legal Services Corporation, which is detailed in the following chapter.

CHAPTER 5

GENERALLY CONTENTIOUS PEOPLE
Legal Services Advocates

In stark contrast to civil service attorneys, who have almost no control over the aims of their work, are Legal Services lawyers—continuously embroiled in fierce battles to protect their mission of defending the interests of the poor. Their well-known militancy has a number of sources: in part it arises from the selective recruitment of activist lawyers; in part it results from the program's highly politicized history; in part it is a response to present necessities. Indeed, as this is being written, the Legal Services community is confronting its most serious challenge to date: an attempt by the Reagan administration to disband the entire program and to repudiate the idea of federally funded law reform efforts.[1]

LEGAL SERVICES PROGRAMS: OLD POVERTY AND NEW

In an earlier day, local bar associations controlled services to indigents, either through the volunteer activities of private attorneys or through donation-supported Legal Aid societies. Such charitable efforts did not attempt to enlarge the rights of the poor; they shunned government money and contented themselves with case-by-case service to persons unable to pay the customary legal fees. In the more

1. For an account of Reagan's animosity toward Legal Services, see, e.g., *New York Times,* 1983, and Taylor, 1983e. For earlier statements of two positions in this controversy, see Chapman, 1977, and Bazelon, 1981.

politicized 1960s, this legal aid philosophy was augmented by a more radical program.[2] An attempt was made by some parts of the federal government and some private interests to declare a "war on poverty." A network of foundation-supported neighborhood law experiments sprang up, designed not just to render services to the poor but also to organize them and to redistribute opportunity in their favor. Eventually, the legal aid and neighborhood law experiments jointly produced the Legal Services Program as a component of the Office of Economic Opportunity, the embodiment of Lyndon Johnson's vision of a Great Society (E. Johnson, 1974). During the more conservative Nixon years that followed, many Office of Economic Opportunity programs were dismantled, but intensive lobbying saved the Legal Services operation, which was separately incorporated in 1974 as a government-funded, private, nonprofit agency: the Legal Services Corporation.

Between 1974 and 1984, local affiliates of the Legal Services Corporation were the most common source of legal advice and representation for poor people in matters of civil law. (Criminal cases were handled by a kindred but completely separate organization: the public defender's office.) The hallmark of Legal Services programs was their attempt to systematically change the balance of rights between the poor and the government and the poor and the private sector (Katz, 1982). For this very reason, their work has become the target of increasingly hostile political rhetoric. In response, the Legal Services Corporation is attempting to lessen its dependency on public funding by enlisting the aid of the private bar, private philanthropy, and individual entrepreneurship to support its work. But this move brings Legal Services full circle back to their origins in legal aid: whereas even a few years ago Legal Services proponents were calling for the expansion of Legal Services to include middle-class clients and to give poor people access to the legislative and executive as well as the judicial branch of government (Cappelletti, Gordley, and E. Johnson, 1975), today Legal Services lawyers worry

2. For three accounts of the historic transformation of legal services to the poor, see Erlanger, 1978a, and Katz, 1982; Earl Johnson (1974) has written the definitive history of the Office of Economic Opportunity's Legal Services Program.

lest their dependence on private philanthropy compromise the vigor of their efforts.

The history of the Legal Services program and the shifting politics in which it is embedded are reflected in the three agencies that participated in this study. All three programs are multicity, regional efforts facing severe cutbacks, staff shrinkages, and centralization. One has been a traditional local program that has relied primarily upon grants from the national parent body for the bulk of its funding. A second agency leans heavily on local law schools by staffing its field offices with student interns and faculty supervisors. The third program is the most innovative in its fund-raising efforts, having developed an aggressive response to the anticipated loss of federal monies. This program now solicits private, United Way contributions; it generates money by writing grants and winning contracts to provide legal aid for specially targeted client groups (women, juveniles, the elderly); and, in a number of instances, it collects fees from the local courts for acting as court-appointed attorney to certain groups of litigants.

Despite these differences in funding, all local Legal Services affiliates are similarly structured by law. They derive at least some of their funds from the national parent corporation and are therefore subject to its rules, which call for the establishment of a board of directors to oversee the work of the affiliate. More than half the board is drawn from the surrounding private bar. This requirement reflects the early hostility of local practitioners to potential competition from Legal Services programs and their consequent attempt to retain some control over legal assistance to the poor (Stumpf et al., 1971). One-third of the board is selected from community leaders who represent the clients served by the agency. This requirement reflects a compromise between the private bar and the founders of the Legal Services program. On the one hand, the early OEO programs demanded "maximum feasible participation" by the poor. On the other hand, private practitioners bitterly opposed client participation on the board in any form. In the end, client representatives were included on the board on the condition that they be outnumbered by lawyers. The remainder of the board is drawn from the ranks of "interested citizens," often representatives of other agencies that deal with the poor. The board, once constituted, appoints an executive director—a lawyer whose job it is to run the program. On paper, each local Legal Services affiliate appears to be controlled by its board. In reality, the executive director nominates candidates for election to the board and thus is almost always able to ensure a group of directors friendly to his administration. If the size of the program warrants it, the executive director may hire a number of associate or deputy directors. Usually, administrative responsibilities in a multioffice program are divided by both geographic and substantive criteria. Branch offices are commonly headed by a member of management and, in the program headquarters units designed to cover certain speciality areas (housing, government benefits work, litigation, and education), are also directed by administrators. The largest programs may even employ some nonlawyers as deputy directors who perform personnel and financial services work for the office.

Below the level of administrators, Legal Services programs commonly distinguish four types of employees: senior attorneys, regular staff attorneys, law students and/or paralegals, and clericals. Senior attorneys, as their title implies, are those with the most experience in poverty law. Typically, they carry their own case loads but are also expected to make themselves available as consultants to other staff members. Sometimes this arrangement is formalized, and senior attorneys are asked to take on supervisory chores vis-à-vis more junior attorneys. In offices with few tensions between staff and administration, a routine pathway into management is thereby created. In offices with deep suspicion and hostility on both sides, senior attorneys resist the blurring between professional and managerial functions and insist that they be viewed solely as the most experienced professionals in the office. Their claim is borne out by the fact that the senior attorneys do whatever law reform work (such as class action suits) the office is able to sustain while regular staff attorneys do the less glamorous case-by-case service work.

The general rule of thumb for staff attorneys is that they are to concentrate their efforts in areas that do not require the attentions of a senior attorney but are too complex for paralegals or law students

148   GENERALLY CONTENTIOUS PEOPLE

to handle. Their primary responsibilities involve court appearances that only bar-certified attorneys can make. Therefore, all cases that must go to court (divorces, for example) are sooner or later turned over to an attorney. Paralegals, and law students when they are available, do all the work that does not require the presence of an attorney: intake, referrals, and document preparation. Law students and paralegals also carry their own specialized case loads: they represent clients in administrative hearings where eligibility for government benefits is determined. Clerical workers are officially responsible for performing secretarial tasks, but in most offices understaffing and underfunding are so acute that everyone seems to do a bit of everything on a catch-as-catch-can basis. Secretaries, for example, wind up doing a considerable amount of intake work while lawyers often do their own typing. Moreover, the semiprofessional role that secretaries play in Legal Services offices is not simply an artifact of staff shortages; it is also a product of the democratic ideology that permeates the program: in every office both administrators and professional staff agree that secretaries should participate in all meetings that determine program priorities and procedures.

Staff unions also play a role in the division of labor in Legal Services programs. Almost all poverty law offices now have unions representing both professional and clerical workers. In general, unionization campaigns date back to the program's heyday, when money was relatively plentiful and programs were expanding from their initial sites into a regional branch office system. In many instances it seemed that the very success of the operation encouraged an ethos of wheeling and dealing among program administrators. Empires grew but staff salaries remained stagnant. Worse, the atmosphere seemed to be one in which petty office politics flourished to the detriment of the due process rights of employees. Coupled with low wages, objections to managerial style often became the source of unionizing drives. In some offices, lawyers and support staff joined separate unions; in others, both groups belonged to the same union. In most, the local unions became affiliated with a national coalition of Legal Services unions. And in all offices where unions existed, the right of management to set policy with the advice of the board came to be a strenuously contested prerogative.

Each local Legal Services office, with all its internal complexities, is also connected to the surrounding private bar in a number of ways. Both national policy makers and local directors insist on a clear-cut division of labor between Legal Services lawyers and private practitioners. In deference to private interests, Legal Services offices are forbidden to take contingency fees or, indeed, any fee-generating case. This edict has recently been expanded to specify that every Legal Services agency must use a measurable percentage of its budget to pay local private practitioners to take cases that would otherwise fall under the Legal Services mandate. In some offices, all such work is referred to a group of sympathetic private attorneys specifically incorporated to handle Legal Services referrals. In other programs, the referral process is much more open and informal, involving many local private practitioners who thereby come to see Legal Services programs as a source of business rather than a source of competition.

In sum, all Legal Services affiliates show the marks of their history. Political controversies between the private bar and Legal Services are reflected to this day in the relationships between directors and programs. Struggles within various offices are recognized in the cleavage between union and management. Most important, disagreements between the poverty law bar and the federal government are revealed in the changing mandate of Legal Services programs and the curtailment of their funding. These difficulties mark the context in which Legal Services affiliates must operate.

EXECUTIVE DIRECTORS AND UNIONIZED STAFF
ATTORNEYS: PROFESSIONALS AS WORKERS

Most programs begin their operations by recruiting staff who, at the very least, have strong commitments to and some experience with poverty law. In the 1970s, when Legal Services programs were more adequately funded, they drew on a heterogeneous applicant pool. Contrary to popular imagery, not all their recruits were graduates of elite law schools, politically leftist or countercultural (Erlanger, 1978a). But today, in a more threatening climate, Legal Services operations do insist on ideological commitment. A recently hired attorney recalls, "When they hired me, they knew that my thinking was pretty much along the lines they were thinking. [I] knew what the philosophy was. We talked a lot about that in my interview. At this point in time, I don't think any Legal Services office can afford to hire someone who's gone to law school to be a Wall Street lawyer and all of a sudden wants to stay in [the area] and maybe will take a Legal Services job. I don't think there's any room for hiring that type of person and then teaching [him or her] what the values are, what the assumptions are." The values and philosophies to which this lawyer refers were also mentioned by several other Legal Services attorneys. A woman who worked for Legal Services while in law school describes her officemates as "mavericks." Her job, she says, is "a great combination of advocacy and yellow journalism." A law professor who supervises a Legal Services office adds, "Legal Services attorneys like to bring down the big guys."

This shared objective among Legal Services attorneys to be advocates for the rights and interests of the poor, to bring down the big guys, does not always produce a shared sense of purpose about running the program itself. Indeed, in some instances, the general Young Turk stance of the Legal Services attorney is directed against the very program in which he or she is employed. A veteran Legal Services attorney describes some of her younger colleagues: "A lot of these people somehow thought it was still the 1960s. They missed the 1960s, they were too young. So they were re-enacting the sixties without having been there . . . a lot of young people who had a lot of free-floating hostility against authority of any kind." In a similar vein, an executive director muses: "I think Legal Services began with just all kinds of ambiguities. Nobody was thinking about management theories so it was all a blur. Also, you are dealing with lawyers, who are just generally contentious people, that's how we get trained and then, Legal Services people come out of a political orientation where there are not very many shrinking violets. And so from the beginning there were always contentions and disputes."

A work force so heavily invested in an antiestablishment posture can be a very difficult one to manage. The fact that Legal Services staffers have solidified their suspicions of management by forming staff unions further underscores this difficulty and points to the fact that Legal Services offices are in some ways dramatically different from other settings in which lawyers are employed. They are, for example, the very opposite of the law firm, not only in the clients they serve but internally as well. Where law firm associates conform closely to the expectations of partners, Legal Services attorneys are prepared to challenge almost every management prerogative.

Nor is the tension between labor and management mere ideological posturing. The difficult conditions under which Legal Services affiliates operate create real incentives for managers to overwork and underpay their employees and for staff to resist such treatment. For example, there is almost always an enormous disparity between the reasonable case loads that staff attorneys are contractually required to carry (about 50 "open and active" cases in the agencies participating in this study) and the enormous numbers that they actually carry. (For example, Katz [1978, p. 279] reports that in a single year, 48 Chicago Legal Services and legal aid attorneys handled 43,803 cases.) A typical account of being overwhelmed is this: "When I was hired [fresh from law school], I was handed 120 cases and told that was my case load. I got training a year and a half later." The issue of productivity is further complicated in two ways. First, there can be no uniform definition of work loads because cases vary enormously: in one office a senior attorney worked on a single massive class action suit for two years while in the same period the lawyer who processed divorce complaints handled hundreds of cases. Moreover, Legal Services lawyers typically do not confine themselves to case work but also engage in education, outreach, and community organizing efforts.

One result of an ambiguous productivity standard is protection of management's latitude to selectively reward friends and punish enemies. One senior attorney has repeatedly turned down promo-

tions into management that would require him to forgo union protections. He describes the way in which managers use ambiguous
rules: "There were always tons of policies that you had to follow and
there were so many ways of fooling around. You'd be operating a
certain way for years. If they didn't like the way you were doing
things somebody would produce the policy that was supposedly
governing the way you were operating and say, 'Well, we sent this
out three years ago.' Not ever applicable other than to just get you in
a situation where you were violating a policy. So it was impossible to
ever say, 'This [is] the way we do things around here.'"

If management maintains room to maneuver by the use of ambiguous rules, however, it is equally true that many of the more conventional management tools have almost no impact on staff behavior. For example, annual evaluations are even more pro forma in
Legal Services offices than they are in the government. Not one of
the 18 Legal Services attorneys in this study was ever evaluated in
the formal, systematic, and timely way the program rules require,
and most had never had any formal evaluation, either in their present
position or in other Legal Services projects from which they had
transferred. Most offices seem to operate on the philosophy that if
no one is obviously floundering it is best to leave everyone alone.

This tendency is strengthened by the fact that tangible rewards
are small and not tied to the outcome of evaluations. The level of pay
is low: starting salaries are less than the national median income, and
even top salaries remain below the entry level pay of law firm associates. Raises are distributed strictly by seniority on the anniversary of
the date of hiring. There can be step increases in salary if a staffer is
promoted into a senior attorney position but otherwise there are no
provisions for bonuses or merit increases and, of course, no fringe
benefits like stock-option plans to be selectively distributed.

Furthermore, the disregard of formal evaluation is not solely a
product of administrative inattentiveness. It is fueled also by the opposition of staff unions to merit ratings. In the words of a union
president: "We were trying to get regularity, predictability, and
union control over salaries, and who gets rewarded. If you say, 'It'll
be done on merit,' or any system other than a purely mechanical one,

the first question is: 'Who decides?' There was no great confidence that if rewards theoretically were done on merit that, *in fact*, they would be done on merit. There was no confidence that management would intelligently exercise those prerogatives and reward the right people on legitimate bases."

Formal, management-dominated evaluations are regarded with suspicion by union representatives, and they also are viewed with a certain amount of disdain by the rank and file. True professionals, they say, are self-starters; they turn to colleagues when they feel the need for advice. "Why supervision?" asks a recent transferee from an out-of-state program. "I don't want a supervisor. What for? I keep hearing, 'I'm not getting enough good supervision.' Sounds very social-worky to me. Doesn't sound lawyerly to me at all. I don't know what it is these people want in the way of supervision. When I say to them, 'Do you have someone to talk to about problems and to discuss cases with?' [they say], 'Oh yes, that's not what I mean by su-pervision.' [In my previous program] nobody went around bleeding about supervision. We talked to each other constantly. There were certain people who were wonderful resources. You got what you needed and nobody went around supervising you like a social work agency. We're lawyers. We're not social workers. That social work model with a supervisor and evaluations somehow doesn't [fit]." These disparaging remarks about social workers are no idiosyncratic choice. Poverty lawyers and social workers have long disagreed about the best way to address the needs of the poor, each group ar-guing for the efficacy of its own services. In a famous article that helped establish Legal Services, Jerome Carlin and Jan Howard (1965) documented the specifically *legal* problems of the poor. They thereby sought to discredit the conventional wisdom that "the poor don't need lawyers, they need social workers."

Yet, despite the disparagement by some staffers of "social-worky" supervision, many in fact do worry about the hidden politics of eval-uation. Indeed, staff members seem more concerned about this issue than do administrators. "The staff wants a system whereby every-body will receive some input on their performance," says one woman who is being pressured to take on supervisory responsibility.

The desire of staff members for feedback on performance is more a procedural than a substantive concern. They fear that where no official record of their performance exists, office politics will prevail despite union attempts to preempt managerial discretion.

In contrast to this staff concern, Legal Services managers seem to know that they can rely on much the same set of constraints that other managers use to ensure productivity. First, there is the staff attorney's own sense of professionalism and duty. Even in the context of severe labor-management dispute and in the shadow of a threatened strike, staff attorneys in one office were making arrangements to do their clients' work in some unofficial capacity. "We have a professional oath to uphold," they said. "None of us [is] going to let our clients down." A woman in another program less riven by strife adds: "You just have to know what's expected of you. It's as though you're in private practice." Many Legal Services attorneys would agree with the woman who said, "I'd found work that I wanted to do for the first time since college. Work [has] always been such an important part of my life that to not have work that I want to do [means] that my life just has no center to it."

These internalized commitments that drive staff attorneys are augmented in Legal Services, as they are elsewhere, by pressure from peers. In all three offices, lawyers do a lot of "talking through a case and brainstorming" together. They routinely read and proof one another's briefs. On more complex cases they often work in teams as co-counsel; every class action suit is staffed in this way. Younger attorneys are supervised here much as they are elsewhere: "Every step of the way, I'm with him," says a supervisor. We "talk about every case, and go over everything he writes. We discuss strategy." If someone were to shirk a reasonable work load in this environment, "you'd hear it real quick," reports an executive director. "The in-house pressure is pretty good. The new lawyers, because they're still kind of go-getters, they give an impetus to everybody else, which is nice."

Also, as in other offices, client pressures keep Legal Services lawyers on their toes. The constant refrain in Legal Services offices is "You have more clients than you have time for. It's very easy to take on too many cases. I don't think the tendency is to shut off too soon. I think it's to not shut off soon enough." The problem of too many clients is exacerbated by the fact that each client represents a multitude of legal problems. "I have never seen a one-problem client walk into this office or any other Legal Services office," notes a veteran lawyer for the elderly. Clients who come in to discuss housing problems often are also being denied government benefits; indigent families whose children need certain social services also face employment discrimination; women fighting for custody of their children also must establish their entitlement to welfare benefits. Clearly, poverty-stricken clients are beset by problems in more than one area of life.

Moreover, in the current political environment, the mismatch between the finite resources of the Legal Services program and the nearly infinite needs of the clients is being steadily enlarged by successive cutbacks in funding. All three of the programs reported in this study have seen fiscally induced staff shrinkages of approximately 50 percent in the past few years. But the demands on their resources have not shrunk concomitantly. Funding sources continue to demand that the number of cases be kept high. Judges who use Legal Services staffers as court-appointed attorneys continue to demand that such offices "either take all the cases or none of them."

In this environment, program administrators put relatively little energy into systematizing staff evaluations. The major battles these days seem to be around mustering the resources to be effective in any way at all. Nevertheless, managerial style is a highly significant determinant of program morale and staff behavior. In a well-run program, acute scarcity leads administrators and staff to set aside their differences in order to present a united front to the rest of the world. In a poorly run program, the same sort of fiscal trauma creates an atmosphere described as "bitter, bitter, bitter . . . a truly Nixonian situation downtown in terms of the paranoia and loyalty [to management] right or wrong."

This study included one program that exemplifies a well-run office and another in which labor-management tensions were greatly inflamed by recent funding cuts. The more tranquil program had lost more than half its staff to budget cuts in a single year and had therefore been reduced from a three-city, multioffice operation to a single small headquarters with peripatetic lawyers and paralegals visiting neighboring cities. The home office is vintage Legal Services: a dark, windowless, noisy room in a building near one of the highways that, not coincidentally, separates an inner-city ghetto from the more prosperous downtown business area. But cutbacks have also led to the defection of those staff members and managers most hostile to each other. The remaining staff seek peace and quiet. They were unanimous in their endorsement of a new manager who, they say, "was chosen not for his lawyering skills, not really for his management skills, but for his ability to relate to people. He's very likable, he's good at making people feel good and working together." "He's holding things together very nicely," they concur. "He's stopping the board from bothering us. He's raising money. He's handling things that have to be handled." In the context of this now tiny program, lawyers view with relief the manager's willingness to do what staffers regard as the undesirable work of office administration. In fact, it is the manager himself who insists that his attorneys keep the union-mandated committee structure alive. When lawyers indicate a desire to forgo certain meetings, he says to them, "I don't want to be trusted. Who's to know I can be trusted? You've got a responsibility to this thing too." In short, this program approximates a collegium in which professionals regard one another as peers and are eager to get on with their work. Often they are almost equally eager to rid themselves of managerial tasks, for which they acknowledge that they have neither the training nor the aptitude.

In stark contrast stands a much larger Legal Services program in which all the antagonists of a bitter union organizing campaign remain in place. The hostility and distrust that originated in the organizing drive are clearly remembered. One woman recalls those days: "Initially, people felt that they wanted respect for the work they did. [But] during bargaining sessions we were treated like shit by management, at the table and in the office—like, they were suddenly demanding that we turn over our files to them for inspection. People watched those negotiations and saw the way management treated us. The attorneys began to realize that in this situation reasonableness and good argument were not working. People began to say, 'They think we're workers!' And then they realized that we *were* workers." This legacy of animosity continues in that virtually every program decision provides fodder for union-management tensions.

The most recent issue to reanimate suspicion on both sides has been a budget cut so serious that it necessitated a massive, program-wide reorganization. Despite the fact that this program was able to avoid layoffs and to shrink entirely by natural attrition, the impact of the budget cuts became an occasion for union/management disagreement. Staff lawyers simply did not trust program administrators: they perceived them to be engaged in highly personalistic office politics, without regard to merit, fairness, or due process standards. Management, in turn, was extremely insistent upon its prerogatives. Under the latest rounds of budget cuts, the executive director and his associates proposed to close branch offices and to reorganize work around subject area specialties in a downtown headquarters. Union members fought to retain neighborhood offices and to resist the "power grab" they perceived as the implicit purpose behind the centralization. The reorganization became a major contract issue. The executive director took the position that "in a unionized structure you are buying into a lot of protections around your job description but you surrender your ability to control the ultimate decisions, because that's why you have management. That's the trade-off." The union leadership argued that the union should have a voice in all aspects of the project reorganization: in deciding on the number and size of the substantive units, their areas of coverage, the job descriptions and policy-making processes within them.

In essence this argument was a dispute about control over the bureaucratic aspects of the workplace. In order to maximize its leverage, management proposed to create a large number of specialty units, each with narrowly defined responsibilities and each headed by a unit supervisor who was a member of management and therefore not subject to union protection. Conversely, the union preferred a smaller number of units, each with broad responsibilities. First, the union reasoned, this would mean a smaller managerial cadre and a larger bargaining unit. Second, units with broad areas of coverage would allow for a more varied workload and, hence, a more orderly pattern of career development for staff.

The staff's distrust of management in general and their own management in particular is exemplified in this office by the account of a housing attorney who has declined a series of offers to move into an administrative position:

> For whatever reason, I was pegged early on by [the executive director] as being someone who he wanted to be part of his management team. For years he was saying to me, "We've got an opening to manage this office. I want you to manage it." And I'd say, "I don't want to be a manager. I want to be a lawyer." And it was at the point where, personally, I was having a hard time saying no and staying a staff attorney.

Then, the staffer continues, a senior attorney position opened up that he accepted with alacrity.

> I think the senior attorneys have increasingly been seen as the top lawyers. There's two status rungs. One is the "management-boys-and-girls" and there's this other whole status group which are "really-the-better-lawyers-around-here." That's been reinforced by the fact that, in the recent round of decisions about the grouping of senior attorneys, myself and [another senior attorney] both chose rather than management positions to stay as senior attorneys, which, I think, helped to reinforce people's feeling that those are important jobs and that people are not using them as promotional positions [but] rather as something desirable in and of themselves.

Although distrust of management is pervasive in this program, the union is the object of only lukewarm enthusiasm. It is widely seen as effective in securing better salaries for professional and clerical staff. Even management concedes this point and admits to buying off opposition to centralization with salary increases. The union has also won important protections for younger staff attorneys, who will no longer be placed in field offices where they do a little bit of everything. By virtue of their last contract, new attorneys have the right to be rotated through the various specialty units to diversify their experiences. More generally, members concede that the union has routinely given staff an at least partially effective voice in the life of the program. Nevertheless, the union commands only a grudging loyalty from most of the staff.

In part, the union is seen as itself the source of unwelcome bureaucratization. This ambivalence is clearly expressed by a senior attorney who says,

> It [the union] has made it less good as a workplace than it was before [but] I'm wondering if, but for the union, this place would have looked much different. The union is at least one thing that allows some pressure to come in—people have to consider staff—whereas without it we wouldn't have that feeling. Although it certainly has made the level of tension much higher than it used to be, [still] it's clearer than before which backs have to get scratched. And it's also a bit clearer that there can be some consequences if people don't play by the rules. Whereas before management was free to say, "We'll do whatever we want! Who's going to stop us?" Now they've at least got to think about, "Well, what's the union position on this? Are we looking for some trouble here? Is there going to be a grievance? Is there going to be a strike?" But the union response to it in terms of seniority and that sort of stuff is just a bunch of junk.

Staff members also are uneasy about whether the division between union and management needlessly polarizes the workplace. Thus a common lament: "There becomes a position that's known as 'the management position' and 'the union position,' even though it doesn't represent even the majority view. And it then becomes more difficult for union members who don't agree with the union position or managers with the management position to be vocal and take a leadership role because they have to deal with their respective leaderships." Many attorneys regret the demise of a more collegial policymaking process, although none denies that management pushed attorneys into the arms of the union by what is repeatedly described as its wheeling and dealing style of administration.

In sum, the Legal Services program is one in which two contradictory models for organizing work are operating simultaneously. For some purposes, participants invoke a professional model of the work. In this model, all lawyers are regarded as peers; rank and deference derive from collective judgments about skill and industriousness. The more junior people willingly acknowledge, indeed emulate, the senior people to whom they are bound by a joint sense of the lawyer's craft and the Legal Services mission. Much of the law reform work, such as class action suits, is accomplished within this framework. A single class action can take years to pursue through a labyrinth of discovery, research, trial, and appeal. The immediate satisfaction of such cases derives less from service to individual clients or from impact on the community (which is often a long time in coming) than from the joys of legal craftsmanship, conducted at a sophisticated level with the support, interest, and encouragement of one's peers.

With respect to many other issues, however, the collegiality of the workplace gives way to an industrial model: one in which management reserves the right to dictate to staff on the basis of superior position, not superior skill. Specifically, managers claim the right to make substantive policy decisions. They see this right as an inherent prerogative of office that derives from neither legal nor administrative talent but exists in and of itself. In the context of Legal Services programs, such assertions of managerial rights have produced counterclaims of workers' rights by the union. Thus, many issues of workplace organization—for example, the demands that staff and administrators may make on each other about such issues as productivity and evaluation—become issues for contract negotiations between two bureaucratic entities: union and management.

Particular offices differ in their relative emphasis on the professional and industrial elements of their programs. These differing emphases, in turn, are highly significant for the quality of life in the program. Clearly, the more professional an office is, the happier a place it is for the lawyers who work there. The more industrial an office is, the more managers insist upon acting as officers who are different in kind rather than degree from other lawyers, the unhappier is the workplace. Yet despite these internal differences, all three offices studied are confronted with a similar external environment. All three, then, have evolved some similarities in their daily operations, overlaid with differences in style and tone.

The primary external constraint that shapes the Legal Services office is the inadequacy of the funds that support its mission. Meager budgets decree that programs must put a premium on cost effective services. To this constraint is added the press of client needs. Like Legal Services themselves, many of the other programs that sustain indigents are being cut back. Appropriations for Aid to Families with Dependent Children, food stamps, and Medicaid are all down. Thus, to the prevalent feeling that "there's always another forty people waiting" is now added a note of panic: "People are dazed and overwhelmed, depressed. Everything's a fucking emergency."

One reason to the general feeling of crisis is to try to do as much work as possible in a standardized way and thereby to encourage fast resolution of individual complaints. Standardization takes two forms. First, certain complaints are processed on boilerplate. For example, two Legal Services programs in this study have developed "divorce mills" in which almost all cases are treated as variants of a basic type. A second form of standardization is the use of paralegals. If a legal problem is straightforward enough to be reducible to a form, it is also simple enough to be handled by support staff. In one program, paralegals do all the divorce work until the moment of court appearances. The attorney who supervises the paralegals comments that, on the day of the court appearance, "some of the uncontested [divorces] I don't even know about. I wouldn't even recognize the name." In another program, a similar divorce mill is staffed by law students. In the third program, domestic relations work is farmed out to the private bar because the staff wish to conserve their resources for the more pressing housing and benefits cases.

As in other offices, the use of boilerplate generally is viewed by staff as a benefit rather than a liability. Most lawyers feel free to suggest changes as they see fit, sometimes even in consultation with the secretaries and paralegals who actually use the forms rather than the supervisors who must approve them. And, as in other settings, lawyers maintain that there are limits to how widely forms can be used, whatever the intentions of management. If the law firm associate departs from the form to produce an individually crafted document at great cost, the Legal Services attorney departs from the form because its provisions do not favor an indigent client's interests. In the present political climate, a housing attorney explains, "the solutions are increasingly hard to figure out because, basically, what we're doing [is] taking the most disadvantaged people with rules that are against them and trying to find some way to make people survive. And we're always going to be the underdog." The underdog often has to argue for a nonstandard interpretation of the rules—a strategy that cannot be pursued by using boilerplate.

Nevertheless, the use of boilerplate in Legal Services programs has an aura of speedup that has no counterpart in other offices. The executive director who says that the thinks of boilerplate "in terms of productivity and quality control a little bit more [in] industrial terms" is wholly unlike the law firm partner who encourages staff to learn the art of drafting documents from scratch. Of all the settings in which lawyers toil as employees, the dichotomy between labor and management is sharpest in the Legal Services office. This pattern is nowhere more evident than in the management view of boilerplate as an industrial instrument for controlling the quality and quantity of work.

The tension engendered by this industrial view of labor relations carries over into the bureaucratic aspects of the workplace. As was discussed earlier, there come to be "labor" and "management" positions on various issues: how large a work load is normal, by what criteria performance is to be rewarded, what voice staff should have in program development and implementation, how specialized work should be, what constitutes the best mix of neighborhood/generalist offices and downtown/specialty offices—all these issues have been the subject of labor-management controversy.

Such controversies not only exemplify the difficulties of applying the industrial model to professional work. They are also significant because they serve to undermine the development of lifetime careers in Legal Service settings. If government and corporate attorneys have to worry about career ceilings, Legal Services attorneys have the opposite concern. On a year-to-year basis they worry about whether their programs will remain in operation. One thirteen-year veteran explains: "It's never been clear, even in the days after the corporation was established in '74. None of us really believed that there was any guarantee that this thing was going to continue forever." Even when programs persist, the attrition rates for individuals are high. Staff burnout results from numerous causes: low salaries, overwhelming case loads, an inauspicious political climate. The effects of a hostile political environment, in particular, are felt not only at the national level but at the local level as well. An attorney who represents the elderly in housing cases describes a local judge who thwarts all her attempts to institute a self-help program among her clients:

> We had one client who had a copy of the statute which dealt with security deposits. He was down in court. He saw another tenant in his building, with the same landlord, who was suing to get their security [deposit] back. And he said, "Oh, here's the statute. You want to look at it?" The other tenant took that copy of the statute and presented it to the judge and said, "This is what we want." And the judge found the person who had given him the copy of the statute in contempt of court for practicing law without a license and wanted to put the guy in jail.

This and similar stories of intransigent judges and uncooperative social service agencies stand in sad contrast to the 70 percent win record reported by the Legal Services Program in 1973 (E. Johnson, 1974, p. ix). Even if, as implied in the previous chapter, lawyers apply self-serving standards in defining the wins and losses of their work, the contrast between past victories and current hopelessness remains poignant.

In such frustrating circumstances, the continual tension over who will control the bureaucratic aspects of the workplace contributes greatly to attrition. A union officer recounts: "The kinds of antagonisms that caused the creation of the union have caused problems since its creation [and] continue to discourage people and drive them away. One of the fundamental goals in the formation of the union was trying to improve the situation so that the job became thought of as a genuine career people would stick with." The union here is expressing two separate aims. First, it wants the program to move from a more patriarchal and capricious mode into a more orderly and bureaucratic one. Second, it wants the bureaucratic order to be one in which staff members are fully enfranchised participants.

Programs vary widely in the degree to which such union hopes are likely to be fulfilled.

In light of the tensions that exist over the financial, technical, and bureaucratic aspects of Legal Services work, one may wonder how such programs continue to function at all. In part, the answer to this question is negative: the tendency of staffers to see Legal Services employment as a way station rather than a career is offset by the difficulties they anticipate in finding other employment. They have trouble being hired by even small firms and government agencies because Legal Services is so isolated from the rest of the bar. "If I go job hunting and say I worked for Legal Services, they don't even know what kind of practice that is. Some of them get it mixed up with public defenders," explains one lawyer. The prospects of establishing an independent private practice also are dim. "The whole trend of the economy is against small businesses. It would be very difficult to get the capital together, pay overhead, etc. I don't really feel that's an option," declares a second.

Another element protects the viability of the Legal Services program, although in some measure at the expense of its staff. Legal Services affiliates are the organizations most hospitable to women lawyers. In fact, they are the only organizations in this study in which professional women are routinely overrepresented. But this openness to women is a two-sided phenomenon. It provides employment to those members of the labor force who have good reason to anticipate discrimination and exclusion. But it also exploits women's vulnerability. Several of those interviewed noted that management can economize on their salaries because other, nonmonetary incentives will secure the loyalty of a female work force. Thus a typical comment: "A lot of women stay here [because] they have fairly good maternity leave policies and a lot of people work part-time. I had a child and then I came back. I work part-time. There aren't many places you can do that."

But Legal Services do not survive entirely with a captive labor force. If there are difficulties and tensions in the workplace, there are also rewards. Primary among them is a sense of political and social purpose that animates virtually all Legal Services attorneys. They may disagree across the labor-management divide on who should run the program, but they agree on the purposes and the clients the program should serve. There are, of course, many unsettled ideological issues in the Legal Services program: disagreements about the relative efficacy of individual service and law reform work, differences in the role that people envision for lawyers in reform efforts, variations in the intensity of commitment to particular client groups. However, none of these issues systematically divides labor from management. More often they unite them in a common struggle against conservative politicians.

In general, there is a growing consensus that in the present political circumstances law reform work, especially the class action suit, is ineffective. One woman tells a typical story:

> I have a very sophisticated case that has been going on for nine years now . . . just an endless thing that's five file cabinets, God knows how many hundreds of thousands of dollars, taken up 25 lawyers' time. [It's] an attempt to get instituted a health care program for 350,000 AFDC children which is mandated by federal law and which state government never put into effect. It's a very worthwhile project. If it ever worked, there would be better preventive health care for a lot of children. Yet you can walk into that courtroom from one minute to the next and you'll never know what screwy thing is going to happen. In the end, it feels very arbitrary.

An increasing number of Legal Services attorneys agree with the woman who says that she spent "25 years doing impact litigation [that is, law reform work], all of which has been rolled back. Every result we had has been rolled back, and it's just a personal decision that I have had it. I get much more satisfaction out of stopping an eviction [or] saving someone's home than out of big impact litigation."

Within each program, sometimes even with each field office, lawyers are free to follow the dictates of their own convictions. Although there are no official, written policies to this effect, lawyers in various offices have made collective decisions about which causes and clients they wish to champion. Typically, housing attorneys in Legal Services offices prefer to represent tenants and to defend people against evictions. Generally they do not take landlords' cases, even when the landlord is himself of limited means. Similarly, most members of family law projects will not defend the custody rights of child abusers or take the part of someone accused of spouse abuse in divorce proceedings. Moreover, these informal understandings are usually constructed not by attorneys alone but by attorneys in consultation with paralegals, secretaries, and client representatives.

Within individual offices lawyers also are able to secure for themselves work that is technically as well as ideologically appealing. One woman who hates negotiation because she believes she caves in too easily does a great deal of litigation. "I like small cases. I like to do things that give me a quick result, in which I can immediately help somebody out of a problem by being a lawyer. I like evictions. I like suing landlords. I like getting apartments fixed up so at the end of the year I can say, 'I got ten apartments fixed up.'" Conversely, the woman in the very next office prefers negotiating to litigating, and her case load reflects this preference. Similarly, a black lawyer who wants to put the bulk of his effort into community organizing and education is permitted to do so. In another office, the woman who handles the more complex custody disputes enjoys the opportunity to construct her cases. "Family law is somewhat different from a lot of other kinds of law. You know, like an accident—it happened, it's over, it's done. You can't control the facts, you can only control how it gets played out. If you're dealing with the custody thing, all the time you're waiting people are doing certain things, visiting or not visiting, [allowing visits or forbidding them]. So you have to say, 'It's going to be held against you. You should [visit or], let them visit.' So, in a sense you really are controlling."

In all these instances the lawyers' loyalty to the Legal Services program is enhanced by their ability to pursue the work they find technically most satisfying—a motivation they share with staff attorneys in other settings.

REFORMERS AND INDIGENT CLIENTS: BALANCING
SERVICE AND SOCIAL CHANGE

The last comment, however, also suggests that the Legal Services lawyer's satisfaction may entail a good deal more control over clients than is given to any other group of staff attorneys. This is an especially curious phenomenon in a setting where a democratic ethos prevails. Legal Services lawyers consult with paralegals and secretaries in ways that are quite unimaginable in a law firm, a corporation, or a government office. Sometimes, when seniority prevails, poverty lawyers will even defer to the claims of nonprofessional staffers on such matters as the assignment of desirable office space. Moreover, Legal Services lawyers are uniquely protective of their own rights vis-à-vis management and, in fact, generally abhor the very concept of managerial prerogative. Given this view, it is somewhat surprising to hear lawyers talking about telling clients what to do rather than giving them advice.

Yet is is not difficult to understand the pressures that create this pattern. Legal Services lawyers are overworked, underpaid, and harried. Most significantly, they draw their clients entirely from a poor, dependent, and powerless population. Often the pressure of "forty more people," every one of whom represents an "emergency," leads the Legal Services lawyer to cut short the consultative process in favor of simply giving orders to clients. One woman explains: "[We] preach client autonomy, but in reality, it's a little impractical when the client isn't educated or doesn't know the system so she can make choices. After the 450th case, where all the clients make the same kind of decision, you've been through it, you feel that you might as well make the decision for the next client, because you're so familiar with the experience. When you take the time to explain all the options, the client still ends up asking you what he should do. I wish all clients were as attractive as their causes."

As this comment illustrates, every Legal Services attorney has a stock of stories to show that, in taking over the decision-making process, lawyers are trying to honor the preferences of their clients. A woman who defends tenants from eviction notes:

> When people come to us, they're in immediate crisis. They literally come in, "My God, what is going to happen to me and my two-year-old kid [who] has muscular dystrophy, my four-year-old [who] is lead poisoned, and me, who has emphysema and 85 percent overweight and can't walk up the stairs?" We're people who have a lot of our clients die on us. There are all these questions and choices they

have to make, and they're crying during the whole time that you talk to them and they just say, "Will you please do what you think is best? You're the lawyer. I don't want to have to do this. You do it." So you take your cue from them.

Only one lawyer sounded a more cautionary note. She insisted that lawyers should defer to the clients' judgment about the social costs of pursuing legal remedies.

> Again and again, we've run up against clients who have rights that are being violated and they will not go to court, they will not pursue their rights. And it does get frustrating. Time and again you hear them say, "My nerves just can't take it." And when people say that, that's probably true. I have one woman who just withdrew from a social security overpayment. She's going to end up paying this money back even though I know we would have won on appeal, because she can't handle it any more. She cannot take the stress of just having this thing hanging over her. It's very important that ultimately the client makes the decision, because it's the client's life. I think a lot of attorneys, particularly in cases where they see law reform potential, will pressure a client to follow through and I don't think that's right.

This suggests that in Legal Services the lawyer's vision of justice may diverge from the client's more sharply than in other settings and that this divergence, in turn, reveals that knowledge is sometimes power—for it enables professional people to substitute their own goals for those of their clients. Sometimes this substitution occurs as a result of a relatively disinterested professional judgment. Lawyers have a much better sense than indigent clients of the possibilities and limitations of the legal process. Thus, a housing attorney tells her client that his wish to drag his landlord into court is inappropriate.

> I'm representing two people, husband and wife, and they have four kids. They have lead paint, they have terrible conditions, I advised them to withhold their rent. I sent a 93A consumer protection letter to their landlord. And I spent a lot of time with them, explaining what all their options are. The husband's biggest thing in the whole world is to drag that landlord into court, no matter what. The wife's concern is her little kid might have lead paint [poisoning], she's real scared about that. The most recent development is, the landlord offered them an apartment next door which is de-leaded, which has al-

most nothing wrong with it. They both called me up and they both agreed that it's really fine and they would like to live there. And the other thing this woman told me is that the test came out clean on the kid. The kid doesn't have lead paint [poisoning]. Then she called me today, very upset, saying, "My husband won't do it. He wants to drag that landlord into court. He wants to see his ass in court." Which exactly fits in with his character. So I'm going to sit down with the two of them and tell them that I'm not willing to do that, that I think the best I can do for them is settle the case.

On occasion, however, the lawyer acts less out of any disinterested professional motive than from sheer self-interest. Thus another housing attorney spoke bluntly:

I think if you look at this organization in particular and you see the contract we just signed in terms of getting much higher salaries at a time when our budget is being cut drastically, the rationale for this is, "We want to be able to encourage people to stick around." In truth folks like myself who've been around for a decade say, "Where the hell else am I going to go?" I've got a mortgage, I've got a family, [I'm] suddenly confronted with the fact that I've got to look out for myself. And I think there is a real putting your own interests at least on a par with the interests of the clients. We have different interests in terms of protecting ourselves.

Those are real conflicts of interests. I've seen times here which seem different from five years ago, ten years ago when I first started, where you would say, "Hey, this client is getting screwed, we've got to appeal this thing. We've got to sue." Now, there's a little bit of more of a, "Well, you know, they contribute a lot of money to the United Way, and we've got to think twice about whether we want to take a chance on suing them because it could ultimately harm poor people because we'd have less money to fund Legal Services." But it really is, I think, saying, "You know, we could do harm to this business we're in."

With this line of reasoning, the prophecy of an impending professional or new class revolution comes closest to being fulfilled. Lawyers who take pay raises at the expense of keeping neighborhood offices open, lawyers who pull their punches to avoid antagonizing contributors, lawyers who pressure clients to persist in cases whose emotional costs exceed the clients' resources—these are instances in which professional people are permitting their own visions of justice to supersede their clients'. Moreover, this substitution clearly goes beyond the ways in which lawyers append their own interests to those of their clients in the business world. In law firms and corporations, lawyers occasionally, perhaps even routinely, "overlawyer" a deal. They counsel unnecessary caution. They run up the bill out of all proportion to the protection they are affording their client. They do not, however, systematically redirect the business person's goals in the way that Legal Services attorneys seem to redefine the goals of the poor.

These observations are not intended to disparage the altruism or the political astuteness of Legal Services attorneys. To the extent that altruism is properly measured by the willingness to pursue a vision of justice in the face of unrelenting political hostility, to work long hours in dingy offices at low pay, to that extent, Legal Services attorneys are certainly the most altruistic lawyers described in this study. Moreover, in the present political climate they are probably correct to retreat from reform efforts, no matter how painful they find this necessity. Granted, then, the altruism and the political savvy of the Legal Services bar. Yet the fact remains that, by their own account, Legal Services attorneys are dedicated to their own vision of their clients' best interest—a vision that, rightly or wrongly, clients do not always share. Put differently, the social distance between poverty lawyers and indigent clients is greater than the social distance between business lawyers and business clients, with a resultingly greater divergence in their understandings of particular cases.

CONCLUSION: THE NEW CLASS AS WORKING CLASS

Thus, we have uncovered a paradox. Business lawyers are the least inclined to voice egalitarian politics, yet they are highly respectful of their clients' wishes and in general they also admire their clients. By contrast, Legal Services attorneys are known for their left-of-center politics. Yet they have substantially less egalitarian relationships with their own clients than do the business lawyers.

This paradox illustrates both the strengths and the weaknesses of the new class argument that professionals are about to become a new elite. Certainly there are instances, as the Legal Services experience demonstrates, in which professional people dominate lay people. But it is also true that those most easily dominated by experts do not form a cross section of the community and include few, if any, of the rich and powerful. Those most easily controlled by experts—the poor, the sick, the dependent, the aged, the handicapped, the homeless, the unemployed—are the same people who can be controlled by almost anyone more fortunate than themselves. They are dominated not only by lawyers but also by police officers who tell them when to "move along," by shopkeepers who extend or withhold credit, by landlords who provide substandard housing, by bankers who redline their neighborhoods, by corporations that relocate their jobs at will. The relative ease with which Legal Services lawyers can tell their clients what to do seems to speak more to the helplessness of the clients than to the power of the attorneys.

Perhaps a better measure of the new class argument is the willingness of professionals to pursue their self-interests through unionization precisely because this movement allows employees to challenge bosses rather than clients—a much better test of class power. But if unionization is taken as evidence that professional people are not only self-interested but also effective in pursuing their interests, the new class theory still receives only tentative and partial support. Very few lawyers in fact are unionized. Among law firm associates and corporate staff attorneys there is virtually no interest in unionization; these lawyers are strongly identified with business values and feel that such an allegiance adequately serves their own interests. Government lawyers, who are less well off financially than business lawyers, are unlikely to unionize, because public sector unions afford little protection to their members in the post-PATCO era.[3] Only

3. The Professional Air Traffic Controllers Organization (PATCO) was a union of public service employees. Its members—air traffic controllers—tested the ban against strikes by civil servants and lost. The union was subsequently decertified and those of its members who persisted in the strike action lost their jobs. For a history of lawyer unionization, see Stavitsky, 1980.

Legal Services attorneys routinely join unions. If unionization, then, is the measure of lawyers' capacity for collective action, it must be said that only a tiny fraction of salaried attorneys, about 1 percent, are acting as members of "a class for themselves."[4]

A more plausible interpretation of unionization among lawyers would emphasize that professionals join unions not because they are part of a new ruling class, but because they are sometimes made to feel very much like the traditional working class. In the three Legal Services offices reported in this study, unionization drives were sparked by low salaries, poor working conditions, and managerial arbitrariness. And in all three settings, the staffs were willing, however reluctantly, to abandon many of the challenges to managerial prerogatives in return for the most traditional of working-class gains—a reasonable wage settlement. Clearly, then, the social location of lawyer unionism suggests that this particular form of collective action arises when lawyers most resemble other workers and least resemble an emerging elite.

The behavior of Legal Services lawyers thus lends only scant support to those who predict the emergence of a new professional power group. Nevertheless, their attitudes in part sustain the argument that professionals have a distinctive way of looking at the world that sets them apart from both labor and capital. One Legal Services lawyer speaks about the differences between her life and her clients': "It's absolutely different. Clients stay where they are. Lawyers go home. We get out of the community. There's no identity. We're not in the same boat as our clients." Another emphasizes the uniqueness of a professional identity: he feels estranged from both business and working-class people.

> My status as a lawyer [is] frequently mentioned when I'm in a social gathering. "We're all lawyers here," or, "You've got to watch what you say." I sometimes do detect a sense of some unease. I think that

4. Karl Marx distinguished between a "class in itself"—i.e., a group of people who, by objective criteria, share a common relationship to the means of production—from a "class for itself"—a class of people mobilized for political action (see, e.g., 1978).

the uneasiness, in terms of non-business people, is probably about equal on both sides. I feel uneasy with them [too]. Am I using terms that are too large? Am I cross-examining someone? But with business people, I feel much more of a sense of them feeling uncomfortable with me and me feeling in control. Legal Services as a breed tend to distrust anyone who's got a profit motive. It would be difficult to find a community of interest there on political issues.

Comments such as these furnish a bit of evidence for the new class theory, although they refer more to the attitudes than to the behavior of salaried attorneys. Even profound feelings of being set apart from others do not necessarily lead to collective action by the people who feel "different." As social scientists have noted repeatedly with some consternation, attitudes and behaviors are by no means closely correlated (Liska, 1974). Among Legal Services attorneys, a unique sense of mission exhausts itself in struggles with an inhospitable environment. Legal Services lawyers serve poor people, and the low status of their clients adheres to them in court. Counsel for the poor often have to work harder than others to establish their credibility before judges and opposing counsel. This effort saps some of their militancy. Further, the financial insecurities of Legal Services work are a significant feature of their reality. In the short run, low salaries spur lawyers to join unions. But in the long run, continued economic stringency produces burnout, high staff turnover, and therefore a lack of steady, cumulative political action by staff attorneys.

An additional force that works against concerted political action by staff attorneys is the widely shared belief that ultimately any lawyer can set up shop independently. "The thing about lawyers is that they always have the potential of leaving that salary and going into private practice" is an oft-repeated refrain. The independent attorney—however hard he or she struggles in reality—remains a point of reference and a model for salaried attorneys. In Appendix A a very small number of private practitioners discuss the question of how realistic the choice of private practice actually is. Suffice it to say here that the difficulties of solo practice, already well established in the literature, seem to be intensifying in the present economy. If the image of solo practice remains widely appealing, its reality seems to offer only temporary escape from the dilemmas of salaried employment.

CHAPTER 6

THE ONCE AND FUTURE PROFESSIONS

A third of a century ago, C. Wright Mills said of salaried white collar people: "Whatever history they have had is a history without events; whatever common interests they have do not lead to unity; whatever future they have will not be of their own making" (1951, p. ix). In the case of lawyers, this statement is largely, though not entirely, correct.

Certainly the history of the legal profession has been one of gradual changes rather than notable events. Perhaps one of the most significant changes in lawyers' experiences is the transformation of a profession of independent practitioners into a profession of employees. In this development, lawyers greatly resemble doctors, and both are coming to be more like engineers, professors, clergy, and scientists—highly trained people who are answerable both to the canons of their profession and to the demands of their employers.

This dual responsibility, in turn, may be no more than a transitional phase in the long sweep of events that led first to the rise of the professions and that is now, perhaps, portending their decline.[1] It is worth recalling that in most societies known to history and anthro-

---

1. The decline of the professions has long been predicted. See, e.g., Toren, 1975. For a similar account specific to the legal profession, see Rothman, 1984. The erosion of professional status is said to have two sources: the increasing expertise of lay people and the subordination of professionals by employers. For a discussion of the first theme, see Haug, 1975, 1976; Haug and Sussman, 1968, 1969 and Lopata, 1976. For a discussion of the second theme, see Aronowitz, 1973, 1979, 1983; Aronowitz et al., 1970; McKinlay, 1973; and Oppenheimer, 1973.

175

pology there have been no professions. Instead, people performed what we now think of as professional tasks—healing, teaching, advocacy, intercession with the supernatural—as part of a more general set of obligations; healing was the task of women or shamans or barbers, advocacy the task of clan or lineage elders, and so on. The development of the modern, fully differentiated profession occurs only when three sets of events converge. First, professionalism seems to require a market economy in which occupational development is left to private initiative. Second, certain occupations must be able to take advantage of the freedoms of the market. Typically they must succeed in organizing themselves into self-interested groups, controlling the supply of practitioners, and gaining public recognition of their status through government licensure. Finally, professions flourish when a small number of powerful patrons is replaced by a numerous middle class of potential clients.[2]

The recent absorption of independent practitioners into a variety of staff positions signals a fundamental transformation of the very conditions that bred and sustained the professions. A numerous clientele is being replaced by a single powerful employer. The hurly-burly of the market is replaced by the long-range planning of such mega-institutions as the national government and the multinational corporation. It may well be that the historic stage is being set, at least in its gross structural features, for the decline of the professions as we currently know them.

Nevertheless, some scholars have argued that, structural changes notwithstanding, professionals in both independent and salaried positions will maintain themselves as powerful figures because of the leverage their expertise provides in dealing with lay people.[3] It certainly seems possible that in one-on-one, "over-the-desk" situa-

2. For an account of the rise of the professions see Johnson, 1977, and Larson, 1977.

3. Several studies suggest that the possession of expertise enables professional people to maintain their power even within bureaucracies. See, e.g., Blau, 1979, and P. Blau, Heydebrand, and Stauffer, 1966. In general this argument—that expertise is a resource which professional people use to promote their own interests within bureaucracies—is but one instance of a more general thesis about life in bureaucracies: people who control areas of uncertainty can turn such control to their own advantage (see, e.g., Crozier, 1963).

tions, individual lawyers frequently prevail over individual clients. Law firm partners may tell a business executive, "You're a god-damn fool. . . . You've got to spend a million dollars . . . or you're going to jail. That's the magnitude of your problem." Corporate house counsel may be able to threaten noncompliant project managers with "kicking the problem upstairs." Legal Services attorneys routinely decide how their clients' interests are best served. Moreover, such over-the-desk domination reveals only part of the lawyer's power, for lawyers dominate lay people more generally through the creation of legal symbols and legal language (Cain, 1979, p. 333). All business people, if not all citizens, are aware of the legislation and regulation—largely written by lawyers—that impinge on their activities. No doubt, then, the new class theorists have their point: at times the expertise of professional people allows them to influence the course of events, often in their own favor.

It is not clear, however, that the control that lawyers sometimes exercise over individual clients or even the general public also gives them control over their own professional lives. Certainly, anyone who interviews staff attorneys can discover concerns and fears among them: law firm associates worry about being partnered; partners worry about the encroachment of corporate law departments; corporate lawyers worry about truncated career ladders; government attorneys worry about mustering the resources to make a respectable showing against corporate attorneys; poverty lawyers worry about the very existence of their programs.

With the exception of poverty lawyers, however, few attorneys seem concerned about the intrinsic difficulties of being employees. They show little inclination to act in keeping with their common interests and experiences as staff people. Indeed, focused as most of them are on the content of their work rather than its organization, they fail to perceive their commonalities.[4] They think of themselves

---

4. On this point Eliot Freidson, referring to doctors, writes: "The occupational organization of the work of one learned profession constitutes a dimension quite as distinct and fully as inportant as its knowledge. . . . The social value of its work is as much a function of its organization as it is of the knowledge and skills it is said to possess" (1970a, p. xi). The same may equally be said of lawyers.

as negotiators or advisers who are very different from litigators, or as poverty lawyers who are very different from business lawyers. For example, even within a single law firm, the corporate lawyer maintains a sharp distinction between himself and a litigator. He is sophisticated, the litigator impossibly naive. "If you've ever seen a settlement agreement written by litigators, it's hysterical. There's never any provision in it for what happens if the contingencies don't happen." Similarly, a law firm associate confides his liking for business people ("They are capable, intelligent, basically interesting people") while a Legal Services attorney disparages them ("Legal Services [lawyers] as a breed tend to distrust anyone who's got a profit motive"). Lawyers' views of one another are so diverse that it is all but impossible to discern any basis for collective action among them. Opinions range all the way from "unethical and incompetent practice is the rule" and "probably 80 percent of all lawyers are people who I wouldn't want to eat lunch with" to "Lawyers have a tremendous respect for logic. If you were to examine 20 professions under a magnifying glass, lawyers would come out the cleanest."

Additionally, lawyers perceive little kinship with other experts. Doctors, they say, are too arrogant and believe that they "participate [in] the divine. In fact, they're decent, ordinary people every bit as capable of being wrong, every bit as loaded with prejudices and hypersensitivities and visceral and gut reaction as anybody else." Engineers are simplistic—they deal with numbers whose meaning is unambiguous and therefore they are unattuned to the subtleties of legal interpretation. Social scientists are too vague—they do not confine themselves to the discussion of observable behavior; they speculate about nebulous concepts like "context" and "impact." Professors have no accountability to anyone and have never known the bottom-line discipline of winning or losing a case, making or breaking a deal.

Thus, it would seem that C. Wright Mills was prescient. Common experiences have not yet given rise to common consciousness or joint politics. But this is not to say that because staff attorneys generally eschew deliberate collective action they have no influence over the course of events in which they participate. As they pursue their careers—from college into law school and thence into summer internships, part-time jobs, first jobs, lateral moves—they must discern what is asked of them and react sensibly to the implicit and explicit expectations of their employers. Sometimes they respond with conformity, sometimes with resistance, sometimes in ways which have consequences that neither they nor their employers have anticipated. Sometimes they respond in ways unique to lawyers, sometimes in ways that seem to be widely shared among staff professionals of all sorts. In every case, however, their reactions to the demands made of them play a key role in determining the course of their experiences.[5]

The first choice that salaried attorneys must make is ideological in character: Whom shall they serve? To what purposes should they lend themselves? Employers exert an enormous but subtle influence over this choice. Applicants seem to be free to apply for jobs when and where they choose. But if they limit themselves to "realistic" applications, they find that the prestige of their law school, their race, sex, class, ethnicity, and religion—as well as their law school record—all play a significant role in making certain jobs available and putting others beyond their reach.[6] Or, to put it diffently, employers' preferences create the reality to which the "realistic" applicant responds.

The choice of specific job, then, is not wholly within the prospective employee's power to make.[7] Nevertheless, the applicant can choose among three easily distinguishable sectors of the job market: the business, individual service, and government bars. The differences among them are partly financial and partly ideological. The

5. For a more general discussion of the role of employees in shaping their own destinies, see Burawoy, 1979.

6. A recent study of four Chicago law firms by Nelson (1983) has shown that firms are becoming more heterogeneous in their recruitment patterns, hiring from previously excluded minority groups. However, the same study shows that while recruitment patterns have become more varied, turnover rates have also increased —leading one to wonder whether the open door of law firm hiring is not, perhaps, a revolving door.

7. For a discussion of how jobs are chosen, see two contrasting accounts: Erlanger (1978b) focuses on the funding patterns that limit the availability of public law jobs; Weisbrod (1983) speaks of job-seeking behavior purely in terms of employee choice.

business bar, as both lawyers who serve it and lawyers who spurn it agree, is dedicated to helping those people who already have money to make more money. Its advantages include the prospect of high income and considerable prestige, of resources adequate to get the job done, of working on problems for which the lawyer's skills and tools are particularly well suited. The individual service bar holds out the pleasures of "working with people" and "helping people" and of being a pillar of the small-town community or local neighborhood. These rewards are almost always counterbalanced, however, by lower incomes and by the experience of wrestling with problems, such as custody suits or landlord-tenant disputes, for which the law does not provide felicitous solutions (Galanter, 1974). The civil service bar once provided considerable security to its members and still offers the challenge of representing the people of the United States. A variety of lawyers have been willing to pay the price of being caught up in endless political and bureaucratic struggles; some are drawn by public policy issues, and others are repelled by the financial difficulties of private practice or the hectic pace of the business bar.[8]

So for the most part, the job market acts as an impersonal mechanism allowing employers and employees of similar proclivities to find each other. Through its operation, partners, general counsel, and executive directors are largely spared the necessity of ordering staff attorneys to perform ideologically repugnant tasks. Moreover, the problem of whom one should serve is further muted by the belief common to almost all lawyers that "everyone deserves representation." The corollary of this belief is that those who do the representing are engaged in an intrinsically worthwhile (if not noble) task and that, this being so, the cause or client they represent in no way reflects on them personally.[9] For those lawyers who specialize in

8. For an account of the values that animate students as they begin their training to be lawyers, see Warkov and Zelan, 1965.

9. Charles Wolfram (1984) raises a further point. He writes: "First and fundamental is the question whether a good lawyer can be a good person. If a lawyer is required or permitted by a law, a professional rule or custom to do something that would be immoral if one were not a lawyer, is the lawyer shielded from ordinary moral judgment about such conduct?" This issue is one that the respondents in this study do not want raised.

business law—well over half the bar—ideological problems are vitiated even further by the similarities between lawyers and business
people. John Donnell (1970) has pointed out this basic compatibility: the work of both groups requires them to analyze situations
quickly, to weigh costs against benefits, and to reach practical conclusions based on imperfect information. Indeed, so pronounced is
the resemblance that even leading law professors do not hesitate to
urge law students to learn from business people and to become more
businesslike (Fried, 1984). And this advice is heeded: the evidence
from corporate law departments shows that a growing number of
lawyers see so little difference between their craft and the business
executive's that they are willing to abandon the law altogether for
business careers.

Nevertheless, the job market does not always guarantee that har-
mony will prevail between bosses and staff attorneys on ideological
issues. In the late 1960s and the early 1970s, for example, law firm
partners were confronted with insistent demands by associates to do
more pro bono work. Today this particular demand no longer seems
to be a pressing issue in law firms; partners and associates have
returned to the consensus that they can best serve the public interest
by making financial contributions to poverty law programs. But in
other settings, ideological issues remain a source of tension. For example, Legal Services lawyers are embroiled in almost continuous
battles to protect their programs from the hostility of conservative
politicians and the suspicions of the private bar. In some Legal Services programs, these struggles produce a high degree of solidarity
within the office, but in others external threats exacerbate labor-
management tensions.

Ideologically motivated discord has been most notable in the
highest levels of the federal government, where political appointees
exercise power over career civil servants.[10] The experience of staff
attorneys in these agencies suggests that salaried lawyers are relatively impotent in protecting their own sense of mission. Their

10. For example, see Penn Kemble's account (1983) of the struggles being waged
at the National Labor Relations Board between Reagan appointees and career civil
servants.

bosses can readily control them with such blunt instruments as budget and program changes or, more subtly, with changes in the philosophies and standard operating procedures of the agencies. The experiences of government attorneys point to one limitation of new class theory: even when professionals have their own agendas, their expertise may not be sufficient to protect their goals. Employers have available a number of stratagems to bring staff professionals to heel.

Confronted with an arsenal of means for keeping them in line, staff attorneys retreat both literally and metaphorically. In the literal sense, they retreat by viewing government positions as an apprenticeship of sorts, to be left behind as soon as suitable private sector positions become available. Metaphorically, civil servants retreat into the "good soldier" stance: they emphasize the technical rather than the substantive features of their work, priding themselves on the skill with which they promote even those policies they consider to be wrongheaded. In assuming this posture, they come to share in one of the most widespread adaptations that employees make to the demands of a bureaucratic environment. They engage in a process that sociologist Robert Merton calls "goal displacement" (1968, pp. 249–260), in which conformity to technical rules becomes an end in itself, eclipsing whatever purposes the rules were originally designed to serve.

Lawyers are especially likely to adopt this mode of dealing with ideological challenges because, as previously noted, it is fostered by their occupational culture. Even in settings where lawyers are free agents and not employees, they can and do argue for the value of advocacy as something that stands quite apart from the merits of what is being advocated. Historian Jerold Auerbach is being more insightful than snide when he repeats the comment that the legal mind is one that "can think of something that is inextricably connected to something else without thinking about what it is connected to" (1976, p. 42). Given this orientation, staff attorneys are unlikely to insist upon promoting any particular ideological position as long as they are permitted to do what they regard as technically adequate legal work.

To aid them in this pursuit, all lawyers resort to the use of standardized forms of one sort or another. Some are commercially marketed in form-books designed for the use of the solo practitioner. Some are distributed through programs in continuing legal education sponsored by various bar associations. Most commonly, however, boilerplate originates in the lawyer's own office and is no more than copies of agreements, briefs, pleadings, interrogatories, or opinion letters that have been written on earlier occasions. There is universal agreement among lawyers, independents, and staff attorneys alike that every deal or case should built on what has already been done. Attorneys differ in how much fine-tuning they do on already existing forms, but none drafts documents from scratch except as a pedagogical exercise.

In the lawyers' experience, then, boilerplate is seen as a way of economizing on the time required to get the job done right. In light of industrial history, however, the existence of boilerplate raises other questions. More than a century ago, where the organization of industry changed from proprietary to corporate forms of capital, relationships between employers and employees also changed. The simple control typical of family businesses (in which an owner or his representative, the foreman, personally supervised production, meting out praise, exhortations, and threats on the shop floor) proved to be an inadequate means of structuring labor relations in larger business units. Corporate managers sought to wrest control of the labor process from workers without using personal, face-to-face domination. The strategy they hit upon was to separate task planning from task execution. This strategy was implemented by both technological and social means (Edwards, 1979) Tools were designed and arranged (for example, on the assembly line) so as to remove as much latitude and discretion as possible from the worker in favor of engineers who took charge of the production process. Similarly, there came to be a sharp social differentiation between the coordinative and supervisory tasks performed by managers and the minutely differentiated production tasks performed by workers.

Today, staff professionals occupy a position made up of contradictions. On the one hand, they possess the expertise required to structure the labor of others. On the other hand, salaried experts themselves are employees and, because of their knowledge, *potentially* the most troublesome of employees. Thus, while there is good reason for employers to safeguard the skills of staff experts, there is equally good reason for them to fear the independence that these skills confer. Boilerplate in law (and its equivalent in medicine and engineering) stands at the confluence of these forces that are simultaneously protective and destructive of professional autonomy. Its very existence speaks to more than simple efficiency. Standardized forms and skeleton drafts of legal instruments are also devices that raise the possibility of separating the design of professional work from its implementation; of structuring work so that a very small number of people can decide what is to be done while a large number confine themselves to filling in forms whose components have been fixed by others. In short, boilerplate presents the possibility of moving the dividing line that now distinguishes the work of lawyers from that of paralegals upward so that it comes to separate the work of lawyers in managerial positions from that of staff attorneys.

One force that militates against the extreme elaboration of this strategy in the case of staff attorneys is the nature of legal knowledge itself. The expertise that undergirds work in the law is very different from the scientific knowledge that sustains medicine. To be sure, medicine and law also have characteristics in common: as in all professions, "art," intuition, common sense, and business sense play a large role in everyday practice.[11] Nevertheless, scientific knowledge is objective, replicable, intrinsically suprahistorical and supracultural,[12] while legal knowledge has none of these once-and-for-all

11. For a discussion of this point as it pertains to doctors, see Freidson (1970a, 1975).

12. The history and sociology of science have demonstrated that the social organization of research activities varies widely. Nevertheless, however produced, knowledge in the hard sciences (e.g., physics) has certain timeless qualities—objectivity, replicability, falsifiability—that cultural knowledge does not possess. For further elaboration of this point, see Ben-David, 1971; Kuhn, 1962; and Merton, "Studies in the Sociology of Science," in Merton, 1968, pp. 585–682.

qualities.[13] Rather, it is cultural knowledge: informed estimates
about which arguments will be persuasive in specific jurisdiction under particular circumstances. By its very nature, this is knowledge
that cannot be entirely standardized, and therefore the work deriving
from it can be prestructured only within certain limits. A number of
scholars have remarked upon the uncertain character of legal wisdom. For example, Edward Laumann and John Heinz comment:
"The procedures dictated by scientific methods, whatever the ambiguities, are more clearly defined than those dictated by due process"
(1979, p. 242). They draw the conclusion that the practice of medicine is dictated by its knowledge base with specialization around dis-
ease processes (for example, oncology) or therapeutic regimens (for
example, surgery), whereas the practice of law is dictated by factors
extrinsic to the law itself, such as the social and economic distinctions between business and individual clients.

   In the present study, the differences between scientific method
and due process are especially important because the uncertainties of
due process serve to protect the staff attorney's freedom to exercise
discretion. If expert knowledge is divided into "technical" and "indeterminate" components, the larger the indeterminate element, the
greater is the professional's freedom from external control.[14] Since
law is a field of expertise in which indeterminacy is marked, it is also
a field in which it is intrinsically difficult to control practitioners by
technical means. Lawyers themselves recognize this point:

> One of the biggest things that law schools have [to do] is disabuse
> many students [of] the notion that words are like numbers. We have
> a lot of trouble with engineers in law school, people whose way of
> expressing themselves and whose mode of thought is in terms of
> mathematical equations. "Five is five." You get another word, they
> don't see that it can change meaning in context so that in one sen-
> tence it means almost the opposite of what it means in another sen-

13. This point has been noted by a number of commentators, among them,
Freund, 1963, and Rueschemeyer, 1964.
   14. The distinction between "technicality" and "indeterminacy" in professional
knowledge was introduced by Jamous and Peloille (1970) and elaborated by Child
and Faulk (1982).

tence. Takes a long time for that to leak through. Even if you had the words that purported to answer [a particular question] you'd have disagreements about what the words mean in that particular context.

To the intrinsically indeterminate, interpretive quality of legal knowledge is added the fact that most legal proceedings are overtly or potentially of an adversarial nature. The combative quality of legal work adds to its indeterminacy since one side can never fully control the allegations of facts or the presentation of evidence by the other (Frank, 1949). The old saw that "one lawyer in a town will starve, but two will find a good living" (Glazer, 1979, p. 90) points to the way in which the law's emphasis on competing claims serves the lawyer's interest, often at the expense of the client's. But it should be observed that the unpredictable course of due process preserves some margin of freedom for attorneys against the demands of employers as well.

Despite the inherent difficulties of controlling staff attorneys by such technical means as the prescriptive use of boilerplate, some employers do attempt to curb their staff in precisely this way.[15] For example, some Legal Services attorneys have little individual choice: administrators in two programs in this study decided that divorces were to be handled in a highly standardized, routinized fashion, and thereafter this is precisely what happened. Further, once the boilerplate has been established, little room remains for pride of authorship and evaluation thereafter increasingly turns on measures of quantity rather than of quality. "What percentage of cases were analyzed within thirty days of being logged in?" "What percentage of 'open and active' cases saw some movement toward resolution in a given period?" Measures such as these come to define adequate employee performance.

Yet the definitions of acceptable or excellent or substandard work do not reside in the forms themselves. Evaluation is a complex process, and controversies about the right to define adequate perfor-

---

15. For a discussion of the degree to which lawyers' work can be "Taylorized," see Engel, 1977.

mance and to measure and reward it draw attention to another aspect of employer-employee relations. Industrial history suggests that workers who cannot be controlled by direct personal domination or by workplace technologies can often be persuaded to serve employers' purposes by bureaucratic manipulation. In essence, bureaucratic control requires the establishment of job descriptions, eligibility requirements, rules for evaluation, reward, promotion, dismissal, and, not least, rules for appealing alleged breaches of the rules by others. If agreement can be reached on all these matters, most of the coercive features of supervision become unnecessary. People work not because of a shop foreman's bullying or a word processor's insistent beeping, but because they know what is expected of them, what rewards accrue to compliance, what penalties attach to defiance of the rules.

Perhaps most significantly from management's point of view, bureaucratic control directs people to try to better themselves individually rather than collectively. The promotion ladders created within organizations invite employees to pin their hopes on a solitary climb rather than a collective effort to improve the quality of life on a given rung. For many reasons, then—its suitability for use in large organizations, its ability to replace focused labor-management conflict with diffuse disgruntlement—bureaucratic control is extensively and increasingly used by employers.[16]

The experiences of staff attorneys illustrate the advance of bureaucratic control. In every setting in which lawyers are employed, the rights and obligations of employees are becoming the subject of increasingly elaborate rules and regulations. In the law firms these rules are systematizing expectations about work loads—the number of billable hours per year that constitute a satisfactory performance, the number of years needed to be eligible for partnership review. In

16. Max Weber believed the trend toward bureaucratization to be irreversible. He wrote: "Once it is fully established, bureaucracy is among those social structures which are the hardest to destroy" (1958, p. 228). Richard Edwards (1979), on the other hand, sees bureaucracies as unstable—a contested terrain whose very orderliness invites both workers and politicians to try to capture it.

corporations the rules are far more minutely detailed and include schedules of vacation benefits, sick-leave entitlements, and the like. Similarly, in that most bureaucratic of settings, the civil service, rules govern all aspects of career development. Even in small Legal Services programs there is a growing attempt to formalize expectations not only concerning pay and promotion, but also concerning such issues as professional growth through job enrichment and continuing education.

Although management's reliance on the elaboration of formal rules is definitely growing, bureaucratization cannot be fully understood as a management scheme unilaterally imposed on a helpless labor force by Machiavellian bosses. Staff attorneys seem to want specification of the rules that govern the workplace every bit as much as their employers do. What young lawyers resent above all is the dominion of patriarchal bosses—bosses whose demands are seen as arbitrary and capricious and whose desire for deference appears to rest on tradition and seniority rather than demonstrated competence. Particularly resented are partners who glower at young attorneys who occasionally flout the unwritten dress code, general counsel who demand unnecessarily that staff attorneys work on Sundays, and executive directors who unilaterally decide to transfer people from headquarters to branch offices. To protect themselves against such practices, staff attorneys pressure employers to specify organizational rules. Thus, staff attorneys contribute to the shaping of their own future—albeit less by collective action and joint politics than by repeated individual decisions.

In opting for the bureaucratization of the workplace, lawyers again have much in common with employees of all sorts—the spread of this phenomenon certainly is not confined to organizations employing lawyers or other professionals. However, the lawyers' commitment to rule elaboration is probably unique in its single-mindedness and intensity, for it expresses not only their short-run interests as employees but also their long-term, deep-seated professional training. Most lawyers would agree with the following statement: "[I] admire attorneys who are courageous leaders of one cause or another, [but] I think it more professional, I have a higher regard for a person's capabilities as a lawyer, when I see that they are able, in effect, to argue either side of any question." In short, among lawyers professionalism requires a commitment to due process as an end in itself. The commitment to rules is divorced from competing visions of a just society. "You can't ensure justice," says a man who has spent half his career teaching law. "The only thing [you] can ensure is a procedural set-up that attempts to make an honest effort to arrive at a just result. But [the law] can't ensure justice." Understandably, people whose highest vision of fairness focuses primarily on questions of procedure are as eager as their employers to promote the bureaucratization of the workplace. Professional and bureaucratic styles, once thought to be antithetical, form a natural partnership among staff attorneys.

Of course, it is not the specification of rules per se that advances or retards anyone's interest; rather, the content of the rules determines who wins and who loses. Associates would be well served by rules requiring fewer hours or years of work; partners by rules that specify the opposite. Staff counsel would be protected by rules creating many opportunities to enter business careers, while the general counsel would then have to find replacements for experienced staff more frequently. Legal Services lawyers would welcome rules giving them the right to set program policy, while executive directors also seek to monopolize this power. In all offices, staff attorneys would like to feel less harried and so would opt for more hiring, whereas bosses prefer to overwork a smaller staff. Thus it seems that staff attorneys and their employers pursue the codification of rules for different purposes: staffers to escape personalistic, unpredictable domination; bosses to set terms of employment that are both favorable to their own interests and accepted without demur by their subordinates.

Who wins the battle of the rules? Almost invariably, the bosses do. In each of the above examples, the rules finally enacted are those that serve management interests. The rule-making process, which appears to be reasonable, fair, and orderly, ultimately serves the interests of employers by allowing them to establish the incentives and constraints that shape the staff attorney's career.

Among salaried lawyers only Legal Services staffers have been willing to challenge the legitimacy of rules whose content they find objectionable. However, their revolt and their willingness to form unions are unlikely to become a model of collective action for other staff attorneys. In the first place, the conditions that promoted Legal Services unionization included severe financial deprivation. Union leaders themselves admit that unionization probably would not have occurred in the absence of salary levels hovering only slightly above the poverty line. Second, the recruits who are attracted to Legal Services programs often are people who already favor antiestablishment politics. It is not only their discovery of their bosses' high-handedness ("People watch[ing] those negotiations began to say, 'They think we're workers.' And then they realized that we *were* workers") but, in some cases, also their preexisting politics, their long-standing interest in "bringing down the big guys," that sustains their union activities. In the absence of both antiestablishment beliefs and oppressive working conditions, staff attorneys probably would not challenge the prerogatives of their employers. So long as employers act through the instrument of duly constituted, fairly administered, impersonal rules, they can almost certainly continue to fix terms of employment favorable to their own interests.

The staff attorney's experience, then, serves to confirm what social scientists have long been saying: bureaucratic domination, in which the appearance of consensus masks real conflicts of interest, is coming to be the primary mechanism by which the more powerful elicit conformity from the less powerful.[17] Unlike technical domination, which is imposed upon lawyers only under conditions of extreme financial scarcity, bureaucratic domination is used in every setting. Moreover, those whose interests are least well served by the

17. In contemporary sociology, the study of complex organizations begins with Max Weber's observation that bureaucracy is a device that is used to legitimate acts of domination under particular historical conditions. Since Weber wrote, there has been a long intellectual detour in which bureaucracies were scrutinized for their internal inefficiencies and inconsistencies or for their departure from the "ideal type" that Weber described. Only recently has the political focus been reanimated, as in the work of Richard Edwards.

advance of bureaucratization are often as eager as its beneficiaries to promote the formalization of relations in the workplace.

However, even the worst-case script, which predicts a precipitous decline in the fortunes of staff professionals, does not suggest that salaried attorneys are about to be reduced to the level of factory workers. Rather, their fate may come to resemble that of engineers or professors: experts who do relatively interesting and varied work, who enjoy a fair amount of prestige, and who earn at least adequate salaries. How does this description of the lawyer's destiny mesh with new class theories that predict the emergence of an elite of professionals and proletarianization theories that predict their subordination?

In part, the new class argument is no more than a specific application of a more general observation: members of all occupations develop self-serving accounts of their place in society; experts tout the value of expertise, business owners the value of risk-taking, workers the value of labor power, and so on. But new class theory goes beyond the observation that experts extol expertise; it predicts also that professionals will succeed in convincing others of the merits of their argument and will thereby obtain positions of power and influence. Some new class theorists, generally those of conservative bent, view the persuasiveness of experts as a form of chicanery; others, usually influenced by Marxism, see it as the unanticipated consequence of business decisions to de-skill workers; but all see it as effective. And, indeed, stated in its most sweeping terms to encompass both professional-client and general, cultural domination, such an argument cannot be discounted from the evidence in this book. It can, however, be modified by an examination of lawyers' experiences. Two caveats are particularly important.

First, few lawyers assert values that are inconsistent with dominant business values, as the willingness of house counsel to accept executive positions demonstrates. If the mass of lawyers can be said to have any unique perspective, it consists of their devotion to rule elaboration, a preoccupation that is cumbersome but not hostile to business interests. Moreover, concern with rules is not limited to the business bar, where, for example, associates demand the codification of partners' expectations. It is characteristic too of the behavior of Legal Services attorneys, who often harbor political beliefs explicitly hostile to the prevailing business ethos. In this vein, Jack Katz (1982) has shown how Legal Services attorneys, for all their good intentions, have done less to eliminate poverty than to bureaucratize it. The real effects of Legal Services, he argues, have been to protect indigents from the distinctive, often capricious methods by which business orders its relations to the poor (garnishment of wages, repossession of consumer goods, summary eviction of tenants) while, at the same time, driving the poor into class-segregated public programs for housing, food, medical care, and the like. Thus even in the most radical segments of the bar much energy is spent in rule elaboration—a process that poses little threat and holds out no alternative vision to the present order.

Second, even were lawyers to be fiercely dedicated to either their own collective advancement or to antiestablishment politics, their will alone would not determine the course of events. Even in broad cultural matters, lawyers have not always been able to protect their interests: the surge in law school enrollment shows that control over the supply of practitioners, essential to the bar's economic interests, eludes them (Curran, 1984), and recent court decisions allowing advertising have helped to drive down even further the prices lawyers charge for their services (New York Times, 1984).

Finally, when lawyers become employees, they find that their bosses are able to control them and to thwart whatever new class goals they might have. The preceding chapters have shown that in all dimensions of work—ideological, technical, bureaucratic—employers can face down staff attorneys' challenges and make their own interests prevail. As yet, this domination by management is a piecemeal affair, for there is no single site in which all three aspects of work are a source of controversy. Nevertheless, data from a broad spectrum of settings reveal no insurmountable barriers intrinsic to legal work that would safeguard the salaried lawyer's autonomy. Thus, theories that emphasize the significance of expertise must be supplemented by theories that recognize the importance of the context in which expertise is put to use. At least in the case of lawyers, professional people can be subordinated by their employers irrespective of their knowledge once employers become accustomed to their presence.[18]

Whether changes in the circumstances of staff attorneys are seen as good or bad depends largely on one's prior values. At least in theory, lawyers have always been accountable to their clients. Nevertheless, lawyers will probably resent the transformation of a numerous, relatively dependent clientele into a single, powerful employer.[19] Business people will undoubtedly welcome any arrangement that permits them to impose their bottom line standards on experts who might otherwise be inclined to do their own thing. And the general public may well assume a plague-on-both-their-houses attitude toward the struggle being waged between property and knowledge elites.

Of course each of these attitudes makes sense to the people holding it. But the present study is an attempt to examine the experiences of salaried lawyers from another point of view—that of the social scientist. From this perspective, the fate of staff attorneys is best un-

18. Using Census Bureau data that describe the entire American labor force, Wright and Singelmann (1982) make a similar argument. They identify two successive processes at work in the American economy that they call "industry shift" and "class composition shift." "Industry shift" describes changes in the economy from labor-intensive to knowledge-intensive enterprises. Fewer people are welding car bodies and more of them are programming computers. Because this pattern of industrial change puts a premium on expertise, the class position of knowledge workers is enhanced by industry shift. But, as new knowledge-intensive enterprises mature, the contributions of various experts come to be better understood. Expertise then becomes less a matter of art and more a matter of routine. This second change marks the beginning of a period in which the class position of experts declines and they become proletarianized.

19. The importance of multiple clients, each relatively dependent upon expert services, to the development of autonomous professions continues to hold true. Of Third World lawyers, Richard Abel (1982, p. 879) writes: "We have seen already that the emergence of a private legal profession is contingent upon the rise of a local bourgeoisie. . . . In Columbia, because tobacco was produced by a few large landholders, it offered an inadequate client base for the legal profession; whereas because coffee was produced by numerous small scale farmers, it provided the mass market necessary for the proliferation of lawyers. A comparison of Ghana and Kenya supports the same hypotheses. In Ghana, small cocoa farmers constituted the ideal clientele for legal services; in Kenya, Europeans (and a few Asians) monopolize the most important cash crops. . . . This small European population generated little demand for legal services."

derstood as part of a larger historic transformation centered in the growth of the bureaucratic corporation and state. In the words of Michael Harrington: "The entire world is inexorably moving toward collective forms of social life" (1979, p. 124).

In the case of the contemporary lawyer, collectivization often takes the form of employment within corporate and government bureaucracies. (Even the independent practitioner must come to terms with these institutions or suffer the penalties of a marginal economic existence.) Collectivization thus appears, from the staff attorney's perspective, as a relatively benign process in which the right to control certain aspects of one's work is forfeited but, in return, many of the administrative burdens and financial insecurities of private practice are also avoided.

Why then is this process of collectivization viewed with such alarm by so many commentators? Max Weber, for example, portrayed bureaucracy as an encroaching iron cage from which there would be no escape or reprieve except in the ephemeral and irrational politics of the charismatic movement (1958a). Similarly, Emile Durkheim warned that the social order would grow increasingly brittle in a mass society without mediating structures between the individual and the state (1951). These arguments, then, focus not on the quality of life within bureaucracies, but on a different question entirely. They ask: Does the growth of the bureaucratic state undermine the pluralism and diversity that are the wellsprings of a vigorous democracy?

Once again, a question of this magnitude cannot be resolved by studying the experiences of staff attorneys. Yet their work histories are not entirely irrelevant either. First, a comparison of salaried lawyers in government and corporate settings suggests that there are few fundamental differences between public and private bureaucracies. If one is thought to be pernicious, the other also must be at least suspect.

To date, Marxist social scientists have been among those most interested in assessing the impact of private bureaucracies on democratic institutions. They contend that the growth of private corporations changes the shape of class conflicts without resolving them.

Clashes that once were played out in the open arenas of the market and the polling place now are moved "indoors": public markets and public government are being displaced by company markets (in the form of company job descriptions and promotion ladders) and company government (in the form of company policies and grievance procedures). In short, the rule of law and the law of supply and demand are being replaced by corporate mechanisms that defeat the democratic safeguards of voter and consumer disaffection operating in the public realm. Thus Marxists conclude: "The historic association between capitalism and democracy cannot be presumed to persist automatically. . . . [T]he central lesson of recent U.S. political history is that . . . *the basic process at work . . . is the substitution of administrative power for power derived from the electorate* . . . in effect, continuing to support the form while abandoning the content of modern democratic government" (Edwards, 1979, pp. 202, 209, 211). (italics mine)

The cogency of this line of analysis is supported by the fact that the experiences of staff attorneys are consistent with changes in the law itself. Just as lawyers increasingly are constrained by administrative authority, so the entire legal system is becoming increasingly administrative in character: policies promulgated by administrative bodies are rapidly becoming a source of law less democratic but no less binding than judge-made or legislatively enacted law. A thorough investigation of the rise of administrative law is a topic beyond the scope of this book.[20] Suffice it to note here that there are certain suggestive parallels between the experiences of those who work in the law and the structure of the legal system in which they are employed.

In light of these sweeping changes, the fate of staff attorneys seems to move somewhat closer to the fate of everyman, that of relatively powerless individuals being absorbed by very powerful organizations. The significance of this process is in no way diminished by the fact that the individuals who are being thus overpowered are not

20. The substitution of administrative action for other forms of political struggle has also been widely noted by lawyers. See, e.g., Freidman, 1966, and Glendon, 1983.

always appealing people. Their claims to expertise and altruism may
well be exaggerated, as the claims of professional people often are.
Sociologist Richard Abel comments that

> Lawyers claim to walk a tightrope (epitomized by the concept of in-
> dependence) between fidelity to client and obligation to society; the
> lawyer's selfish interests are supposed to play no part. Yet structural
> changes in the lawyer-client relationship have made it difficult, if not
> impossible, to maintain this balance. On the one hand, lawyers serve
> massive clients (the state and large corporations), which employ
> them or provide a significant portion of their income; self-interest,
> disguised as loyalty to client, is likely to outweigh obligation to soci-
> ety. On the other hand, lawyers serve one-shot, legally aided clients;
> self-interest, disguised as obligation to society (which, as the state, is
> also paymaster) is likely to outweigh loyalty to the client. (1981, p.
> 1185)

Similarly, Bryant Garth (1983) points out the hidden self-interest in
the bar's call for reform through increased competence rather than
increased accountability. Nevertheless, the subordination of professionals is significant to the extent that it represents the silencing of
one voice in a plural society.

Perhaps it is especially ominous that staff attorneys, who are
uniquely qualified to defend their own interests, should be so easily
controlled. Their professional training attunes them to the play of
competing interests and equips them to be persuasive advocates and
formidable adversaries. Nevertheless, they are becoming corporate
men and women with hardly a struggle. If these legal experts can be
subordinated, anyone can.

Moreover, the response of staff attorneys to their employers' initiatives reveals the limits of rationalist political remedies to social
problems. Both the leftists and the liberal variants of rationalist politics are inclined to assume that people reflect on their objective circumstances and then take appropriate action to promote their individual or collective interests (Mills, 1951, p. 298). This is not a political vision that allows much room for unforseen contingencies and
unintended consequences. The response of staff attorneys to the circumstances in which they find themselves suggest the inadequacy of
the rationalist view. Attorneys are slow to attend to their objective

circumstances. They pay a great deal of attention to the substance of their work but relatively little to its organization. And when they do attend to their own interests as employees, they try to protect themselves by calling for ever greater elaboration of rules and procedures. In so doing, they contribute to the growth of precisely those organizational patterns that make it all but impossible for ordinary individuals to exercise significant control over their lives. The story of the staff attorney is thus a quintessentially modern and ironic story, one in which the very measures people employ to protect themselves become the means for their subordination. It is also, perhaps, one chapter of a much longer and bleaker chronicle that foretells the decline of pluralism and the emergence of a mass society.

APPENDIX A
Solo Practitioners

The life of the independent practitioner stands in sharp contrast to the experiences of salaried attorneys. Whereas staff attorneys are constrained by their employers, independent practitioners need consult only their own preferences when arranging their work life. However, their freedom is won at considerable cost: their income is precarious, and they must shoulder all the administrative burdens of maintaining their own offices.

In American popular culture the lawyer who practices on his own is a familiar yet elusive figure. Sometimes he is portrayed (the masculine pronoun is used deliberately) as a curious blend of individualism and conformity: a fearless, even heroic champion of the underdog, yet one whose very actions vindicate the system of which he is a part. In Harper Lee's *To Kill a Mockingbird* the lawyer-protagonist, Atticus Finch, personifies the "constant elevation of reason over prejudice and passion" (Bok, 1983, p. 38) as he steadfastly defends a black man in a racist town. Yet the solo practitioner is not always shown in this admirable light. Sometimes he is depicted as a sleazy ambulance-chaser—Paul Newman scrounging business from the recently bereaved in the opening scenes of *The Verdict*. And on still other occasions, his very skill at the law makes the solo practitioner a figure of heartlessness, sophistry, and chicanery: "Too many ifs and buts and howevers / Too much hereinbefore, provided, whereas," in the words of Carl Sandburg (1950, p. 189).

The scholarly literature does little to sustain these images of the

199

independent practitioner as either heroic or base. Instead, research shows the independent practitioner to be a middling sort of man: he attended a law school of moderate prestige, he works in a middle-sized city, his income is modest, his work seldom breaks new ground in jurisprudence, but he is well integrated into the civic life of his community (Carlin, 1962, 1966; Handler, 1967; Ladinsky, 1963a, 1963b; Landon, 1982; Lortie, 1959).

Despite his civic standing, however, the solo practitioner's niche has long been a precarious one with ethical and financial pressures often at loggerheads. Individual clients, "one-shotters," bring the solo practitioner a meager stream of business (Galanter, 1974). Since he relies primarily on word-of-mouth to further his practice, he is compelled to maintain his reputation for helpfulness under even the least promising circumstances.[1] Hence he is often tempted into dubious behavior (Carlin, 1962, 1966). For example, when divorce laws were highly restrictive, lawyers routinely connived at the creation of fictitious adultery complaints to facilitate their clients' objectives (O'Gorman, 1963). In other circumstances, economic considerations may compromise the performance of the solo practitioner. Often it seems that neither he nor his client can afford to have him do a really good job. Personal injury lawyers, for example, have been found to urge upon their clients settlements that maximize the lawyer's income but not the client's recovery (Rosenthal, 1976). Almost always, the independent lawyer is eager to maintain the goodwill of the local business community that brings him his most lucrative work. To this end, he may at times compromise the interest of individual clients, as in consumer-protection cases that pit private persons against small businesses (McCaulay, 1979).

The plights and joys of the private practice attorney are fairly well established in the literature. In this study, interviews with five randomly selected solo practitioners were focused on the contrast between self-employment and working for others. The reader should be warned, however, that the very small number of respondents and

1. For a discussion of the role of personal networks in maintaining a clientele, see Ladinsky, 1976, and Landon, 1982.

the unscientific mode of their selection make the evidence of this appendix little more than suggestive. First, the decision to interview only solo practitioners means that the interviewees' comments probably overstate the economic difficulties of private practice—small partnerships of two or three lawyers are almost certainly less financially precarious than one-person offices. Second, interviewing independent lawyers in a city with many large firms also tends to overstate the difficulties of private practice—not everyone who hangs out a shingle does so in the shadow of enormously wealthy and prestigious competitors. Nevertheless, the respondents' comments are worth repeating because they suggest, however tentatively, how little independent practice can serve as a satisfying alternative to salaried employment.

In general, the respondents' comments, while consistent with previous research, suggest that the solo practitioner's financial position is becoming increasingly bleak. Though the real effects of changes in the law and the economy are a matter of dispute among scholars, the respondents unanimously feel that both law reform efforts and the vagaries of the business cycle are eroding their already marginal position even further.

They insist that criminal defense work, once a mainstay of their case load, has been diminished by public defender programs for the indigent. And although they readily admit that low income people were never their preferred clients, they still lament the passing of the good old days when poor people, faced with the threat of incarceration or eviction, somehow scraped together the money to retain private counsel. In the area of civil law, the creation of no-fault automobile insurance and no-fault pro se divorce procedures has also substantially reduced the amount of work available to them, they claim. None of these changes alone destroys the private practitioner's livelihood, but taken together, the lawyers insist, they substantially diminish their income.

Along with these changes in the law go economic changes that impinge on attorneys with small private practices. The last two Republican administrations, for example, have nullified tax breaks that solo practitioners once enjoyed for hiring people new to the labor force as support staff. Large corporations are beginning to offer employees prepaid group legal plans, thereby taking middle-class consumers out of the private attorney's orbit. As interest rates have risen, real estate work has become less plentiful, depriving the private attorney of yet another source of revenue. Unlike the business attorney who handles both acquisition and bankruptcy cases and therefore flourishes whatever the state of the economy, the independent practitioner is very dependent upon upswings in the business cycle (Pashigian, 1978).

Finally, the recent flood of law school graduates has made economic survival more difficult for many lawyers. Increased competition has produced, among other things, increasing recourse to advertising. From the consumer's perspective, advertising has worked to drive down the cost of legal services (New York Times, 1984). But, for this very reason, advertising is a mixed blessing from the solo practitioner's point of view. Often it seems to exacerbate the very problem that independent attorneys wanted it to alleviate: when some lawyers publish a fixed fee schedule, they make the general economic climate more competitive for many other attorneys. One of them explains: "As long as attorneys are willing to sell their services for a pittance, then this is what we're faced with. We allow these young men and women to advertise divorces for $100 plus $38 for the costs and people are actually willing to engage their services and think they are going to get an acceptable job done. There's nothing you can do. I feel that when I do a divorce, spend my time to treat the life of a person who is going to be living [with the agreement] for the next fifty years, think about the problems he or she is going to have, for $100 fees [there] is no way that I can sell that person sufficient time to do my job properly. [But] the public doesn't want to believe that."

The economic difficulties that private practice attorneys confront are compounded by the social structure of the organized bar. Clearly those who participated in this study felt alienated from bar association activities, as did Jerome Carlin's respondents two decades ago (1962, 1966). As one put it:

The bar association works against the interests of the independent practitioner because it's staffed [by] people that have their time subsidized to do their bar work . . . people from the larger firms. And there's a reason why the larger firms want this. They get a lot out of it: visibility, the pretense of public service, they get their people on influential committees, they're involved with rules changes, they get to rub elbows with court administrators, judges and so forth. There are a lot of reasons why the bar serves the large firms and the large firms serve the bar. The bar has never done anything for me in all the years I've been in it.

The large law firms, by virtue of their bar association activities, have disproportionate influence in creating the list of bar-approved candidates for judicial appointments. Often the judges themselves are drawn from the ranks of firm partners. Solo practitioners perceive such judges to be partial to business lawyers and hostile to independent practitioners. So convinced of judicial disdain are they that they sometimes are even hesitant to add their names to the roster of lawyers available for court-appointed work, assuming that such assignments will go to members of small firms or to lawyers in community service agencies. In a network of "old boys" the private practice lawyer feels himself to be an outsider.

The specific legal and economic handicaps that beset the private practitioner are augmented by what lawyers describe as a nebulous climate of contempt for lawyers and distrust in the institutions of the court. Despite the fact that decades of research into occupational status show lawyers to be highly regarded (Hodge, Siegel, and Rossi, 1964), they report many complaints from lay people. "I get tired of people [who] say all lawyers are corrupt . . . people you meet at parties [who] always want to tell you their bad experiences with lawyers. I can't think of an instance where they've come up and said, 'I just want to tell you how much I respect the legal profession.' It's always a negative thing." On occasion, independent practitioners are the butt not only of the lay people's cynicism and distrust, but also of the contempt of other lawyers. Insists one lawyer:

Unethical and incompetent practice is the rule. The way we get a lot of parasites who are lawyers is: you feed them ambition. "You want to be a ditchdigger or you want to be someone?" So now they come out of this middle or lower middle class home . . . they're not quite smart enough to be doctors . . . [they] don't have a business to step into. What's an obvious choice? A lawyer. Now you send these guys to law school. And the law schools want as many as they can get because they got their faculty to pay and they want to be a bigger law school, a better law school, a better-funded law school, a well-known law school. So keep them coming. Now you can't keep those people coming unless you're going to let them out. So you can't flunk too many of them. Now the bar association, what if they humiliate 25,000? See, they got to pass them [too].

Moreover, independent practitioners deal with clients under circumstances least likely to promote trust or admiration. Business people use lawyers routinely and so come to know what to expect of them. Individual clients usually resort to legal aid only under crisis conditions. "If somebody comes in here, it's always with a problem they can't handle in their own life. It's never for a check-up, or because they have a sprained finger. It's usually something they've wrestled with for a long time," explains a young man who bitterly resents the disdain for lawyers that has been expressed to him. He speaks for many attorneys when he insists that clients are more often the problem than lawyers. Each of the five interviewees told some variant of the following story, differing in detail but not in substance:

> The small practitioner is in jeopardy because we get two types of clients. Either they're in serious trouble or they're looking for money. Either way [they] don't understand, [they] almost feel that you're the enemy if things aren't proceeding properly. And the result is that you seldom get thanks. If they win the case they feel that they should have won anyway. If you lose the case, then of course it was your fault that you screwed up. Most of the time that person has contributed to his or her problem. [For] example, this week a case has come into the office of somebody who hired a contractor to renovate the kitchen. That's a typical case that comes in here. It's not thrilling, it's not an intellectual challenge, it's just bread and butter stuff that's all boring for a lawyer, to be perfectly honest. Well, the contractor got 75 percent of the total contract price before the work started, and then, of course, took another job because there's no incentive for the contractor to even come and finish it. So these people are in big

trouble. It's four months later and now they come to me. "What can we do, the contractor had our money all these months?" Sure, I can file suit. But it's very expensive and very time-consuming. And maybe two years down the line they're going to ultimately get their money. And maybe not. Because maybe the contractor by then will have done a half-assed job on it and they'll be fighting over whether it was a workman-like condition or not. But, really, the client was stupid for giving 75 percent down, truly. That's a typical case.

On the other hand, I feel lawyers as a group are extremely trustworthy. Lawyers I know have a tremendous respect for logic. They're holding a lot of money in escrow all the time, they're dealing with heavy business transactions [with] very little shenanigans, given the circumstances.

The tensions that this anecdote reflect have long been implicit in the relationship between attorneys and clients. British sociologist Maureen Cain describes these tensions as arising from the "translation" that lawyers perform as they recast clients' commonsensical, lay demands into appropriate legal terms. In a typical instance of the translation process:

A clien told Lawyer D that she wished to bequeath her money to her children, including her share of a house owned jointly with her husband. She was particularly concerned to secure these monies for her children in the event of her husband remarrying after her death. Lawyer D told her that a jointly owned house would become the sole property of her husband after her death, and she could not in any way guarantee her share of the money invested in it for her children. However, the woman was pressing. Lawyer D then suggested to her that changing the ownership of the house to a tenancy-in common would enable her half to be secured for the children. . . . The lawyer's discourse was donimated by conceptions of relations involving ownership potentialities and capacities. Thus the husband and wife became joint owners and possible tenants; the children became beneficiaries; the possible future spouse did not figure at all. The house which in everyday discourse the wife and husband regarded as "theirs" turned out in legal discourse to be capable of being theirs in many different ways. (Cain, 1979, p. 340)

But the tensions between lawyers and clients in this study go beyond those depicted in this case. An inauspicious economic and social environment has heightened distrust on both sides. Clients try to avoid lawyers whenever possible and are resentful when they discover that they cannot always do so. And this feeling is hardly lessened by the trend toward do-it-yourself law, as described by a lawyer: "When people send away for a form book, or they do their own things, they usually wind up botching it up so badly that some lawyer gets that fifteen hours of billable work just to unbotch it before he even starts to help. There's been a terrible amount of public pressure to make things simple. Public policy is saying they don't want the lawyer to use his tools. And the more simple we make things, the more general the words, the more litigation is caused."

Some lawyers react to client demands and suspicions with considerable personal hostility. One interviewee who does a great deal of commercial collection work describes both his clients and their adversaries as "the scum of the earth." Although most lawyers use gentler language, they nevertheless view their clients' grievances with a jaundiced eye. "The spear carrying attitude—'let's go get those bastards, they've ruined my life'—lasts for a certain curve. It starts out slow, then it gets up to a peak and it might stay there, depending on the personality involved, for a month or two years, and then it goes down."

Private practice lawyers differ among themselves, as do business lawyers, concerning the management of recalcitrant clients. One of them says, "I will stop a lot of people from filing suit, even if it means I may be cutting my income by 75 percent. But I do feel that I have some principles. I'd rather make much, much less money and have less aggravation. I impose that value, I guess, when possible, on a client and say, 'Look, what will ultimately bring you happiness?'" More common, however, are lawyers who are unwilling to settle for less money and less aggravation, who will countenance almost anything from a client as long as the bills get paid. "I don't look at my function as being responsible [for the client's behavior]," declares another attorney. "If someone wants to do something opposite to my advice that's their life, they can do it. I might get a little pissed [but] that's probably just my pride being hurt. If they want to go to the defendant's house and threaten his wife, then they go. Everything I say or do, I document with a follow-up letter so that they can never come back and say, 'Well, he said it was ok to go and beat the wife up.'"

The solo practitioner's tolerance for combative client behavior is directly related to his survival. The young man who spoke of super-imposing his "less-is-more" view of conflict resolution on his client's desire for vengeance has given up his practice since he was inter-viewed. His colleague, who is only mildly offended by a client who assaults his adversary's wife, is beginning to build a steady income. Even he, however, is abandoning his self-conception as a traditional solo practitioner serving individual clients. To augment this source of income, he and other private practice attorneys are testing a vari-ety of business arrangements. Two of our five interviewees derive the bulk of their income from work farmed out to them by large law firms. One specializes in handling real estate matters for firms with long-standing ties to both parties in particular transactions. The sec-ond specializes in commercial collections work that firms are reluc-tant to do for themselves. Independent attorneys who have no ties to large law firms seek to develop comparable arrangements for a secure income. One specializes in representing disabled workers on a con-tingency fee basis in workmen's compensation cases. In addition to client word-of-mouth he enjoys a steady stream of referrals from unions and other employee groups. Some independent lawyers do a substantial amount of teaching in law schools and adult education programs to supplement their income and their exposure to poten-tial clients and sources of referral.

Despite such attempts to stabilize their income, the solo practi-tioners who participated in this study lead a marginal economic exis-tence. Their offices are shabby, their secretaries are part-time, and their earnings are modest. The question clearly arises: Why do they choose to arrange their careers as they do?

Part of the answer seems to be the relatively low cost of entering practice for themselves. Hanging out a shingle is a much less expen-sive proposition in law than it is in medicine. There are almost no ir-reducible costs. Four of the five men interviewed split the rent on their offices with others. Two of them have fairly straightforward ar-rangements with officemates to divide the rent on a suite of rooms opening off a common reception area. Another man rents his own room within a small partnership, and a fourth has a kind of peripatetic arrangement in which he pays a partnership a small percentage of his income in return for access to whatever office is unoccupied on a particular day. Similarly, secretarial costs can be shared under a variety of arrangements. At least two of our lawyers carried no malpractice insurance: one because he dealt only with routine matters farmed out to him from firms and did not feel himself to be exposed to any risk, the other because he possessed so few assets that he needed no protection against their seizure. The fact that disgruntled clients would be unable to make any recovery against these two men only underscores the point: cost-cutting is possible in establishing a law practice. Some private practice attorneys also find that they can manage without a professional library if they are willing to take the time to use the libraries available in state and federal courthouses or to get a computer and modem with access to Lexis, a computerized legal research tool. Even for solo practitioners who carry the highest overhead—rent on a two-room office, wages for a part-time secretary, malpractice insurance, and office equipment—the total cost of setting up a practice seems to be about $20,000 as of mid-1982. The financial burden of solo practice, then, is less in the outlay and start-up costs than it is in the uncertainty of income.

Indeed, the strongest lure of solo practice is not primarily economic. Rather, private practice attorneys portray themselves as the last of the rugged individualists—the satisfaction that they seem to value most highly is a sense of independence. They deplore the office politics and the subordination within an elaborate hierarchy that they assume to be the lot of the staff attorney. Some see the value of independence in essentially negative terms. "Well, you see," explains one, "when you start getting into partnerships and associations what you're really buying is responsibility for someone else's fuck-ups. Not to mention their morals. So that's why I stay away from them." Others phrase their desire for independence in more positive, if pompous, terms: "I would prefer to accept the onerous burdens of proprietorship and retain my independence, as opposed to giving up the worry of those burdens and giving up my independence as well."

Independence, in turn, seems to carry two meanings for solo practitioners. First, and more obviously, it means the freedom to incur the financial costs of setting one's own hours, of sleeping late or leaving early, of scheduling vacations to suit oneself, and so on. Correlatively, it means the freedom to turn away or accept clients as one wishes—although economic considerations require that this right be exercised with extreme restraint. But independence also has a meaning for the lawyer's work itself. Solo practitioners need to answer to no one but themselves in pursuing cases that appeal to them for religious, political, or even quixotic reasons. For example, the lawyer who handles disability cases describes his efforts to secure benefits for a woman who, because of a technicality, was clearly ineligible for them:

> I believe in the hereafter . . . [that] I'm going to have to account [for] just how I have conducted my life and whether or not I've acted honorably and not only selfishly and greedily. [So] there are times when I will take a case and I will spend a lot of time on it, whatever it requires, even though I know there's little hope, because I know it's important to this particular client.

> I had one I just ran through. A man's wife has muscular dystrophy and she now can't even feed herself. Her problem was that she had muscular dystrophy—and it tends to be this way—for many, many years before it was accurately diagnosed. [For] social security disability you have [to be in the work force] twenty of the forty quarters before you become disabled. Here is this person with crushing medical bills, and I mean crushing. She goes into the hospital, she's in there for three months. The medical bills are $30,000 and $40,000. Crushing need, decent guy, decent person and we had to establish the fact that she manifested disabling symptoms of the disease prior to the end of 1957. That's twenty-five years ago. That had very little hope. But I thought for these two people I'd give it a shot because I didn't want them to feel that the mechanism had failed them and turned a deaf ear to them and that nobody really cared. And that kind of thing, I do in situations because I like to think I'm a decent human being. Many of us do this and you don't talk about it.

We don't have time to do that too often, but this was an exceptional case.

As predicted, the lawyer lost this particular case. But his independence allows him, on selected occasions, to pursue not merely legality and due process but some private sense of justice as well.[2]

Every solo practitioner can recall times when his work provided this kind of satisfaction. Yet moments such as these are not the norm. The more common reality seems to be one of working for clients who understand little about the legal process, whose behavior is often inappropriate, and whose expectations are unrealistic. Worse, the law does not seem to furnish the attorney with a tool that lends itself to resolving the clients' problems. "Law is vulgar pragmatism," says one. "It's the representation of the current balance of forces in society." That balance of power is not one that favors the interests of middle or low income private citizens. "There are very few cases that come through this office that would justify why we thought we became lawyers," concludes another.

It would appear that many if not most solo practitioners derive neither great income nor great professional or intellectual satisfaction from the bulk of their work. Were they to be confronted with similar problems in a staff position, they might be able to construct some remedies. For example, the staff unions in Legal Services programs campaign not only for higher salaries for their members but also for more interesting and varied work. However, the strong value that solo practitioners place on independence militates against the development of any collective strategy to improve their lot. For the most part, solo practitioners are people who do not want even the entanglements of jointly owned office supplies. Clearly, they are unlikely to undertake such complex, long-term joint actions as would be needed to change the laws with which they work, the number of new lawyers with whom they compete, or the general public's perception of lawyers' ethics. Rather, solo practitioners are driven by their individualism to make their separate peace with the institutions

2. For a more systematic discussion of *pro bono* work by private practitioners, see Lochner, 1975.

(law firms, courts, labor unions, adult education programs, and so forth) upon which they rely for business referrals.

So the questions recur: Is independence enough? Have solo practitioners struck a good balance between autonomy and financial rewards? Between autonomy and efficacy? Is their independence perhaps more apparent than real? In large measure, the answers to these questions are dictated by individual values.

It is worth noting, however, that not one of our five solo practitioners has made a lifelong commitment to this form of practice. None of them conforms to the traditional image of the private practice attorney as a man who graduates from law school, hangs out a shingle, and gradually builds an ever-more-solid practice in his community. Although half of all recent entrants to the bar continue to try solo practice (Curran, 1983, p. 82), the data in this study suggest, however tentatively, the difficulties of persevering in that choice. Instead, it seems that solo practice is becoming a phase in an attorney's career rather than its entirety. Each of the men whose experiences are reported in this chapter has been a staff attorney at some time in his career. They had accepted employment in government work or in a small firm as their first jobs out of law school. Often the breakup of a small firm of five or ten partners precipitated the decision to strike out on their own. On the other end of this process, one man has recently decided against continuing in private practice, a second derives the bulk of his income from his position as an adjunct law school professor, and a third and fourth are expressing increasing restlessness over the financial limitations of their practices. Only one seems committed to his present form of practice for an indefinite period, and he has little need to deal with individual clients since he functions virtually as a satellite real estate lawyer for several law firms.

These interviews, though few in number, suggest that the solo practitioner more nearly resembles a small businessman than a big-time lawyer.[3] The failure rate for such lawyers, as for small business-

---

3. For a startlingly similar account of the trajectory of the small business practice, see Chinoy, 1955.

men, is high. Going into business for oneself seems to be part of the cycle: while holding a modest staff position, the attorney dreams of setting up shop on his own. When he has saved enough money or when a crisis deprives him of salaried employment, he establishes his own office. He then struggles along for a number of years on his own, perhaps in loose association with a group of similarly situated attorneys. Sometimes such an independent practice can be stabilized at an acceptable economic level. Sometimes it, too, unravels and the solo practitioner is forced back into salaried employment. Rarely are even moderately successful private practices secure in the face of a prolonged downturn in the national economy. Thus, although private practice remains a source of popular imagery, for a great many lawyers it is not a viable life-long alternative to salaried employment.

APPENDIX B
Interview Schedule

Confidentiality; permission to tape; explanation of the study of salaried professionals.

BACKGROUND

1. When did you decide to become a lawyer? What was your image of the profession at that time? What did you think you would especially like and dislike about being a lawyer? Did you imagine yourself to be a particular kind of specialist? Did you anticipate any specific rewards such as high salary, the opportunity to help people, respect/status, interesting work?

2. Did you consider other careers: for example, medicine, business, education? If yes, what decided you on your eventual choice of law? Could you imagine yourself, under any circumstances, having a second career not in the law? What would it be?

3. Did your family support the choice you made? Were there other lawyers in your family? Other professionals?

CAREER HISTORY

1. What was your first job in the law? Do you associate particular experiences with this job that altered or confirmed your previous images of work in the law?

2. Please list briefly all subsequent jobs preceding the present one.

3. For each job: Why did you make the change? What were the most significant adjustments required of you in the new setting?

PRESENT JOB

General Characteristics

1. How did you come to take this job? Did you know anyone in this organization who sponsored you? When you were interviewed, how did you assess this organization? How would you describe the atmosphere here to another candidate?

2. How is your time allocated at this point in your career? What percentage of your work time is spent on client-related work, office administration, scholarly efforts, pro bono work, bar activities?

3. Does this allocation of effort satisfy you? If you wanted to do significantly more or less of something, who would object? What would the penalties be?

4. Among your present tasks, what portions of your work do you like best? Be specific. Do you get to do enough of the kind of work you enjoy most? What would you have to do to get more assignments that you particularly like? Have you ever made such an attempt? Did you succeed or fail?

5. Among your present tasks, what portions of your work do you like least? Be specific. How often do you have to do things you dislike? If you particularly wanted to avoid an assignment, could you? Have you ever tried to? Did you succeed or fail?

6. Overall, how varied or diversified is your work? Are you satisfied with its diversity?

7. Are you satisfied with the range of work this organization as a whole takes on? In your view, are there types of work this organization should be doing which it is not doing? Does this organization do certain kinds of work which you think it should not be doing? Have you tried to influence organizational policy in this area? If so, what happened?

Working on Cases

1. How do you get assignments to cases or deals or clients? How much control do you have over the content and quantity of your assignments?

2. Overall, how large is your work load? How many hours do you work each week? Why so many? Would it be possible to reduce the number of hours you work? What would be the costs or penalties if you did so?

3. Is it possible to spend as much time as you need to do a good job on each assignment? If not, does the pressure to move on to the next thing usually come from your bosses or your clients?

4. In the course of your work, are there standard operating procedures that are suggested or required by the organization? How much of your work involves the use of boilerplate? Has the use of standard operating precedures

and boilerplate increased over the years you have been here? How much of your work is circulated in scrutiny files? Do you approve of the standard operating procedures which are in place here? How were they devised—by management or professionals? How were you taught about them when you came here? How much room do you have to devise your own routines?

5. What are the more informal ways in which the quality of work is ensured among professionals here? How did you learn about them? Do you have a formally assigned mentor or sponsor? If so, what was his or her role when you came here? What is it now? Are you mentor or sponsor to someone younger than yourself? Whom do you do most of your brainstorming with—are these people above, below, or lateral to you in the organization? What percentage of your work is co-counseled? How often do you see what other people do? How often do other professionals in this organization see your work? Is this a very social office—do people who work together also see each other outside the office?

6. How is your work evaluated? By whom? How often? Are the criteria by which you are evaluated clear to you? Do you think they are appropriate? Does the formal evaluation system really have "teeth" in it—that is, does it affect the way you work on a daily basis? Please give examples. If you were responsible for evaluations, what kind of system would you create?

Clients

1. Who are your clients? In general, do you find them to be appealing people, people you enjoy working with?

2. How knowledgeable and sophisticated are your clients about their legal problems? How does your work differ to accommodate a very well-informed or a very naive client? Which kind do you prefer? How much effort do you put into educating your clients about the legal dimensions of their problems?

3. What do you do when clients do not follow your advice? Under what conditions would you consider withdrawing from representation? Could you do so on your own, or would you have to get permission to do so from someone else?

4. What do you see as the role of self-help groups for the nonprofessional public? What areas of your professional work do you think could never be taught to lay people?

Managers

1. How does one rise through the ranks in this organization? How does one become a manager? Are managers generally the people with the most seniority? The best lawyers? Do you possess real administrative talent?

2. Would you hope to become a manager yourself? Why or why not?

3. What is the pay differential between managers and staff professionals in this organization? Do you find this differential appropriate?

4. Is it important to you to have input on such broad policy issues as budget, technology, staffing? Which ones? Why or why not? Are there barriers that prevent you from providing this input? What are they? How do you deal with them?

5. Would a union be a useful vehicle for expressing your interests as a professional person in this organization? Why or why not? In general, how do you feel about the prospect of professional people joining unions? Ideally, what structure would you devise to allow professional people to have input in the organizations that employ them?

Support Staff

1. What types of support staff do you work with most closely? For what purposes? What parts of your work can you delegate to secretaries? Paralegals? Interns?

2. Do you have direct line authority over your support staff—for example, does your secretary report directly to you or to an office manager? Do you evaluate the support staff who work for you? Do you provide career development planning for them?

3. In addition to higher incomes, what special forms of recognition are given to professionals but not support staff—for example parking privileges, dining rooms, office space, club memberships?

4. What role do support staff play in the life of this organization? Are secretaries and paralegals important in showing newcomers the ropes? Are they invited to most office parties and functions?

Intellectual Basis of Work

1. How much of your work really requires legal training? How much is common sense? How relevant and useful do you now find your law school training to be? What other kinds of knowledge (for example, in finance, medicine, social work) do you need to do your job?

2. All occupations claim specialized knowledge relevant to their work. How does your knowledge compare to that of doctors, engineers, professors, business executives, social workers? How does your knowledge compare to that of craftsmen like carpenters or plumbers?

BEYOND THE WORKPLACE

1. Are many members of your family professional people? What percentage of your friends and social acquaintances are also professionals?

2. Do you notice any differences in the way you relate to friends who are professional people and those who are not? Are there any important differences between professional and nonprofessional people that make friendships between them more difficult?

3. Do you have children? [If respondent has children] Do you think that your children will pursue professional careers? What messages do you think you and your spouse are transmitting to them about professional work? Are you sending/planning to send your children to private schools? How would you feel if they chose a technical school rather than college? How would you feel if they chose a business career rather than a profession?

4. What are the essential differences between professionals and working class people? What are the essential differences between professionals and business people?

5. What role would you like to see professional people play in policy making—for example, on issues of nuclear war or crime and delinquency? Should experts be running things in industry or in government? Does the idea that a new class of professional people is gaining power in society make sense to you? If forced to make a choice, would you rather be governed by the first 200 people in the Boston telephone directory or the Harvard faculty?

REFERENCES

Abel, Richard. 1980. "The Sociology of American Lawyers: A Bibliographic Guide." *Law and Policy Quarterly* 2:335–391.
———. 1981. "Toward A Political Economy of Lawyers." *Wisconsin Law Review* 1981:1117–1189.
———. 1982. "The Underdevelopment of Legal Professions." *American Bar Foundation Research Journal* 1982, no. 3 (Summer): 871–893.
Abel, Richard (ed.). 1982. *The Politics of Informal Justice.* Vol. 1: *The American Experience.* Vol. 2: *Comparative Studies.* New York: Academic Press.
American Business Lawyer. 1978. "A Businessman's View of Lawyers: A Program." *American Business Lawyer* 33 (Jan.):817–845.
Aric Press et al. 1984. "The Big Law Business." *Newsweek* (Apr. 18):87–91A.
Aronowitz, Stanley. 1973. *False Promises.* New York: McGraw-Hill.
———. 1979. "The Professional-Managerial Class or Middle Strata." In *Between Labor and Capital,* edited by Pat Walker, pp. 213–242.
———. 1983. *Working Class Hero.* New York: Pilgrim Press.
Aronowitz, Stanley; Bennet, Roy; Berger, Bennett; and Friedenberg, Edgar Z. 1970. "Strategies for Radical Social Change." *Social Policy* (Nov.–Dec.):9–23.
Auchincloss, Louis. 1963. *Power of Attorney.* Boston: Houghton Mifflin.
———. 1977. *The Great World and Timothy Colt.* New York: Queens House.
Auerbach, Jerold. 1976. "A Plague of Lawyers." *Harpers* (Oct.):37–44.
———. 1983. *Justice Without Law.* New York: Oxford University Press.
Banks, Robert. 1983. "Companies Struggle to Control Legal Costs." *Harvard Business Review* (Mar./Apr.):168–172.

219

Bazelon, David. 1981. "Let's Keep Legal Services." *New Republic* (June 13): 17–19.

Becker, Howard, et al. 1961. *Boys in White*. Chicago: University of Chicago Press.

Bell, Daniel. 1973. *The Coming of Post-Industrial Society*. New York: Basic Books.

Ben-David, Joseph. 1971. *The Scientist's Role in Society*. Englewood Cliffs, N. J.: Prentice-Hall.

Berends, Miek. 1981. "Modes of Lawyer-Client Interaction: Translation, Transformation and Social Control." Paper presented at the annual meeting of the Law and Society Association.

Berger, Peter L. 1978. "Ethics and the Present Class Struggle." *Worldview* 12 (Apr.):6–11.

———. 1979. "The Worldview of the New Class: Secularity and its Discontents." In *The New Class?* edited by B. Bruce-Briggs, pp. 49–55.

Berle, Adolph, and Means, Gardiner C.. 1932. *The Modern Corporation and Private Property*. New York: Macmillan.

Bernstein, Peter. 1978. "The Wall Street Lawyers Are Thriving on Change." *Fortune* 97 (Mar. 13):104–112.

Blau, Judith. 1979. "Expertise and Power in Professional Organizations." *Sociology of Work and Occupations* 6, no. 1 (Feb.):103–123.

Blau, Peter; Heydebrand, Wolf; and Stauffer, Robert. 1966. "The Structure of Small Bureaucracies. *American Sociological Review* 31, no. 2 (Apr.):179–191.

Blaustein, Albert, and Porter, Charles. 1954. *The American Lawyer*. Westport, Conn.: Greenwood Press.

Bledstein, Barton J. 1976. *The Culture of Professionalism*. New York: Norton.

Blumberg, Abraham. 1967. "The Practice of Law as a Confidence Game: Organizational Cooptation of a Profession." *Law and Society* 1:15–39.

Bok, Derek. 1983. "A Flawed System." *Harvard Magazine* (May–June): 38–45, 70–71.

Braverman, Harry. 1974. *Labor and Monopoly Capital*. New York: Monthly Review Press.

Brint, Steven. 1981. "Is There a 'New Class' Ideology?" Paper read at the annual meeting of the Eastern Sociological Society.

———. 1984. "'New Class' and Cumulative Trend Explanations of the Liberal Political Attitudes of Professionals." *American Journal of Sociology* 90, no. 1 (July):30–71.

Brown, Peter M. 1983. "Misguided Lawyers." *New York Times* (Dec. 6): A31.

Bruce-Briggs, B. (ed.). 1979. *The New Class?* New Brunswick, N.J.: Transaction Books.

Burawoy, Michael. 1979. *Manufacturing Consent.* Chicago: University of
Chicago Press.

Burnham, James. 1941. *The Managerial Revolution.* New York: John Day.

Businessweek. 1984. "A New Corporate Powerhouse: The Legal Department." *Businessweek* (Apr. 19):66–71.

Cain, Maureen. 1979. "The General Practice Lawyer and the Client: To-
wards a Radical Conception." *International Journal of the Sociology of
Law* 7:331–354.

Cappelletti, Mauro; Gordley, James; and Johnson, Earl. 1975. *Toward
Equal Justice.* Dobbs Ferry, N.Y.: Oceania Press.

Carlin, Jerome. 1962. *Lawyers on Their Own.* New Brunswick, N.J.: Rutgers
University Press.

———. 1966. *Lawyer's Ethics.* New York: Russell Sage.

Carlin, Jerome, and Howard, Jan. 1965. "Legal Representation and Class
Justice." *UCLA Law Review* 12:381–437.

Chapman, Stephen. 1977. "The Rich Get Rich and the Poor Get Lawyers."
New Republic (Sept. 24):9–15.

Chayes, Antonia, et al. 1983. "Managing Your Lawyers." *Harvard Business
Review* (Jan./Feb.):84–91

Child, John, and Faulk, Janet. 1982. "Maintenance of Occupational Control: The Case of Professions." *Sociology of Work and Occupations* 9,
no. 2 (May):155–192.

Chinoy, Ely. 1955. *Automobile Workers and the American Dream.* Boston:
Beacon Press.

Clinard, Marshall, and Yeager, Peter. 1980. *Corporate Crime.* New York:
Free Press.

Cohen, Marcia, and Wagner, David. 1982. "Social Work Professionalism:
Reality and Illusion." In *Professionals as Workers,* edited by Charles
Derber, pp. 141–164.

Collins, Randall, and Makowsky, Michael. 1984. *The Discovery of Society.* 3d
ed. New York: Random House.

Crozier, Michel. 1963. *The Bureaucratic Phenomenon.* Chicago: University
of Chicago Press.

Curran, Barbara. 1983. "Lawyer Demographics." In *Lawyers Almanac, 1982–
1983,* pp. 81–82. New York: Law and Business, Inc.

———. 1984. "The Legal Profession in the 1980's: Selected Statistics from
The 1984 Lawyers' Statistical Report." Paper read at the Annual Meeting of the Law and Society Association.

Dacey, Norman. 1965. *How to Avoid Probate.* New York: Crown.

Daniels, Arlene Kaplan, 1972. "A Subspecialty within a Professional Specialty: Military Psychiatry." In *Medical Men and Their Work,* edited by Eliot Freidson and Judith Lorber, pp. 145–162.

———. 1975. "Advisory and Coercive Functions In Psychiatry." *Sociology of Work and Occupations* 2, no. 1 (Feb.):55–78.

Davies, Celia. 1983. "Professionals in Bureaucracies: The Conflict Theory Revisited." In *The Sociology of the Professions,* edited by Robert Dingwall and Philip Lewis, pp. 177–194.

Derber, Charles (ed.). 1982. *Professionals as Workers: Mental Labor in Advanced Capitalism.* Boston: G. K. Hall.

Dingwall, Robert, and Lewis, Philip (eds.). 1983. *The Sociology of the Professions.* New York: St. Martin's Press.

Donnell, John. 1970. *The Corporate Counsel: A Role Study.* Bloomington: Indiana University Bureau of Business Research.

Durkheim, Emile. 1951. *Suicide.* New York: Free Press.

Edwards, Richard. 1979. *Contested Terrain.* New York: Basic Books.

Ehrenreich, Barbara, and Ehrenreich, John. 1979. "The Professional-Managerial Class." In *Between Labor and Capitol,* edited by Pat Walker, pp. 5–48.

Eisenstein, James, and Jacob, Herbert. 1977. *Felony Justice: An Organizational Analysis.* Boston: Little Brown.

Engel, David. 1977. "Standardization of Lawyers' Services." *American Bar Foundation Research Journal* 1977, no. 4 (Fall):817–844.

Epstein, Cynthia Fuchs. 1980. "The New Women and Old Establishment: Wall Street Lawyers in the 1970s." *Sociology of Work and Occupations* 7, no. 3 (Aug.):291–316.

———. 1981. *Women in Law.* New York: Basic Books.

Erlanger, Howard. 1978a. "Lawyers and Neighborhood Legal Services: Social Backgrounds and the Impetus for Reform." *Law and Society Review* 12, no. 2 (Winter):253–274.

———. 1978b. "Young Lawyers and Work in the Public Interest." *American Bar Foundation Research Journal* 1978, no. 1 (Winter):83–104.

Frank, Jerome. 1949. *Courts on Trial.* Princeton, N.J.: Princeton University Press.

Freed, Roy N. 1983. "The Demands of High-Tech Lawyering." *New York Times* (Oct. 2):C3.

Freidman, Laurence. 1966. "On Legalistic Reasoning: A Footnote to Weber." *Wisconsin Law Review* 1966, no. 1 (Winter):148–171.

Freidson, Eliot. 1970a. *The Profession of Medicine.* New York: Dodd Mead.

———. 1970b. *Professional Dominance.*Chicago: Aldine

———. 1973. "Professions and the Occupational Principle." In *The Professions and Their Prospects,* edited by Eliot Freidson, pp. 19–38.

———. 1975. *Doctoring Together.* New York: Elsevier.

————. 1983. "The Theory of Professions: State of the Art." In *The Sociology of the Professions,* edited by Robert Dingwall and Philip Lewis, pp. 19–37.

Freidson, Eliot (ed.). 1973. *The Professions and Their Prospects.* Beverly Hills: Sage.

Freidson, Eliot, and Lorber, Judith (eds.). 1972. *Medical Men and Their Work.* New York: Atherton.

Freund, Paul. 1963. "The Legal Profession." *Daedalus* 92, no. 4:689–700.

Fried, Charles. 1984. "The Trouble with Lawyers." *New York Times Magazine* (Feb. 12):56–63.

Galanter, Marc. 1974. "Why the Haves Come Out Ahead: Speculation on the Limits of Legal Change." *Law and Society Review* 9, no. 1 (Fall):95–159.

————. 1983. " Mega-Law and Mega-Lawyering in the Contemporary United States." In *The Sociology of the Professions,* edited by Robert Dingwall and Philip Lewis, pp. 152–176.

Galbraith, John Kenneth. 1958. *The Affluent Society.* Boston: Houghton Mifflin.

————. 1967. *The New Industrial State.* Boston: Houghton Mifflin.

Gallucio, Nick. 1978. "The Rise of the Company Lawyer." *Forbes* 123 (Sept. 18):168–181.

Garth, Bryant. 1983. "Rethinking the Legal Profession's Approach to Collective Self-Improvement: Competence and the Consumer Perspective." *Wisconsin Law Review* 1983:639–687.

Gerth, Hans and Mills, C. Wright. 1958. *From Max Weber.* New York: Oxford University Press.

Gilb, Corinne. 1966. *Hidden Hierarchies.* New York: Harper & Row.

Gilboy, Janet. 1981. "The Social Organization of Legal Services to Indigent Defendants." *American Bar Foundation Research Journal* 1981, no. 4 (Fall):1023–1048.

Girth, Marjorie. 1976. *Poor People's Lawyers.* Hicksville, N.Y.: Exposition Press.

Glazer, Nathan. 1979. "Lawyers and the New Class." In *The New Class?* edited by B. Bruce-Briggs, pp. 89–100.

Glendon, Mary Ann. 1983. "The Sources of Law in a Changing Legal Order." TePoel Lecute, delivered at Creighton University Law School, Sept. 1, 1983.

Goffman, Erving. 1959. *The Presentation of Self in Everyday Life.* New York: Doubleday.

Goldner, Fred; Ritti, R. Richard; and Ference, Thomas. 1977. "The Production of Cynical Knowledge in Organizations." *American Sociological Review* 42, no. 4:539–551.

Goulden, Joseph. 1972. *The Superlawyers*. New York: Webright and Talley.
Gouldner, Alvin. 1964. *Patterns of Industrial Bureaucracy*. New York: Free Press.
———. 1979. *The Future of Intellectuals and the Rise of the New Class*. New York: Seabury Press.
Halberstam, David. 1969. *The Best and The Brightest*. New York: Random House.
Hall, Richard. 1963. "The Concept of Bureaucracy." *American Journal of Sociology* 69, No. 1:32–40.
———. 1968. "Professionalization and Bureaucratization." *American Sociological Review* 33, no. 1:92–104.
Halmos, Paul (ed.) 1973. *Professionalization and Social Change*. University of Keele, England: Sociological Review Monograph 20.
Handler, Joel. 1967. *The Lawyer and His Community*. Madison: University of Wisconsin Press.
Harrington, Michael. 1979. "The New Class and the Left." In *The New CLass?* edited by B. Bruce-Briggs, pp. 123–138.
Haug, Marie. 1975. "The Deprofessionalization of Everyone?" *Social Focus* 8, no. 3 (Aug.):197–213.
———. 1976. "The Erosion of Professional Authority: A Cross-Cultural Inquiry in the Case of the Physician." *Health and Society* (Winter):83–106.
Haug, Marie, and Sussman, Marvin. 1968. "Professional Autonomy and the Revolt of the Client." *Social Problems* 17, no. 2 (Fall):153–161.
———. 1969. "Professionalism and the Public." *Sociological Inquiry* 39:57–64.
Heinz, John, and Laumann, Edward. 1982. *Chicago Lawyers*. New York: Russell Sage.
Higgins, George V. 1985. "Tyrannosaurus Lex." *New England Monthly* 2, no. 2 (Feb.):28–36.
Hodge, Robert; Siegel, Paul; and Rossi, Peter. 1964. "Occupational Prestige in the United States, 1925–1963." *American Journal of Sociology* 70 (Nov.):286–302.
Hoffman, Paul. 1973. *Lions in the Street*. New York: Saturday Review Press.
———. 1982. *Lions in the Eighties*. New York: Doubleday.
Homer, Julia. 1984. "Private Court Systems: Discount Decisions." *Inc.* 6, no. 8 (Aug.):34.
Horobin, Gordon. 1983. "Professional Mystery: The Maintenance of Charisma in General Medical Practice. In *The Sociology of the Professions,* edited by Robert Dingwall and Philip Lewis, pp. 84–105.
Hosticka, Carl. 1979. "We Don't Care About What Happened, We Only

Care About What is Going to Happen: Lawyer-Client Negotiations of Reality." *Social Problems* 26, no. 5 (June):599–610.

Illich, Ivan, et al. 1977. *Disabling Professions.* London: Marion Boyers.

Jackson, J. A. (ed.). 1970. *Professions and Professionalism.* New York: Cambridge University Press.

Jamous, H., and Peloille, B. 1970. "Changes in the French University Hospital System." In *Professions and Professionalization,* edited by J. A. Jackson, pp.111–152.

Jenkins, John A. 1983. "Experts Day in Court." *New York Times Magazine* (Dec. 11):98–106.

———. 1984. "Outside the Law." *TWA Ambassador* (Aug. 14):18.

Johnson, Earl. 1974. *Justice and Reform.* New York: Russell Sage.

Johnson, Terence. 1972. *Professions and Power.* London: British Sociological Association.

Kanter, Rosabeth Moss. 1977. *Men and Women of the Corporation.* New York: Basic Books.

Katz, Jack. 1978. "Lawyers for the Poor in Transition: Involvement, Reform and the Turn-Over Problem in the Legal Services Program." *Law and Society Review* 12, no. 2 (Winter):275–300.

———. 1982. *Poor People's Lawyer in Transition.* New Brunswick, N.J.: Rutgers University Press.

Kemble, Penn. 1983. "The New Anti-Union Crusade." *New Republic* (Sept. 19, 26):18–20.

King, Nick. 1983. "The Law Gets Down to Business." *Boston Globe* (May 17):37.

Kinsley, Michael. 1983. "Conspiracy by Newspaper: Overly Friendly Skies." *New Republic* (Oct. 17):12–13.

Kolko, Gabriel. 1963. *The Triumph of Conservatism.* New York: Free Press.

Kornhauser, William. 1962. *Scientists in Industry.* Berkeley: University of California Press.

Kristol, Irving (ed.). 1978. *Two Cheers for Capitalism.* New York: Basic Books.

Kuhn, Thomas. 1962. *The Structure of Scientific Revolutions.* Chicago: University of Chicago Press.

Ladinsky, Jack. 1963a. "Careers of Lawyers, Law Practice and Legal Institutions." *American Sociological Review* 28, no. 1:47–54.

———. 1963b. "The Impact of Social Backgrounds of Lawyers on Law Practice and the Law." *Journal of Legal Education* 16, no. 2:127–144.

———. 1976. "The Traffic in Legal Services: Lawyer Seeking Behavior and the Channelling of Clients." *Law and Society Review* 11 (Special):207–223.

Lancaster, Hal. 1982. "Companies Expanding Legal Staffs as the Cost of Outside Work Soars." *Wall Street Journal* (Mar. 1):25.

Landon, Donald D. 1982. "Lawyers and Localities: The Interaction of Community Context and Professionalism. *American Bar Foundation Research Journal* 1982, no. 2 (Spring):459–485.

Larson, Magali. 1977. *The Rise of Professionalism*. Berkeley: University of California Press.

———. 1980. "Proletarianization and Educated Labor." *Theory and Society* 9, no. 1 (Jan.):131–171.

Lasch, Christopher. 1978. *Haven in a Heartless World*. New York: Basic Books.

Laumann, Edward, and Heinz, John. 1977. "Specialization and Prestige in the Legal Profession: The Structure of Deference." *American Bar Foundation Research Journal* 1977, no. 1 (Winter):155–216.

———. 1979. "The Organization of Lawyer's Work: Size, Intensity and Co-Practice of Fields of Law." *American Bar Foundation Research Journal* 1979, no. 2 (Spring):217–246.

Lee, Harper. 1960. *To Kill a Mockingbird*. New York: Lippincott.

Leventman, Paula. 1981. *Professionals Out of Work*. New York: Free Press.

Lewin, Tamar. 1982. "Biggest Firms Mostly Grow." *New York Times* (Sept. 21):D2.

———. 1983a. "A Gentlemanly Profession Enters a Tough New Era." *New York Times* (Jan. 16):C1, C10.

———. 1983b. "The In-House Legal Staffs." *New York Times* (Apr. 5):D2.

———. 1983c. "Chain of Legal Clinics Is No. 1." *New York Times* (May 9):D1, D10

———. 1983d. "Hiring Away Legal Talent." *New York Times* (July 12): D2.

———. 1983e. "Fall in Income at Big Firms." *New York Times* (Nov. 15): D2.

———. 1984. "Retaining Valued Attorneys." *New York Times* (May 29): D2, D4.

Liska, Allen. 1974. "Emergent Issues in the Attitude-Behavior Consistency Controversy." *American Sociological Review* 39, no. 2 (Apr.):261–272.

Lochner, Philip. 1975. "The No-Fee and Low-Fee Legal Practice of Private Attorneys." *Law and Society Review* 9, no. 3 (Spring):431–473.

Lopata, Helena Z. 1976. "Expertization of Everyone and the Revolt of the Client." *Sociological Quarterly* 17 (Autumn):435–447.

Lortie, Dan. 1959. "Laymen to Lawmen: Law School, Careers and Professional Socialization." *Harvard Educational Review* 29:352–369.

Magaziner, Ira, and Reich, Robert. 1982. *Minding America's Business*. New York: Harcourt Brace Jovanovitch.

Marglin, Stephen. 1975. "What Do Bosses Do?" *Review of Radical Political Economics* 6:60–112; 7:20–37.

Martindale-Hubbell, Inc. 1984. *Martindale and Hubbell Law Directory*, vol. 3. New York: Martindale-Hubbell.

Marx, Karl. 1978. "The German Ideology." In *The Marx-Engels Reader*, 2d ed., edited by Robert C. Tucker, pp. 146–200. New York: Norton.

Mayer, Martin. 1966. *The Lawyers*. New York: Harper & Row.

Mayhew, Leon, and Reiss, Albert J. Jr. 1969. "The Social Organization of Legal Contacts." *American Sociological Review* 34, no. 3:309–317.

McCaulay, Stewart. 1979. "Lawyers and Consumer Protection Laws." *Law and Society Review* 14, no. 1:115–171.

McKinlay, John. 1973. "On the Professional Regulation of Change." In *Professionalization and Social Change*, edited by Paul Halmos, pp. 61–84.

Meiksins, Peter. 1982. "Science in the Labor Process: Engineers as Workers." In *Professionals as Workers*, edited by Charles Derber, pp. 121–140.

———. 1985. "A Model for Engineering Professionalism: The Wickenden Report." Paper read at the Annual Meeting of the Eastern Sociological Society.

Merton, Robert K. 1968. *Social Theory and Social Structure*, enlarged ed. New York: Free Press.

Mills, C. Wright. 1951. *White Collar*. New York: Oxford University Press.

Montagna, Paul. 1968. "Professionalization and Bureaucratization in Large Professional Organizations." *American Journal of Sociology* 74, no. 1 (Sept.):138–145.

Nelson, Robert. 1981. "Practice and Privilege: Social Change and the Structure of Large Law Firms." *American Bar Foundation Research Journal* 1981, no. 1 (Winter):95–140.

———. 1983. "The Changing Structure of Opportunity: Recruitment and Careers In Large Law Firms." *American Bar Foundation Research Journal* 1983, no. 1 (Winter):109–142.

New York Times. 1983. "More Lawlessness in Legal Services." *New York Times* [editorial] (Nov. 29):A26.

———. 1984. "F.T.C. Sees Lawyers Ads as Beneficial." *New York Times* (Dec. 7):24.

Nobel, David. 1977. *America By Design*. New York: Alfred A. Knopf.

———. 1979. "Social Choice in Machine Design." In *Case Studies in the Labor Process*, edited by Andrew Zimbalist, pp. 18–50.

O'Connor, James. 1973. *The Fiscal Crisis of the State*. New York: St. Martin's Press.

O'Gorman, Hubert. 1963. *Lawyers and Matrimonial Cases*. New York: Free Press.

Oppenheimer, Martin. 1973. "The Proletarianization of the Professional." In *Professionalization and Social Change*, edited by Paul Halmos, pp. 213–227.

Osborne, John Jay. 1979. *The Associates*. Boston: Houghton Mifflin.

Pashigian, B. Peter. 1978. "The Number and Earnings of Lawyers: Some Recent Findings." *American Bar Foundation Research Journal* 1978, no. 1 (Winter):51–82.

Perrucci, Robert, and Gerstl, Joel. 1969. *Profession Without Community*. New York: Random House.

Quirk, Paul. 1981. *Industry Influence in Federal Regulatory Agencies*. Princeton, N.J.: Princeton University Press.

Ratner, Ronnie Steinberg. 1980. "The Paradox of Protection: Maximum Hours Legislation." *International Labour Review* 119 (Mar.–Apr.):185–198.

Reich, Robert. 1981. "The Liberal Promise of Prosperity." *New Republic* (Feb. 21):20–23.

Ritti, R. Richard. 1971. *The Engineer in the Industrial Corporation*. New York: Columbia University Press.

Rohatyn, Felix. 1984. *The Twenty Year Century*. New York: Random House.

Rosenthal, Douglas. 1976. *Lawyers and Clients: Who's in Charge?* New York: Russell Sage.

Rothman, Robert. 1984. "Deprofessionalization: The Case of Law in America." *Sociology of Work and Occupations* 11, no. 2 (May):183–206.

Rueschemeyer, Dietrich. 1964. "Doctors and Lawyers: A Comment on the Theory of the Professions." *Canadian Review of Sociology and Anthropology* 1, no. 1:17–30.

———. 1973. *Lawyers and Their Society*. Cambridge: Harvard University Press.

———. 1983. "Professional Autonomy and the Social Control of Expertise." In *The Sociology of the Professions*, edited by Robert Dingwall and Philip Lewis, pp. 38–58.

Sandburg, Carl. 1950. "The Lawyers Know Too Little." *Collected Poems*, p. 189. New York: Harcourt, Brace.

Schwartz, Murray. 1980. "The Reorganization of the Legal Profession." *Texas Law Review* 58:1268–1290.

Shaffer, Thomas. 1981. "Henry Knox and the Moral Theology of Law Firms." *Washington and Lee Law Review* 38:347–375.

Shakespeare, William. 1971. *King Henry the Sixth, Part II*, pp. 550–591. In *The Complete Works of Shakespeare*, edited by Irving Ribner and George Kittredge. Lexington, Mass.: Xerox Publishing Co.

Skolnick, Jerome. 1967. "Social Control in the Adversary System." *Journal of Conflict Resolution* 11, no. 1:59–67.

Slovak, Jeffrey. 1979. "Working for Corporate Actors: Social Change and Elite Attorneys in Chicago." *American Bar Foundation Research Journal* 1979, no. 3 (Summer):465–500.

———. 1981. "The Ethics of Corporate Lawyers: A Sociological Approach." *American Bar Foundation Research Journal* 1981, no. 3 (Summer):753–794.

Smigel, Erwin. 1960. "The Impact of Recruitment on the Organization of the Large Law Firm." *American Sociological Review* 25, no. 1:56–66.

———. 1964. *The Wall Street Lawyer.* New York: Free Press.

Spector, Malcolm. 1972. "The Rise and Fall of a Mobility Route." *Social Problems* 20, no. 2 (Fall):173–185.

———. 1973. "Secrecy in Job-Seeking Among Government Attorneys." *Urban Life and Culture* 2, no. 2 (July):211–229.

Springfield Morning Union. 1983. "Lawyers Turn to Boutique Merchandizing." *Springfield Morning Union* (Sept. 23):36.

Stavitsky, Bruce. 1980. "Lawyer Unionization in Quasi-Governmental Public and Private Sectors. *California Western Law Review* 17:55–74.

Stewart, James B. 1983. *The Partners.* New York: Simon and Schuster.

Stinchcombe, Arthur L. 1959. "Bureaucratic and Craft Administration of Production." *Administrative Science Quarterly* 4:168–187.

Stumpf, Harry et al. 1971. "The Legal Profession and Legal Services: Explorations in Local Bar Politics." *Law and Society Review* 6, no. 1: 47–67.

Sudnow, David. 1965. "Normal Crimes: Sociological Features of the Penal Code in A Public Defender's Office." *Social Problems* 12, no. 3:255–276.

Taylor, Stuart Jr. 1983a. "Of Lawyers, Ethics and Business." *New York Times* (Feb. 6):C4.

———. 1983b. "Lawyer Confidentiality vs. Disclosing Crimes to Be." *New York Times* (Feb. 14):A9.

———. 1983c. "Law Firms Squirm, Then Turn to Public Relations." *New York Times* (July 27):A18.

———. 1983d. "Ethics Code Isn't Open and Shut." *New York Times* (Aug. 7):E7.

———. 1983e. "New Rules on Legal Aid: Two Views." *New York Times* (Dec. 24):A9.

———. 1984. "When Goals of Boss and His Staff Lawyers Clash." *New York Times* (June 22):A14.

Toren, Nina. 1975. "Deprofessionalization and Its Sources." *Sociology of Work and Occupations* 2, no. 4 (Nov.):323–337.

Udy, Stanley. 1959. "Bureaucracy and Rationality in Weber's Organizational Theory." *American Sociological Review* 24, no. 6:791–795.

Useem, Michael. 1984. *The Inner Circle.* New York: Oxford University Press.

Veblen, Thorstein. 1921. *The Engineers and the Price System.* New York: B. W. Huebsch.

Walker, Pat. (ed.). 1979. *Between Labor and Capital.* Boston: South End Press.

Warkov, Seymour, and Zelan, Joseph. 1965. *Lawyers in the Making.* Chicago: Aldine.

Weber, Max. 1958a. "Bureaucracy." In *From Max Weber*, edited by Hans Gerth and C. Wright Mills, pp. 196–244.

———. 1958b. "Politics as a Vocation." In *From Max Weber*, edited by Hans Gerth and C. Wright Mills, pp. 77–128.

———. 1959c. "Science as a Vocation." In *From Max Weber*, edited by Hans Gerth and C. Wright Mills, pp. 129–158.

Weisbrod, Burton A. 1983. "Non-Profit and Proprietary Sector Behavior: Wage Differentials Among Lawyers." *Journal of Labor Economics* 1, no. 3:246–263.

Wilson, Sloan. 1955. *The Man In The Grey Flannel Suit.* New York: Simon and Schuster.

Wolfram, Charles. 1984. "The 'Ethics' of Lawyers." *Cornell Law Forum* 11, no. 1 (June):10–14.

Wright, Erik Olin. 1979. *Class Structure and Income Determination.* New York: Academic Press.

———. 1980. "Class and Occupation." *Theory and Society* 9, no. 1 (Jan.): 177–214.

Wright, Erik Olin, and Singelmann, Joachim. 1982. "Proletarianization in the Changing American Class Structure." *American Journal of Sociology* 88 (suppl.):176–209.

Wright, Erik Olin, et al. 1982. "The American Class Structure." *American Sociological Review* 47, no. 6 (Dec.):709–726.

Wutnow, Robert, and Shrum, Wesley. 1983. "Knowledge Workers as a New Class." *Sociology of Work and Occupations* 10, no. 4 (Nov.): 471–487.

Zimbalist, Andrew (ed.). 1979. *Case Studies in the Labor Process.* New York: Monthly Review Press.

INDEX

Abel, Richard, 20, 193*n*, 196
Administrative rationalization. *See* Bureaucratic control
Adversary character of law, 43, 113, 186. *See also* Destandardization
Associates in law firms: career development, 36, 39–40, 46, 53–56; competitiveness, 39; as apprentices, 43–46; evaluation of, 53–55; attrition of, 54; and loyalty to firm, 59, 66; as constituency for administrative rationalization, 66–67, 188. *See also* Permanent associates
Attrition: from law firms, 54; from corporate law departments, 83, 85–86; from civil service agencies, 111–13, 123, 139; from Legal Services affiliates, 162–64, 173. *See also* Career ceilings.

Boilerplate, 183; in law firms, 48–50; in corporate law departments, 89; in civil service agencies, 128–30; in Legal Service affiliates, 161. *See also* Deskilling; Technical control
Bureaucracies: as workplaces, 16, 188–97 passim; compatibility with professions, 17, 31, 189
Bureaucratic control, x, 19, 187–91; in law firms, 65–69; encouraged by staff attorneys, 66–67, 187–91; in corpo-

rate law departments, 81–85; in civil service agencies, 115–18, 122–23, 125–28, 130–32, 134–36, 142; in Legal Services affiliates, 151–54, 157–62 passim

Career ceilings: in corporate law departments, 82–83, 85–86; in civil service agencies, 123; in Legal Services affiliates, 152, 164
Civil service law departments: types, 108; structure of, 108–09; regional and home offices, 108–09, 119–22; mandate of, 108–10; poverty of, 108, 115–16, 120–21, 138; and Justice Department, 110–11; ideological control in, 110, 113–14, 120–21; attrition to industry, 111–13, 139; political character of, 114–15, 129–30, 133–41; rewards in, 114, 121–22; staff evaluation, 115–17, 130–32, 135–36; bureaucratic control in, 115–18, 122–23, 125–28, 130–32, 134–36, 142; office morale, 116–18, 121; de-skilling, 118; informal social life, 118, 124; comparison to law firms, 119–20; career ceilings, 123; peer pressure, 124, 127–28; boilerplate in, 125, 139–41
Clients, relationships to, 7–8, 15, 176–77; in law firms, 60–64; in cor-

231